LIFE BEFORE THE WAR

LIFE BEFORE THE WAR

Britain in the Later 1930s

Michael Alpert

PEN & SWORD
HISTORY
AN IMPRINT OF PEN & SWORD BOOKS LTD.
YORKSHIRE – PHILADELPHIA

First published in Great Britain in 2025 by
PEN AND SWORD HISTORY
An imprint of
Pen & Sword Books Ltd
Yorkshire – Philadelphia

ISBN 978 1 39905 389 1

A CIP catalogue record for this book is available from the British Library.

Typeset in Times New Roman 11/13.5 by
SJmagic DESIGN SERVICES, India.
Printed and bound in the UK by CPI Group (UK) Ltd.

The Publisher's authorised representative in the EU for product safety is Authorised Rep Compliance Ltd., Ground Floor, 71 Lower Baggot Street, Dublin D02 P593, Ireland.
www.arccompliance.com

For a complete list of Pen & Sword titles please contact
PEN & SWORD BOOKS LIMITED
George House, Units 12 & 13, Beevor Street, Off Pontefract Road,
Barnsley, South Yorkshire, S71 1HN, England
E-mail: enquiries@pen-and-sword.co.uk
Website: www.pen-and-sword.co.uk

or

PEN AND SWORD BOOKS
1950 Lawrence Rd, Havertown, PA 19083, USA
E-mail: uspen-and-sword@casematepublishers.com
Website: www.penandswordbooks.com

MIX
Paper | Supporting responsible forestry
FSC® C013604

Contents

Introduction

My parents and most of their siblings were young marrieds in the latter years of the 1930s. They lived through the tensions and the crises of the age and responded to the values of that time. A large amount of investigatory work has been published about those years, in particular on international politics and diplomacy. Much social history has also been produced, though it tends to deal with the entire age between the two World Wars. My intention is to concentrate on the latter 1930s, as Britain emerged from the Great Depression of 1929–33 and as the European crisis deepened after Hitler came to power in Germany in January 1933.

Social history is about general conditions and changes that affect large numbers of people. This book aims to offer a picture of British society in the second part of the decade of the 1930s, approximately from 1935 until the outbreak of war in September 1939. It begins with a picture of population and general demography. It then looks at the world of work, of unemployment and employment, of incomes and prices and thus about the standard of living. This is determined largely by the housing and the food one can afford for oneself and one's family. It is also affected by the medical care people receive and the education that they or the State can provide for their children. At a more optional level of consumption, people's standard of living is reflected by the clothes they can afford, the entertainment they can enjoy and the holidays they can take. Overall looms the question of values, which may vary between the classes, or are themselves a defining factor of class differentiation. Class structure and perception were clearly marked in the years before the Second World War though the limits were beginning to fray at the edges. Class, income, religion and values in general also affected the question of the relative positions of men and women, and attitudes to family, marriage and sex.

Social history is never-ending; each subject chases each other's tail, and it is difficult to know where to begin. Nevertheless, certain emotions in the latter 1930s were general and few people would have escaped them. Among them was anxiety, created by the growing international crisis. Although this book is not a political or diplomatic history of the European crisis, which culminated in the British declaration of war against Germany on 3 September 1939, it was a constant background to people's lives and their reaction to it is part of the history of British society.

Until Britain went to war again with Germany in 1939, the 1914–18 conflict was termed 'the Great War'. It was indeed 'great' because in the later 1930s it was the major event in the memory of most adults over 30; and children growing up knew about it from their parents. Britain had lost approximately 750,000 of the 6 million men who served in the armed forces during the 1914–18 war. Many people in their twenties and thirties by 1935–39 had lost their fathers, uncles and older brothers in the fighting. Some men and women, ageing by the late 1930s, had lost sons. Among young men, the slaughter was immense. Additionally, 1.7 million men from Great Britain and Ireland had been wounded and very many were permanently crippled or unable to function in other ways. War-disabled men could be seen everywhere, begging and doing what they could to scrape a few shillings together to supplement their pensions. Widows were legion.

Inevitably, fear of another war dominated the minds of many, for while universal peace had seemed to have arrived in the 1920s, by halfway through the 1930s Fascism had begun its aggressive expansionism when Mussolini's forces attacked Abyssinia in October 1935. In 1938, the Czech crisis, caused by German demands for territory, created near panic, assuaged by the Munich agreements of September 1938, after which speeded-up rearmament and in 1939 real preparations for war brought tension to a height.

The strains of daily life also created pervasive anxiety among large numbers of people, at a time when social security was limited. The suffering caused by unemployment and low wages, at its height in the early part of the 1930s, continued even when new industries and rearmament brought prosperity, particularly to the Midlands and the South-East of England, but unemployment figures were still high in the depressed areas of Britain when war began in September 1939. Even in relatively prosperous parts of the country, unemployment was greater than would be considered acceptable in postwar Britain. The fear of unemployment marked another great difference between the classes. For most middle-class salaried people, unemployment was an unfamiliar experience. This had a political effect. From the 1935 elections onward, the Conservatives, whose ideas on how to deal with economic problems were thought by many to be the only reliable ones, maintained a dominant majority in the House of Commons. Moreover, in the minds of many people in the upper middle and upper classes, working-class demonstrations against high unemployment and poor working conditions were thought to be threatening a revolution. The horror felt by the events of the Russian Revolution, a bare score of years earlier, and which had brought the confiscation of private property and the murder of the Russian royal family, was still vivid.

While anxieties were widespread, life went on. Between 1921 and 1941 Britain increased its total population by 3,836,600. Although the loss of young men had created a surplus of women, the rate of marriage rose. While the birth rate fell drastically to 14.7 per 1,000 in 1936–40 from 23.6 per 1,000 in the immediate pre-1914 generation, advances in medicine and other improvements in health had also lowered the death rate in the same years from 14 per 1,000 of the population to 12.2. Sixty per cent of the population increase was absorbed by the economically prosperous South-East. Greater London's population was over 8.5 million by 1939. It was estimated that a million people of working age moved to the South-East, and a large number also to the newer industrial centres in the Midlands, while the depressed areas of the North, of parts of Scotland and South Wales lost population.

Britain was a highly urbanised country. A study made in late 1938 for the purpose of providing air raid shelters calculated that 20 million people lived in cities of over 100,000 inhabitants, to which were to be added the 4.25 million who lived in towns of between 50,000 and 100,000. British industry absorbed nearly half the working population, while the equivalent figure in France was 37 per cent and in the US 47 per cent. Only just over 5 per cent of the working population of Britain laboured in agriculture, compared with nearly 40 per cent in France and 21 per cent in the US.

Britain was thus a highly industrialised and urbanised nation, with a healthy birth rate, experiencing a major population shift. For all that, unemployment during the later 1930s, with its concomitants of depression, poverty and illness, was widespread, particularly in the older industrial, cotton, shipbuilding and mining regions, and was being reduced only by rearmament as Britain faced the European political crisis of 1936–39.

A Note on Currency

The change brought about by the decimalisation of the currency in 1971 was not merely a question of making it easier to calculate sums of money, but also of the vocabulary and even the oral expression of how much something cost.

In the 1930s, there were banknotes for five pounds, one pound and half a pound or ten shillings. The pound was divided into twenty shillings (the 'guinea', much used to quote the prices of high-class items, was the sum of one pound and one shilling). Each shilling was divided into twelve pence. There were quarter-pence called 'farthings', and half-pennies, pronounced 'hayp'nce' ('hayp'ny' in the singular). Pence were abbreviated in writing to d., thus a price would be marked as 2d.

Shillings were abbreviated to *s* or /-, so one pound and five shillings was written £.1.5s or 25/-. One usually said 'twenty-five shillings'. An account might total, say, £1.5.4½d., or one pound, five shillings and fourpence and one halfpenny. People would say 'One pound, five and fourp'nce hayp'ny' or 'twenty-five and fourp'nce hayp'ny'.

If shillings or pence were mentioned together the sum would be expressed, for example, as 'seven and six', that is seven shillings and six pence. The shilling was called a 'bob' and the sixpence a 'tanner'.

The silver (actually only 50 per cent) coinage consisted of the 3d., 6d. and shilling (twelve pence) pieces. There was a florin, worth two shillings, and the half-crown, which most people called 'half a crown', worth two shillings and six pence, or one eighth of a pound.

The following table shows equivalent values for pre- and post-decimalised British currency (approximate for amounts under 6d.)

'Old' money	***Decimalised***
1d.	½p
2½d.	1p
6d.	2½p
1/-	5p
2/-	10p
2/6d.	12½p
5/-	25p
10/-	50p
15/-	75p

Inflation has made sums of money mentioned nearly a century ago meaningless unless we know people's incomes. £5 a week or £250 a year was the minimum on which one could live a 'lower' middle-class life. A working man who had a regular £4 a week could live with some ease, but many earned far less and suffered occasional or even regular unemployment.

I must thank the many friends with whom I have discussed the matters dealt with in this book. I am in great debt to my wife, who listened to me reading the chapters aloud and picked up errors in syntax and doubtful statements. The helpful London Library has been the source for almost all the books quoted in the Bibliography.

MICHAEL ALPERT
December 2024

Chapter 1

The World of Work

Unemployment

Not work, but lack of it, and unemployment was characteristic of the 1930s. In the depressed regions of Britain – South Wales, Central Scotland, and much of Northern England – worklessness hovered threateningly over tens of thousands of families like a lowering storm cloud.

Most working men and some women over the age of 16 and earning under £250 a year or £5 per week were covered by unemployment insurance, which by 1937 protected 13.25 million of the 19.5 million workers aged 16–64. For almost the entire period between 1919 and 1939 at least 10 per cent of the insured population were out of work. The number of unemployed reached its maximum of 2.74 million in June 1932. It did not fall to 2 million for three years. By December 1936 it had dropped to 1.68 million. In June 1939 it had fallen to 1.35 million. Many, however, were not covered by unemployment insurance. Among the unprotected were those who earned over £250 a year, including married women, nurses, teachers, civil servants and police. However, in 1938 insurance cover was extended to domestic servants and agricultural workers. There was also a substantial number who had been denied benefit. As late as 1 January 1939, the Labour Party's newspaper *Daily Herald* thought that some 200,000 people not covered by the benefit scheme were seeking work. Unemployment was the shadow that darkened the lives of many families over substantial parts of Britain until the end of the thirties.

The bald statistics of unemployment represented wasted lives, poverty, poor diet and housing and a restricted life. Over the entire United Kingdom, one person out of eight of the insured working population was workless in 1938. Many had not worked in years. This, however, concealed the regional variation in the proportion of unemployed working people. In mid-1937 Wales had no jobs for over 20 per cent of its insured workers; in the north-west, the north-east and parts of Scotland there was no work for between 12 and

16 per cent, and in the East Midlands unemployment affected 7.5 per cent of the working population. In Wales the rate of unemployment never fell below 9 per cent in the decade between 1929 and 1939 and was as high as 36.5 per cent in 1932. In Greater London, in contrast, 1932 was the highest year for unemployment at 14 per cent of the insured population, while over the whole period unemployment in the capital averaged 6 per cent. In the prosperous South-East the figure was 5 per cent. The contrast was huge. In St. Alban's (Hertfordshire), just under 4 per cent were out of work when at the same time in Maryport (in northern Cumberland) the figure was 57 per cent; in Merthyr (South Wales) it was 52 per cent and in Jarrow in the North-East it stood at a colossal 68 per cent. Unemployment hit primarily men who had earned mostly between £2 and £3 a week in the depressed industries. The middle classes, which in broad terms can be defined as those who received more than £250 a year, were less affected. So it seemed, but the middle classes were not entitled to benefit. Middle-class jobs attracted large numbers of applicants, but figures for the difficulty of obtaining employment rather than for losing it are not available. Nevertheless, a minor clerical or local authority office post could attract hundreds of applicants.

The recovery of the economy in the later 1930s took place largely in the Midlands and the South-East, but the statistics that indicated a fall in the percentage of the workless masked the experience of long-term unemployment. In the years right up to the Second World War, entire regions in South Wales, the North-West of England, Lancashire and Central Scotland were economically and socially devastated.

Older and basic industries in Britain, fundamentally coal, shipbuilding, textiles, and iron and steel, were technically backward compared to those in Japan, Germany and the US. This was reflected in the numbers unemployed in 1937. A quarter of shipbuilding workers, 16 per cent of miners and 14.5 per cent of building workers were unemployed, compared with just over 3 per cent of workers in the electrical industry, 6 per cent in the motor industry of one kind or another and just under 7 per cent in the chemical sector, so that at the same time as production was recovering in areas with newer industries, involving in particular chemical, motor and electrical engineering, the population that lived in the depressed areas continued to suffer massive unemployment in the interwar period to a degree never before experienced in its length and in the number of people, often skilled men, who were affected. This tragedy became imprinted on the national consciousness to such an extent that 'full employment' became a mantra in political discourse and a major ambition for the post-1945 period. In comparison, over the recent half-century, that is the years 1971–2023, average unemployment in Britain has been 6.75 per cent of the insured population, with a minimum of 3.5 per cent in December 1973 and a maximum of just under 12 per cent in April 1984.

Even as the British economy began to revive in 1936, stimulated by the first steps in rearmament, 25 per cent of coalminers and 30 per cent of men who had worked in shipbuilding lived without work, wages or a meaningful life where they might pride themselves on maintaining a wife and family. In certain places where workpeople were dependent on one industry, for example in Crook (County Durham), figures for November 1936 revealed that 71 per cent of the insured workers had not earned a wage for five or more years. Women workers found and kept their employment more easily than men, because they earned much less (the average women's wage in 1935 was 27/2d. per week, compared with the men's 56/5d.). School-leavers might be able to get a job paying very low wages as errand boys or shop assistants, but employers would sack them when they reached the age when they had to pay higher insurance contributions. As late as 1938, the long list of offers of employment in the January numbers of the *Willesden Chronicle*, a newspaper covering a wide spread of built-up suburbs just outside the boundary of north-west London, were almost all for young people. The fictional Harry Hardcastle in Walter Greenwood's never-out-of-print novel *Love on the Dole* of 1933 starts work in a northern city at 14 as a pawnbroker's assistant. He is paid a pittance of a wage and must work very long hours. Then he becomes an engineering apprentice, but he is dismissed as soon he reaches the age of 18 when he merits a skilled man's wage. An older man who lost his job might never work again. Long-term unemployed men lost their skills and often their physical ability to do a day's labour.

Shipbuilding was possibly the most depressed of all British industries. Just before 1914, shipyards were building about 2 million tons of shipping per year. In 1932, the figure was only 188,000. Ninety per cent of capacity was unused. Of all the places that the novelist J. B. Priestley visited in his *English Journey*, published in 1934, Jarrow, the Durham town of 35,590 inhabitants, from which the historic 'hunger march' of unemployed men to London would set off on 5 October 1936, had 'thick air, heavy with enforced idleness, poverty and misery'. One out of every two shops had closed. Life was 'a perpetual, penniless, bleak Sabbath'. Men's faces were 'drawn masks'. In this 'grimy wilderness of grim despair' there was coal dust everywhere, and the houses were unrepaired and tumbledown. Palmer's Shipbuilders had been the majority employer. It had closed and only a handful of skilled men were employed in the town. While this was perhaps the most appalling example of the destruction of the life of an entire community, a similar tragedy had befallen the Dowlais steelworks in Wales, which closed, taking with it not only the steelworkers' employment but also the jobs of the miners of the coalfield that had supplied Dowlais with fuel.

How Much Unemployment Benefit Did They Receive?

According to the National Insurance Act which had been passed in 1911, the benefit payable by May 1934 was 17s. per week for a single person. A married man was granted an additional 9s. per week for his wife and 3s. for each child. Thus, the weekly total for a family of husband, wife and two children was £1.12s. per week or somewhat over half the average wage. By the end of the thirties the cover had increased by a further shilling for the wife. A family with three children then received £1.16s. In most cases, living on this sum reduced the family standard of living to bare subsistence. This was intentional, because it was thought wrong that anyone should receive more in benefit than at work. Nobody did, in fact, except perhaps men earning the lowest of wages and with large numbers of children.

Unemployment benefit was paid only for the first twenty-six weeks. Then the unemployed worker had to 'sign on' for 'transitional payments'. It was the system for calculating these, known as the 'Means Test', that became the label by which living in the 1930s without income from a job was and still is described. The relief was known as the 'dole', a mediaeval term for a charity donation reintroduced by the right-wing *Daily Mail* in June 1919. The term 'on the dole' was soon applied to unemployment benefit as well, though officially this was called 'covenanted benefit'. The relief payment was administered by the Public Assistance Committee or PAC, a local body that, depending on its political complexion, might be more or less sympathetic to the plea of the shabby, thin man who came before it as a supplicant. PACs knew that their job was to keep the amount they handed out as low as possible, and to restrict it to those who could be described as 'genuinely seeking work'. Skilled and experienced men could find themselves treated like beggars.

The Experience of Unemployment

To draw the dole meant that a man had to demonstrate that he had no means, no savings or non-essential possessions that could be sold. The earnings of his wife and children were deemed to be his own assets. Thus, thrift was discouraged, and men were humiliated by being given a few shillings by their working wives or children. A result of this was that either the working children, or sometimes the father, moved away. The plight of families living on the dole was pictured in Walter Greenwood's novel *Love on the Dole*, based on the author's experiences and set in Hanky Park, a poor part of Salford. This book was made into a highly successful play and a film during the Second World War. In it a workless man must live on the contributions of his daughter, who is the mistress of a bookmaker.

To qualify for the dole, one had to be, as the regulation said, 'genuinely seeking work', but this phrase was harshly used to deny income to unemployed men, who would call regularly at factories even where signs proclaimed: 'No Hands Needed'. Stringent attempts were made to limit the qualification for benefit and to limit the amount granted by the hated Means Test in a way that created significant hardship and resentment. A skilled man who refused to take unskilled work was denied the dole, so occasionally skilled craftsmen took a few days' work doing labouring jobs. But sometimes the work on offer was not a realistic alternative, as William Woodruff describes in his *The Road to Nab End* when a painter goes to the Labour Exchange to collect the dole:

'"Ow t'be?" the clerk said.

"Nicely," Gordon lied, expecting to sign his name, take his money and push his way out again.

"I've got a job for thee," the clerk went on, shuffling some papers.

"Th 'as?"

"Yes."

"Wher' is it?"

"Cornwall.'

"Wher's Cornwall?" asked Gordon. "It sounds a long way."

"That it is. A very long way."

"What kind of painting is it?"

"It isn't painting."

"It isn't?"

"What is't then?"

"It's digging tin down a mine."

"Ah'm not a tin miner. Ah'm a painter."

"Does t'refuse to go to Cornwall?"

"Ah do."

"Then tha's just lost thee dole."

"Tha can't mean it."

"Aye, but I do. If tha not 'genuinely seeking work' and obviously tha' not, benefits have to be stopped."'

Love on the Dole includes a vivid scene in Chapter 10 where a man is told that he is no longer entitled to the dole because the Public Assistance Committee has judged the household's aggregate income as sufficient for its needs:

'"You've a couple of sons living with you who are working, haven't you?"

"Aye," the man answered, "One's earning twenty-five bob [shillings] and t'other a couple of quid [pounds], when they work a full week."

"In view of these facts," the manager interrupted, "the Public Assistance Committee has ruled your household's aggregate income sufficient for your needs: therefore, your claim for transitional benefit [the formal name for the 'dole'] is disallowed."'

The man protested that his sons were saving to get married, but to no avail. Even more resented was the habit of officials entering homes uninvited and telling the unemployed householder to sell cherished family items, such as pianos, if he wanted to keep his dole.

Searching for work was an aimless task. For many it became physically difficult because their diet was insufficient to maintain the strength to cycle or walk over the hills and moorlands to the next town. At best they might find an odd job, a bit of painting or a minor repair or looking after a barrow or a shop, which would have to be concealed in case the relieving officer found out and suspended the dole. Men wandered or cycled about sometimes from the early morning. Some public opinion regarded the unemployed as lazy scroungers or unemployable, but several official enquiries confirmed that most of the workless people of the depressed areas were indeed actively seeking work. After all, jobs when available were swiftly filled.

For men who had been unemployed for a very long time, their very reason for existence and their pride as men who kept their wives and families were gone. Many reported a sense of impotence, while others felt humiliated and cowed. They had lost their authority as husbands and fathers. Their skills were worthless. They no longer frequented the pub, which was for many the social centre of their lives, not only because they could not afford to drink there themselves but also because they could not say 'This round's on me'.

'That's one thing that makes us human,' said one man, 'we don't wait for things to happen to us; we work for them. But if you can't find any work to do you have the feeling that you're not human. You're out of place.'

While a sense of worthlessness and habits of idleness such as lying late in bed, often to keep warm, overwhelmed many, others devoted themselves to cultivating their allotments and bringing home basic vegetables for their families, repaired their boots and the children's shoes and, if they could collect the necessary materials, tried to improve their houses. The major mental stimulation for some unemployed men came from reading, particularly in mining regions where Miners' Institutes were well stocked with books. In Pontypridd (South Wales), where 6,500 men had no work, library borrowing figures surged. Groups of men would assemble in the public library, trying to keep warm in the winter and combing the Vacancies pages in the newspaper. Cinema attendances also kept up. The reason was easy enough to discover: the cinema was cheap and warm, performances were continuous and nobody told you to leave when you had seen the film through once.

Food, Diet and Health

An enquiry conducted in 1933 concluded that a family consisting of a man, his wife and two children required a minimum of 16/8d. per week for food alone. In 1934 special investigators were appointed to find out about conditions in the Distressed Areas, as the regions where unemployment was heaviest were known. Their reports revealed appalling social and economic breakdown. Unemployment meant a grim life of scrimping, pawning often essential clothing, trying to repair shoes and household items, picking up cheap items in jumble sales, waiting till markets were about to close late on Saturday nights and picking up spoiled cabbages and carrots from under the stalls, collecting fuel from slag heaps and railway tracks, and occasional poaching. Once food, rent and fuel were paid for, hardly anything was left for other essentials, such as clothes, shoes, heating more than the main living room, and the cheapest amusement, or even a daily newspaper or postage stamp when applications for work required a letter. Another enquiry in 1934 stated that a man, wife and five children of the ages of 5, 6, 7, 9 and 11 received considerably less than they needed. One London woman with nine children received 48s. per week. She died of pneumonia, but the coroner said that had she had sufficient and proper nutrition she would have survived.

The shortage of money led to a decline in health. In 1936 a report on the Durham coalfield where miners' wages, assuming they had work, were particularly low, reported that 94 per cent of the children showed signs of rickets, a deficiency disease. Several enquiries into calorific needs were carried out, but there was no recommended and agreed standard by which malnutrition could be accurately identified. There was no doubt, however, that better feeding of pregnant women reduced the maternal death rate, as was measured in the Rhondda Valley of South Wales in 1934–35 when the rate fell from 11 deaths per 1,000 to slightly under five when extra food was provided. The best known of a number of investigations into the adequacy or otherwise of the income of an unemployed man and his family to eat healthily was Sir John Boyd Orr's *Food, Health and Income: A Survey of Adequacy of Diet in Relation to Income*, first issued in 1936 by the publisher and MP for the depressed town of Stockton-on-Tees (and postwar prime minister) Harold Macmillan, and with a second edition in the following year. John Boyd Orr was a biologist and physician who became an expert in the relation between income, food and health. A leading international civil servant, he would be awarded the Nobel Peace Prize in 1949. While advisers of the government, among them the British Medical Association, insisted that the sample budgets they calculated were sufficient to avoid any major increase in sickness or mortality, and thus that the 'dole' was enough to cover essential needs, John Boyd Orr disputed these reports and insisted that, at the best, the diet of an unemployed family was monotonous and heavily dependent on bread and potatoes, margarine, the cheapest cuts of meat, condensed milk, other vegetables – if the man had an allotment – and very little fresh fruit. Stomach ailments and other illness caused by poor feeding were widespread. The official claim was that ill health was not a result of unemployment alone, but arose rather from general poverty and poor, insanitary housing. It was proclaimed that the average death rate had fallen from 14 per 1,000 in 1919 to 11.5 per 1,000 in late 1938. Infantile mortality had also fallen markedly even in the depressed areas. Other investigations suggested that the opposite was true and that the death rates were markedly higher in the most depressed areas. Certain specific statistics were alarming, particularly the rates of deaths of mothers in childbirth and of infantile malnutrition. If a family head was unemployed and little income was coming into the family budget, they would not share equally in the general improvement in living standards. Within poor or unemployed families, investigators concurred that it was the wives and mothers who suffered most, because they denied themselves food to keep up the strength of their growing children and their husbands, who might need their strength if work became available, or for walking or cycling to search for work in order to fulfil the criterion of 'genuinely seeking work'. Chronic indigestion and anaemia were often diagnosed. When John Boyd Orr constructed an adequate diet, that is one that not only maintained life but allowed those who lived on it to live healthily, he calculated that 10 per cent of British people ate inadequately in every respect, in calories, protein, fat, calcium, iron, phosphorus and vitamins A and C. The diet of the next 20 per cent who had slightly higher incomes was adequate only in fat and protein. In all, half the population was below the required standard for one or more essential nutrients. The poorest of the unemployed easily fell prey to deficiency diseases such as rickets, anaemia, tuberculosis and rotting teeth. They were not literally starving, because basic foodstuffs were indeed cheap. In 1935 a parliamentary answer to Mr. Gallagher, the Communist MP for West Fife, quoted the following prices: milk at 2½d. a pint, cheese at 8½d. a pound, sugar at 2½d. a pound. Bacon could be found at 11½d. a pound, potatoes at 6¾d. for seven pounds and butter at 2¼d. a pound. A newspaper cost a penny. A typical budget, for a Lancashire family of six, consisting of an unemployed mill worker, his wife and four children, was:

Rent	8/8d.
Coal	3/6d.
Gas and water	2/6d.
Insurance and Trade Union	3/1d.
Subscription Co-op club	1/0d.
Clothing	6d.
Meat	2/0d.
Milk	2/6d.
Bread	4/8½d.
Margarine	2/0d.
Jam	7d.

These items totalled £1.11.0½d. The family received a dole of £1.11.6d. This left 5½d. for any other costs. Pawning some items produced another few shillings, but this could be done only once.

The Perception of Unemployment

Unemployed men usually went to the Labour Exchange, to which employers would notify vacancies, but the novelist Norman Collins's character Mr. Puddy, in his novel *London Belongs to Me*, published in 1945 but set in 1938, considers himself a cut above this and attends Bowman's Employment Agency. It costs him 5s. to register as well as half his first week's pay of £2.5s. as a night watchman in a London warehouse. In relatively prosperous Coventry, in the Midlands, the author J. B. Priestley recounted what he might have seen a century earlier when a 22-year-old man who, together with his father, had been unemployed for many years and was not entitled for some reason to the dole, carried the author's luggage to a hotel, for which Priestley gave him a generous two shillings. Priestley also describes teenagers who had never worked. They seemed to have no anxiety or loss of self-respect. Undisciplined and carefree, they had no sense of responsibility and so, in the author's view, would not make reliable employees. These were perhaps two extremes: one, Puddy, considers himself a class above the unemployed because he has a job, though with a low wage, while the others, the teenagers, joyfully seize the opportunity not to work.

How much did people who worked and lived outside the depressed areas know or care? John Stevenson, a leading historian of the period, remarks that the protest or 'hunger' marches were not supported by the Labour Party or the Trades Union Conference. Moreover, in the absence of the instant journalism and television of later times, the public was not always aware of the situation in the depressed areas. The result was that unemployment was considered by many as a regional rather than a national matter. There was not enough political pressure to insist on an American-style 'New Deal' expansion of the economy, and the weak Labour Party refused to accept a Popular Front alliance of the Left and Centre such as had won the June 1936 elections in France.

Moreover, unemployed workers themselves were rarely militant. No lives were lost in British industrial disputes, in contrast with the United States where police had fired on militant strikers. The Communist Party of Great Britain had received only slightly over 27,000 votes in the 1935 general election. It achieved its highest membership ever – a mere 18,000 – in December 1938. Throughout the latter 1930s there was only one Communist MP. This was Willie Gallagher, a militant who represented West Fife in Scotland where his personal popularity earned him over one-third of the votes in the 1935 election. Public opinion was, broadly speaking, equally divided. The Conservatives had received 48 per cent of the votes at the general elections of November 1935, while Labour had attracted just under 40 per cent, but the electoral system gave Labour only 154 seats. The Liberal and Liberal National parties had received just over 5 per cent each, which meant that the Conservative government maintained a sizeable parliamentary majority. Despite mass unemployment, unions were rarely militant, and overt protest was limited to little more than minor scuffles. William Woodruff describes a demonstration by unemployed men in Blackburn (Lancashire) in 1931, when he himself, a 15-year-old boy pushing a grocer's cart, was accused of being a lackey because he had a job delivering bread and other items of food to middle-class homes. Walter Greenwood's famous novel *Love on the Dole* describes a protest march that the police break up brutally, but whether it actually happened is unknown. In mid-December 1938 a group of unemployed men staged a sit-down in central London's Oxford Circus, demanding work building air-raid shelters, but dispersed peacefully. In February 1939, Professor J. B. S. Haldane, a prominent socialist, led eighty unemployed men to Primrose Hill, a high point in North London, in an appeal for similar work. Other unemployed men conducted a well-mannered sit-in in the Ritz Hotel, ordering afternoon tea from bemused waiters. Their intention was to awaken consciousness, which suggests that middle- and upper-class people who lived in the capital had little awareness of the plight of the workless. Even if the bulk of the population of Britain were vaguely aware of the condition of the unemployed, they came to accept it as inevitable, perhaps as overpopulation in India was seen.

To visitors from more prosperous areas, the unemployed, standing in small groups on street corners, leaning on lampposts, kicking empty cans and puffing on cheap cigarettes, or playing pitch and toss or setting dogs on rats, seemed apathetic. George Orwell, in his famous *The Road to Wigan Pier*, in which he recounts his experience of life among the unemployed, put their passivity down to

> fish-and-chips, art-silk stockings, tinned salmon, cut-price chocolate (five two-ounce bars for sixpence), the movies, the radio, strong tea and the Football Pools

However, Orwell seems to be referring here to low-waged rather than unemployed workers, for whom the dole would allow few of the pleasures he mentions. In prosperous London one saw unemployed miners, accustomed to chapel choirs, singing in the streets for money, while

October 1936 witnessed what became the iconic image of unemployment: the Jarrow March, when 200 unemployed men marched to the capital from that town in North-East England where the local shipyard had closed. The Jarrow marchers were cheered, but they were not received by the prime minister. Their petition for work was received by Parliament, but not debated. The plight of the unemployed in the depressed areas was rarely in the ken of the more prosperous South, even though novels such as Walter Greenwood's *Love on the Dole*, travel books such as J. B. Priestley's *English Journey* and journalistic-type documentaries such as Orwell's *The Road to Wigan Pier* were widely read. An exhibition in Charing Cross Underground Station about unemployed life in the depressed areas was visited by 80,000 people.

There was even resentment, often underlined in the press, on the part of people who were earning enough to pay income tax, at the 'hand-outs' as they called them, given to unemployed men. Some people wondered why compulsory work camps undertaking public works could not be created. Some indeed were, though they were voluntary and created to help young unemployed men to gain skills and maintain their health. Reports varied; some found them a stimulating experience while others described them as resembling concentration camps, with poor material conditions and unsympathetic staff. One telling statistic for 1937 contrasts the 1.5 million unemployed with the 2.5 million people who held driving licences, and the nearly 2 million private cars that were on the road. The world of the unemployed was far distant both physically and in the awareness of the man washing his car in a treelined outer London suburb.

Recovery

Hope for a limited recovery arose when in 1934 the government introduced the Special Areas Act. The Act appointed commissioners for South Wales, Tyneside, West Cumberland and Scotland, and invested in projects such as the new integrated iron, steel and tinplate plant in Ebbw Vale. There were further measures taken in 1935, followed by the Special Areas (Amendment) Act of 1937. This provided some direct limited State investment in the depressed regions and offered taxation and rental concessions to encourage industry to start up in the areas of high unemployment. Government grants were used to set up training centres, often run by philanthropic interests, in areas where unemployment was severe. Up to a thousand such centres were in operation by the end of the

1930s and between 150,000 and 200,000 men were involved at various times. However, Conservative economic policy forbade any major drive to soak up the tens of thousands of unemployed men by large investments in public works such as those that Franklin D. Roosevelt's presidency created in the US. The substantial increase of 46 per cent in industrial production that did come about took place mostly in the Midlands and South-East England. Chemicals, electrical industries and motor vehicle output surged, and the building industry boomed, giving rise in its turn to demand for labour, bricks, tiles, cement, timber, gas and sewer pipes, glass, and furniture, as well as expansion in local and central government departments and in commercial offices. By 1937 the index of industrial production had climbed to 147 (taking 1925–29 as 100), and 1.3 million more people were employed than in 1932. Profits had increased by 10 per cent over the same period, and wages by 7 per cent.

Great optimism was created by the transatlantic liner *Queen Mary*, as it glided down the Clydeside slipway in pouring rain on Tuesday, 26 September 1934 after Queen Mary had launched it in the presence of 200,000 people. Construction of the ship had begun on 27 December 1930 but had been suspended for two years at the depth of the Depression. On Friday, 10 December 1931, 3,000 shipbuilders were laid off and 10,000 other Glaswegians working in auxiliary trades lost their jobs or went on short time. Clydeside was dead. The rusting hulk of the new liner became symbolic of the Depression.

The government had now agreed to make credits available. As the crowds of workmen poured into the shipyard on the day that work began again, they were cheered on their way by bagpipers. The *Queen Mary* provided a great boost of optimism, but this was hardly justified yet. Things would be different on 27 September 1938 when the *Queen Mary*'s sister ship, the *Queen Elizabeth*, was launched, for by then rearmament was roaring ahead. As William Woodruff recounts in *Beyond Nab End*, the sequel to his *The Road to Nab End*, his father, unemployed for years when cotton weaving collapsed, was at work once more, no longer in a Blackburn mill, but with Rolls-Royce in Derby. Other men and their families had migrated to where work was available. One hunger-marcher from Wales tramped through the boom town of Slough, twenty miles west of London. He recalled that 'The Welsh accents were so thick that I thought I was in the Rhondda, with this difference: instead of silent pits, the massive factories all lit up were in full go'. The population of this Berkshire town, 33,612 in 1931, had risen with migration from the depressed regions to 50,000, 620,000 by 1939. Another 1930s boom town to which people flocked from the depressed areas was Luton (Bedfordshire). The prosperity that Vauxhall Motors and the other firms brought to Luton helped the town pass through the depression of the 1930s with very little of the hardship for which the period is remembered. In 1934 the *Luton News* proudly announced that Luton had the lowest percentage of unemployed workers in the country. This made the town a huge magnet from all over the country for those seeking work and a better standard of living. Families from depressed areas, including Tyneside in England and Clydeside in Scotland, moved to Luton, triggering yet another wave of expansion as houses were built for the newcomers.

Work

Between 1923 and 1938 the number of coalminers fell from over 1.25 million to 700,000; cotton workers totalled 439,000 in 1923 but only 251,000 in 1938. In the iron and steel industry the total fell from 185,000 in 1923 to 152,000. In shipbuilding, the 282,000 of 1920 had fallen by half to 129,000 in 1938. Where had they gone? If not still on the unemployed register, workers had moved to motor vehicle building, bicycle and aircraft construction, the electrical trades, other industries and building, as well as the various distributive trades that gave work and income to close on 2 million men and women. More and more men were working in large modern factories with over 500 workers each. Public works contracting, general engineering and what official statistics described as 'miscellaneous services' included activities where the numbers employed between 1923 and 1938 doubled. In 1933 the completion of the National Grid, a network of power stations connected by high-voltage transmission lines carried by pylons, had brought widespread electrical power and had encouraged the growth of light industry and manufacturing in the suburbs around large cities away from the coalfields. London and the towns around it saw dramatic growth in the production of a varied panorama of small items, among them radios, batteries, vacuum cleaners, electric lamps, radiant fires, extractor fans, gas and electricity meters, ladies' stockings, cameras, photographic materials, scientific and surgical instruments, paints and an endless list of finished goods. Numerous service industries flourished, among them huge and luxurious new cinemas, dog racing in massive stadia, hairdressing and tailoring, as well as catering in bright new restaurants and milk bars for an increasing number of people who ate out. Girls were able to find employment in factories where their nimble fingers and ability to concentrate and work accurately on repetitive tasks were demanded, such as in assembling radio or telephone parts, electrical items and fuse boxes. In 1938 70 per cent of school-leavers began work when they reached their fourteenth birthday, but very many had been working for several hours a week already in shops and delivery services. The demand for juveniles was high and continuous in the 1930s because they were cheap. In some ways, jobs for boys tended to be dead-end such as errand boys, messengers or newspaper sellers. But the fall in the birth rate during the Great War had reduced the numbers of teenagers in the early 1930s. One teenager, Harry Simons, living in Hackney in East London, whose elder brothers had gone into tailors' workshops or factories, now found a job as a dispatch clerk in a shoe factory. Now there were jobs for machine-tool setters, motor-car fitters, skilled craftsmen in factories producing both military and civil aircraft, domestic machines such as gas and electric cookers, refrigerators, vacuum cleaners, table lamps, wirelesses, gramophones, water heaters and electric irons. There was work for drivers of delivery lorries and vans, who were steadily replacing horses and carts. J. B. Priestley, driving along the new arterial Great West Road, noted that he saw bright new factories producing potato crisps, perfumes, toothpaste and fire extinguishers. In 1936 the Chancellor of the Exchequer, Neville Chamberlain, proclaimed in his budget speech that industrial output had increased by 29 per cent, Britain had increased its exports by £50 million, and £70 million of National Debt had been redeemed. Additionally, growing international tension persuaded the British government to spend an annually increasing budget on rearmament, which contributed to rising employment. Among the many firms that were reanimated was Cammell-Laird of Birkenhead. Idle in 1932, in 1934 it was awarded a £3 million contract to construct the Royal Navy's new aircraft carrier *Ark Royal*, giving work and wages to hundreds of men and bringing prosperity back to streets and shops.

In the latter 1930s the economy was rapidly expanding. Out of the mergers of the interwar years rose giant concerns such as Imperial Chemical Industries, Unilever and Shell, which had thousands of employees. The Ford factory at Dagenham (Essex) set up the mass production of motor vehicles and gave work to 7,000 employees. Austin and Morris did likewise in the Midlands. Chain stores multiplied: Marks and Spencer, defying the depression, opened 129 stores in the early part of the thirties. Between 1929 and 1939 its annual turnover rose from nearly £2.4 million to nearly £23.4 million. It joined other stores such as Woolworth's, Sainsbury's, Boot's Chemists, which added 200 more outlets to the thousand it had opened by 1933, and clothing chains such as Montagu Burton and British Home Stores. By 1939 the department and chain stores were selling British people 15 per cent of their clothes and shoes. By 1935 half of the largest British companies had headquarters buildings in London. These large companies – Shell, ICI, London Transport and others – employed huge staffs in their offices and on their shop floors. Particularly in the South and the Midlands, openings appeared for shop workers, office staff, transport employees, and the service sector in general. Middle-class 'white-collar' employees became business executives, bookkeepers, insurance clerks, operators of business machines, telephonists and shorthand typists, so that by 1939 white-collar jobs employed a quarter of the working population. Nevertheless, any steady job was valuable and enjoyed status. Robert Barltrop, a schoolboy in Walthamstow, a London outer suburb, had an aunt whose boyfriend had been a public lavatory attendant. On marriage he became the respected caretaker at the public library. Robert remembered that he always wore a well-pressed suit and highly polished shoes.

Working Conditions

At the same time, the Shops Act of 1934 and the Factories Act of 1937 improved working conditions for women and young people. The reforms laid down that young people under the age of 16 could not be employed for more than forty-four hours a week, and if between 16 and 18 years old they were limited to forty-eight weekly hours. All the same, in some casual trades, survivors of Victorian 'sweated' conditions, small workshops, agriculture, whenever work was available or if there was a 'rush' on, perhaps before Christmas, or in seasonal trades, employees worked very long hours, sometimes quite legally. In 1938 the average weekly number of hours worked by adult men in the 'principal' industries, that is those which were inspected, was almost forty-eight and women laboured for forty-three and a half hours weekly. Ten- or twelve-hour shifts were not rare. Except for enlightened firms such as Marks and Spencer's and Cadbury's Chocolate 'village' at Bournville, near Birmingham, canteen, washroom and lavatory provision was not high up in employers' concerns, while accidents and sickness were caused by working conditions, bad lighting, high or low temperatures, and absence of safety regulations (men filmed at work in the building trades or constructing the Tube in London in the 1930s do not appear to be wearing protective clothing or helmets). Consequently, the number of fatal accidents at work in Britain between the wars was almost twice what it would be in the 1960s.

Women at Work

Even though social pressure encouraged women's role as housewives, and only 10 per cent of married women worked, over 30 per cent of single women of working age were earning a wage. As late as 1939 the largest number of working women were domestic servants, although this figure had fallen from its highest point in 1931. Domestic service, where the difficulty of finding servants was a frequent complaint by prospective employers, was seen by government as a way of offering jobs to unemployed women. An average of 4,000 to 5,000 women were trained each year between the wars in residential courses. However, being a kitchen maid or a 'cook-general' in a middle-class home where you had a tiny room and had to carry out almost all the domestic labour, with little time off, no privacy, and you endured another woman ordering you about in a high-class 'la-di-da' voice, was not to the taste of most young women. Even the Ministry of Labour accepted that refusal to accept a job as a 'skivvy' – and most of the women offered domestic work did not have the knowledge to do more than the least skilled household tasks – ought not to be a reason to deny them unemployment benefit, and so in 1938 domestic servants came at last under the shelter of the insurance scheme. Before then a woman who was dismissed or walked out had nothing to fall back on. She had no protection against an unfavourable reference. Nevertheless, in the 1930s domestic service was still the major female occupation. The 7 January 1938 issue of the *Willesden Chronicle* carried very few adverts by domestics offering their services, but many long columns announcing vacancies and promising all sorts of good conditions. But conditions were hard and the wages low: perhaps £1 a week rising to as much as 27/6d. for a skilled cook, although accommodation and food were provided. A pound a week might have been more than a girl working in a shop or a factory would have had left after rent, food, bus fares, fuel and other outgoings. The maid might even be able to send a few shillings back to her family in one of the depressed areas of the country. On the other hand, the servant might have to pay the cost of her uniform. And her hours were long and her days off were rare. You would not be a domestic if you had a reasonable alternative.

Other women found new openings. Office jobs and work in new factories were thought suitable for women, who could be paid less than men. Perhaps the nearest to domestic service was in catering. Lyons's Corner Houses employed a host of waitresses, called 'nippies', and the expansion of restaurants, cafés and milk bars offered work that was preferable to domestic service, not only because the employer did not seek to control a woman's life away from work, or change her name to suit her social class, as was not unknown in private domestic employment, but because there was some legal protection for her wages and conditions, she had company of her own age and she met new people, which might increase her marriage opportunities. Moreover, her hours were fewer than in domestic service. Next in preference would be factory work. It had long been accepted that even married women could work in some industries, notably cotton and in the Staffordshire Potteries. In the cotton mills, the non-managerial staff was almost completely female. They worked long hours, usually from 7.30 a.m. to 5.30 p.m. Working conditions were bad, the mills were noisy, the atmosphere was humid, and the women's earnings peaked at about 38s. per week. A study the Mass-Observation organisation of the cotton town of Bolton (Lancashire) in 1937 reported that 30,000 women were working in 120 still-active mills. The huge buildings dominated the skyline, pouring out their smoke. Inside the mills it was warm and damp, dusty and noisy as the looms clattered. But at least work in the cotton mills offered some sort of career progression as one's skills increased. It was better than the unpopular alternative of being a kitchen maid for most girls when they left school. Even better, girls in Bolton aimed to work in the big stores, such as Woolworth's. Marks and Spencer's was particularly popular because it ran a progressive staff welfare service. But office work for women offered higher pay and status than either factory jobs or domestic service, as was reflected in the large and growing number of women working in offices by 1938. A mother might insist that her daughters attend classes in shorthand and typing so that she would step up in social status by leaving the 'common' factory floor or the demeaning wearing of uniform and formal subordination of domestic service. She would join the lower middle classes and perhaps meet a middle-class marriage partner.

In general, women were not expected to see their jobs as more than an intermediate step between school and marriage, when they would, if family income allowed, devote themselves to their husbands and children. Both employers and trade unions saw this as desirable. Management was almost entirely male. Yet women provided around 30 per cent of the labour force in 1931. By that year, out of between 5.5 and 6 million working women,

1.5 million worked in public administration, commerce, and 500,000 in the new, expanding light industries. Even in the professions, which as well as being restrictive required long training with the support of parents, that was often denied, by 1935 there were 135 women solicitors, 79 barristers and 2,810 doctors, almost all general practitioners.

Britain was highly industrialised. Only 5 or 6 per cent of the labour force worked on farms. British agriculture, deeply depressed because of the competition of cheap food imports, was backward. Wages were low. One-quarter of rural parishes had no piped water supply, while only a minority of farms were connected to the National Electricity Grid. In 1939 horses were much more frequently seen than tractors. Farm workers had little access to shops or any of the steadily improving benefits of town life.

Chapter 2

Incomes, Outgoings and the Cost of Living

Widespread unemployment bore heavily on both the skilled and unskilled working class in the 1930s, particularly for coalminers, cotton-industry operatives and shipbuilders, and in the older industrial regions of the North of England, parts of Central Scotland and South Wales, but men who retained their jobs profited by the even greater fall in prices. There was no great collapse of wage rates, except in areas of high unemployment where people who sought work would have to take what employers offered. Rates of pay were reduced by substantial percentages in the cotton, wool, shipbuilding and construction industries, in many cases in a desperate effort to keep the industry or business solvent. This reflected sometimes small employers' greed, but also, and especially in the case of shopkeepers, the reduction in their turnover in places where their largely unemployed customers had little to spend. But for people who were in work, wages were maintained even during the crisis of the early 1930s; the 1931 budget-balancing cuts in the salaries of teachers, police and civil servants were restored in 1934, and wages started to rise as recovery began halfway through the decade. Historians have pointed out that social and revolutionary disturbances were avoided in Britain because even the dole for a family man was not far below the lowest wage, though the latter was very low indeed. Nevertheless, by 1936 wages had regained the losses suffered during the acute period of the Depression, and from then till 1938 the average tendency was upward. It seems likely, then, that for those who managed to stay in full-time employment in the 1930s standards of living rose significantly.

The average, however, concealed wide differences in earnings. In 1937 agricultural labourers, at the bottom of the scale, earned (to the nearest shilling) about £1.14s. a week, though they might have the doubtful benefit of a damp and crumbling 'tied' cottage that they would have to vacate when they retired. In his *English Journey* J. B. Priestley cites the case of a night watchman in the cotton town of Blackburn (Lancashire). He was paid £1.16s. a week, slightly more than and his family might have received in benefit if he had no job. Goods porters on the railways earned £2.7s. Building labourers and labourers employed by local authorities earned £2.15s. A Bradford warehouseman in the wool business, who had earned between 27s. and 30s. before 1914, was now on 50s. Coalminers, who were subject to notably variable earnings, earned about £3 in a good week. London bus and tram conductors earned £4.3s. Workers in the Potteries got about £3.6s a week, engineering fitters received over £4, compositors slightly more. The average for working men was just under £200 a year or £3.15s. a week. Some, such as wiremen in the newer electrical installation industry, earned more. Agricultural labourers and shop assistants, in contrast, earned much less. Yet no men in the major industries, except railway engine drivers, seem to have reached the magic figure of £4.10s. a week, though workers in the motor-car and motor-cycle industry, centred on the Midlands and London, might reach very close to this figure. Overall, according to an analysis of incomes in 1938, 88 per cent of working men had incomes of less than £5 per week, and 31 per cent of these earned less than £2.10s. The average for men over 21 in manufacturing industries covered by Ministry of Labour surveys was £3.9s. in 1938. Overtime could increase the weekly take-home pay, and those aristocrats of the working-class, the senior engine-drivers and the printers, might draw up to around £5, but in many industries, short-time working and seasonal layoffs would reduce the average figure of take-home pay.

Rather than averages, however, the incomes and outgoings of individual people in different jobs are perhaps more illustrative of the standard of living in the years just before the Second World War. Several budgets of employed family men were described in *The New Survey of London Life and Labour*, of 1935, produced by researchers at the London School of Economics. A railway goods train guard in London received £3.6s. He lived in a very small flat but had a bathroom with a hot water supply. He ate a cooked breakfast and bought his groceries from the Co-op. His hours were irregular, so he had to live near his work, but he did not have to pay fares. He had an allotment on which he grew vegetables. Railwaymen enjoyed privileged free or reduced-fare travel, so he took his holidays in the country, travelling by rail. A goods checker at King's Cross main-line station in London earned £4 a week. Hs rented a flat for himself, his wife, two sons and a daughter. He had a coal shed, an important advantage since his heating and possibly his cooking might have been all with coal. Another checker, probably of a lower grade, earned £3, while his daughter, also employed by the railway, received £1.5.6d. He gave his wife £2.11s. for housekeeping. They went to the cinema and, using their rail travel privileges, travelled occasionally to walk by the Thames at Richmond or visit Kew Gardens (admission to which cost a mere penny) and to the sea at Westcliff in the Thames Estuary. He lived on the London County Council's Becontree estate in Essex, so he had a long journey to work and back. He also worked shifts of nine hours which might begin at 6 a.m. and last till 11 p.m. A senior postal sorter, working at Mount Pleasant in North London, did not have private transport and being obliged to work the night shift in alternate months, had to go home by night bus to Paddington main-line station and catch a train out to Southall in Middlesex, where his income had allowed him to buy a new house. He often missed the train and had to wait for an hour before he could get home and catch up on lost sleep. Similarly, an engine driver earned £4.5s. but if he was on late turn he had to take an all-night bus to get home. His daughter earned 18s. a week. The family occupied a council house with three bedrooms and a bathroom with a hot water supply. He enjoyed free travel on the railway so took two holidays a year and stayed with relatives. A couple where the husband was a docker earning close on £3 per week, if he was not on short time, paid 8/6d. per week for two rooms in a house in Rotherhithe, in London's dock area. They did not spend money on entertainment. In the summer they went hop-picking in Kent as did many poor Londoners. The *Willesden Chronicle* of 7 January 1938 carried an invitation for men to apply to be firemen. Wages in the first year were £3 per week, £.3.5s in the second year, rising by annual increments of 2/6 to £4, then by increments of 2/ a week until they reached £4.8s after eleven years' service. A driver enjoyed an allowance of an extra 2/6 and there was a rent allowance of 10s. This would bring the senior fireman driver up to just over £5 per week. His job carried a pension, for which 5 per cent of his wage was deducted. This was good pay indeed, but dangerous work.

When looking at these examples of mostly low-waged and sometimes irregularly working men, the investigators were struck by how well their wives seemed to have managed to keep the families out of debt, fed, clothed and clean. They noted that a common practice was to save a few pence a week for purchases of occasional needs such as clothing from mail-order firms and paying for them by instalments on low interest. It was a way of buying long-lasting items such as garments and household hardware. Another custom was to shop at the Co-operative Wholesale Society.

The 'Co-op', with its hundreds of local shops, paid an annual dividend based on the amount that had been spent, and this might act as a welcome windfall.

The *New Survey* was offering examples of men working in London. In contrast, in the depressed areas, though unemployment benefit and the dole were supposed to be low enough to make it always worthwhile to work, they did not necessarily do so because some wage rates were abysmally low to start with. A school-leaving girl, 'Mary Smith', not entitled to benefit, was glad to get a job even though it demanded long hours in a seaside town where she would be laid off when autumn came. 'Mary' was paid as little as 6s. a week and was evidently afraid to give her real name to the investigator. In those conditions, the average fall in weekly hours of work was of little relevance to her.

When the novelist J. B. Priestley drove around England in 1933, writing as a social observer and commentator, he selected specific instances to illustrate among other things poverty and social contrasts. He did this in a very personal way when he attended a reunion in Bradford of men of his Great War regiment. Some survivors felt that their clothes simply were not in good enough condition, so they did not come to the reunion, even though the more prosperous veterans had ensured that no charge would be made for their less well-off old comrades. Priestley also visited the mining community of Seaham (County Durham) where he records that one in five men had suffered injuries and that their income rarely topped £2 weekly. In due course, these men would reach the age of 65 and be entitled to the old-age pension of 10s. a week, or somewhat more if they were married. This was, of course, nowhere near enough to live on and one must suppose that their children were expected to help.

Some noted novels of the time describe the earnings and spending of their characters. In Patrick Hamilton's well-known *Hangover Square*, published in 1941 but set in prewar London, the hero, George Harvey Bone, lives, largely in an alcoholic haze, on £4 a week but has £300 in War Loan which would provide £10.10s. a year or about 4s. a week.

In his bestseller *London Belongs to Me*, published in 1945 but relating to 1938–39, Norman Collins's character Mr. Josser retires as the novel begins. He is granted a pension of £2 a week by his firm. His daughter Doris, aged 21, earns a healthy £4 as a London typist. She lives at home as younger, unmarried children, especially girls, did in general, being expected to contribute to the household expenses. However, in the novel she decides to leave home and share rooms with another girl. School-leavers might give all their money to their mothers to help out with living expenses and receive only pocket money and bus fares in return. Fourteen-year-old Esther Simons, living in a poor part of East London in the 1920s with her often unemployed father, two younger siblings and one older working brother, vividly described running home excitedly with her first wage packet of 15s. and handing it over to her mother. It made her feel 'grown-up'. So also, a first-born might be expected to delay marriage until the younger children left school and began to contribute to the household expenses. Such a situation might well go on until the children became adults and could afford to live alone, or even until they married. Mr. Josser's son Ted, who is older and the manager of a Co-op grocery, is paid £6.5s. a week. He has achieved a middle-class income. Similarly, Esther Simons's husband, a milkman who worked for a small private dairy supplying milk to families in East London, earning £5 or sometimes £6 a week in his demanding job, which meant getting up very early, doing two rounds with a waggon and two shire horses in all weathers, and manhandling heavy churns, was even able to buy a very cheap second-hand car, but when his employer went bankrupt, his firm was taken over by one of the big national dairies, and his wage fell drastically.

Middle-Class Incomes

In contrast, middle-class occupations enjoyed incomes of between £4 and £10 a week. As income increased, it would permit employing a domestic cleaner, known as a 'charwoman', and perhaps buying a second-hand car. The very well-off one-fifth of the population, prosperous businessmen and high-ranking professionals, enjoyed an income of over £10 a week or £500 per year. This allowed them to enjoy luxuries such as holidays abroad. Most of these occupations had the inestimable advantage of stable incomes and were not at risk of short-time working, as was common in the building trade, for instance, or of being laid off completely. Salaries in private industry and commerce remained stable at annual averages for a civil service clerical officer of £260 in 1935, £224 for a railway clerk and £368 for a bank clerk, although the female civil service shorthand typist received only £162. Managers in industry earned an average of £440 per year. The civil service and teaching had salaries that were incremental, that is they increased annually over about a dozen years and were pensioned. Benjamin Kimp, a clerk in the office of the Post Office Savings Bank, stationed in London, had spent twenty years rising through the stages of a lower to a higher grade, and then enjoyed promotion to supervisory status, at which stage he had retired at the age of 60 in 1927 with a pension based on his final salary of about £490 per year. He lived in a house in a London suburb for which he paid £38 a year rent. While he had just been able to afford this when his salary had reached £204 at the beginning of the century, the rent was a minor item in his budget thirty-five years later. In the latter 1930s, as he reached the age of 70, he and his wife could enjoy the lower costs of essential goods and discretionary spending.

For teachers, average salary in 1930 for men in secondary schools was £424, and for women £322, somewhat over twice what working men earned. As for professional men, such as barristers (average earnings £1,090 per year) and general medical practitioners (average earnings £1,094), these had more than doubled their incomes since 1914. Middle-class men, nevertheless, had to spend more on clothes, had to save for their retirements if their posts were not pensionable, and had to contribute to private insurances or pay for their medical costs, for which they were not covered by the National Insurance contribution. Middle-class families also paid for their children's education, usually in private schools.

Women who had clerical skills earned considerably more than factory or shop workers. Single women in London and other large cities, such as Pamela Frankau's Sally Fisher in her 1939 novel *The Devil We Know*, 'lived the life of all the straightened, practical young women in London, with meals in a Lyon's teashop, travelling by bus, cheap seats at the cinema, buying "bargain" dresses and shampooing her hair at home on Saturday nights: with severe economy practised from Thursdays onward and two weeks holiday every year. Readers are not told if Sally gets holiday pay. Yet she has a responsible and senior post as secretary to the editor of a monthly magazine, and is well paid, earning as she does £5 a week. Most young women of the time would not have described Sally's life as 'straightened'. Lilian Matfield, in J. B. Priestley's 1930 novel *Angel Pavement*, working for a firm that sells veneers and inlays to cabinetmakers, lives in a hostel for single women where for 25s. or 30s. a week, depending perhaps on the quality and size of the room, she has her accommodation, breakfast and an evening meal provided, as well as lunch at weekends. She had begun her office job in London's financial centre, the City, at a salary of only £3 a week. By the end of the novel, the expansion of the firm has raised her salary to £4.10s a week. Later, as the firm prospers her wage increases to £5, to which she can add the allowance of £6 a month that she receives from her father, a retired medical practitioner. As the narrator comments:

> Any girl at the Burpenfield [the hostel for single women where Lilian Matfield lives] would have instantly appreciated the profound contrast between five pounds a week and four pounds ten shillings, for whereas on four pounds ten you still have to be careful, on five pounds you can really begin to splash about a bit.

Miss Matfield has middle-class expectations, so does not seem to realise that many a working-class family would consider itself comfortably off with £4.10s a week.

Priestley introduces a scene early in the novel in which Smeeth, the chief clerk or office manager, and the firm's owner, Mr. Dersingham, are discussing the need to cut expenses. They list the salaries of the employees. The commercial traveller for the business has a salary of £200 a year and earns commission, while Smeeth himself gets £315 a year. Poppy, Miss Matfield's very junior assistant, earns £2.10s a week. Mr. Turgis, the clerk in his early twenties, is on £3.10s a week. Middle-class office workers like these did not belong to trade unions, nor were they entitled to unemployment benefit once they had incomes of over £250 a year. Consequentially, if business declined, they would have to take a cut in salary. If it failed, they had no protection at all.

Most women and girls, however, earned far less than Miss Matfield. The average for female earnings in 1935 was 27/2d. per week. At a lower level, girls who did not possess clerical skills, but who were considered sufficiently well-spoken and -mannered to deal with the public, could avoid the 'common' females in the workshop or factory and take a job as a waitress at, for example, Quality Inns, one of the new modern high-quality but economical eating places in the larger cities, where the wages were low, though they might make between £1.15s. and £2 a week in tips. Even so, since a London rent for one room could be as much as 14s. a week, not much was left over. The ideal, which was highly sought after, was a job as a 'nippy' in J. Lyons and Company's Corner Houses, which paid 26s. a week and extra for weekend working, and where one might well meet a desirable marriage partner. In contrast, in 1934, the barmaid Ella Dawson in Patrick Hamilton's *The Plains of Cement* earns 22s. a week, but she has her room included and probably her food also.

Rents varied enormously, from a few shillings for poor-quality Victorian cottages and back-to-backs in northern cities, to luxury flats in the West End of London. Some were in purpose-built blocks, such as the 'mansions' built for young couples in late nineteenth- and early twentieth-century London, which were rented for about 30s a week, while a large number of houses were still let at pre-Great War rents which various rent control acts had pegged at levels at 15s. a week or less. In cities a family might occupy part of a house, in which a kitchen had been installed on an upper floor, while the bathroom had to be shared. The cost in London might be 25s. a week but less in the provinces. Smaller flats or a couple of rooms might be let, depending on the area, for 8s. or 10s. a week. Rent, in fact, was a high part of expenditure for a working-class budget, and sometimes a high rent was unavoidable if a man was to live close to his work, as was the case with Esther Simons's husband, the milkman.

If you were prepared to live further away and pay the public transport fares or cycle to work, then for the middle class and for the skilled working class with secure employment, you could buy your house with a loan from a Building Society. The loan was secured by mortgaging the house to the society. Mortgage repayment interest attracted income tax relief so that house purchase became a desirable form of saving. For other small savings, at a day-to-day level, the Post Office Savings Bank offered its almost 10 million (in 1930) account holders an interest rate of 2.5 per cent annually or 6d. in the pound, which was not taxed. This was not as low as it might seem at a time when prices were tending to fall, and it came with the facility to make very small deposits and withdrawals without charge and at any post office in the country. Unsurprisingly, in 1930 33 million transactions took place in post offices, processed by an army of 4,000 clerks.

As for income tax, only 3.7 million people paid it in the 1930s. While a married man earning up to £350 per year with a wife and three children paid little or no income tax, the rates were quite high for those who did come into the tax-paying bracket: the standard rate was 4/6d. in the pound, raised to 5/6d. in 1938 and in 1939 to 7/6 or 37.5 per cent. Surtax affected about 100,000, who enjoyed grand incomes of over £2,000 a year. This was the stratum of luxury spending.

Spending

Even in 1932, with official unemployment standing at the horrifying figure of close on 3 million, a statistic which meant that, considering wives and children, between 6 and 7 million people were living 'on the dole' or not even entitled to it, consumer spending actually staged a limited recovery from its collapse in the previous year. This was not surprising, for prices had hit rock-bottom. In fact, prices of commodities had collapsed. It was said that wheat was being traded in Liverpool at the lowest price since the reign of Charles II in the seventeenth century, and sugar, tobacco, hemp, jute, silk, wool, copper, tea and lead prices had collapsed. Rumour even had it that coffee was being burned in the fireboxes of Brazilian locomotives to try to keep the price up.

As the economist John Maynard Keynes, who advocated inflating the money supply, proclaimed on the wireless on 11 January 1931, 'Therefore, O patriotic housewives of Britain, sally out early tomorrow in the streets and go to the sales … for never were things so cheap … and have the added joy that you are increasing employment …' He was right. Whiteley's in London had reduced the price of men's raincoats from 14/6 to 10s. Ponting's in London's elegant Kensington High Street proclaimed that prices in its spring sale had been cut to the levels of 1914. Artificial silk frocks could be had for 10s., as could ladies' walking shoes. A coat was on sale for a mere pound and a nightdress for 3/11d. The *Willesden Chronicle* of 7 January 1938 carried an advertisement by B. B. Evans, a very large department store in the busy Kilburn High Road in north-west London. Men's dressing gowns could be had for 12/11d., to be worn over pyjamas at 3/11d., while ladies could keep warm in the winter with combinations for 2s., and boys could look smart in three-piece tweed suits for 14/11d. Given that average annual earnings rose sharply from 1936 onward and considering the falling cost of living, in 1938 real earnings were calculated as being 7 per cent higher than in 1930. Another way of looking at the relation between earnings and spending is the calculation made by the historian John Stevenson, that the fall in the prices of many basic foods, such as sugar, flour and meat, and articles such as clothing and furniture, meant that a working-class family which had spent three-quarters of its income on rent and food in 1914 was spending less than half on those items in 1937–38 and thus had money available for elective spending. On the other hand, the official cost of living indexes may have suggested that prices were dropping more than they were or that the falls were in items, such as candles, which were not significant in the spending of a working-class household. Nevertheless, from a base figure of 100 in 1906–10, the index of prices had risen to its highest point after the Great War to 186 in 1925, but then had fallen back to 148 in 1933.

However, the fall in prices was of little importance to the unemployed, because they had money only for the basic necessities, even if cheapness of some items made life markedly more pleasant for people in regular work. On the other hand, it allowed a family where the breadwinner was unemployed to maintain life, but this would be on a diet that consisted of a monotonous minimum of basic foodstuffs, such as bread, potatoes, margarine, tea, and now and then fish and chips. There was certainly no margin for extras. A close examination of the population of Sheffield showed that two out of five working-class people were suffering serious hardship. So, while several surveys, notably in Bristol in 1937 and in York in the previous year, concluded that absolute poverty was less common in the 1930s than before 1914, up to 30 per cent of the population, particularly in areas of high unemployment, found it hard to maintain a life that could satisfy more than basic human needs.

Yet generational changes were beginning to take place behind the dark curtain of unemployment or low incomes. Families were becoming smaller, so wages would go further. In 1933 the birth rate fell to its lowest level ever of 14.5 per 1,000 of the population. The overall population nevertheless increased because improvements in public health, medical advances and better nourishment led to a reduction in the death rate. While in 1900 this had stood at just over 18 per 1,000, and there had been 154 deaths per 1,000 of children in their first year of life, by 1938 these figures had fallen to 11.5 and 54.

In the 1930s, wages in the depressed areas were low, and often not much higher than what a married man with children could claim on the dole. At least 12 per cent of the insured population were without work for considerable amounts of time and were living on rates of benefit and 'dole' that Sir John Boyd Orr in his influential report described as not providing enough for adequate nourishment. Yet there were more cars on the road, more new houses, and wireless sets, and food was very cheap, having fallen by more than the average rate of deflation: sugar by 50 per cent, frozen meat by 17 per cent, and flour by 14 per cent. Average standards of consumption, of food and a range of other consumables, increased in the later 1930s, particularly for the employed worker, though not for the unemployed man and his family. For most middle-class salaried people, however, unemployment was an unfamiliar experience.

The middle-class family with an income of over £250 a year could consider buying a house with the aid of a loan from a building society. In addition, however, they had to pay municipal rates, water rates and insurance. To keep up with the neighbours and be 'respectable', they had to keep their house in good condition. So, before the age of do-it-yourself, they had to pay for repairs and indoor and exterior decoration, and they also had to bear the cost of maintaining a garden which would be a matter of pride and competitiveness. A house cost more to heat than a couple of rooms, so coal, electricity and gas charges had to be allowed for in budgeting. The season ticket on the train to the office cost perhaps £20 a year and you bought at least two newspapers every day to read on the journey. Another daily periodical might be delivered for your wife to read at home. Its delivery had to be paid for and the paperboy, as well as sundry other people such as the postman, the dustman and the butcher and grocer's boys, would expect Christmas boxes. The middle-class wife of course did not work and expected regular domestic help from a charwoman. Once the man of the family was receiving a sufficiently healthy salary she would expect a live-in servant. A cook and a maid are commonly pictured in novels of the 1930s set in a middle-class context. Mr. Brown, father of the notorious William in Richmal Crompton's highly popular series of humorous novels about William the schoolboy and his upper middle-class family and their friends, published from the 1920s onward, employs a maid and a cook. He pays for William's education, and subscriptions to various local clubs, as well as a gardener. William's brother Robert is 'at college', for which it may be assumed that Mr. Brown is also paying fees. If medical or dental treatment were required, it had to be paid for. Surgery and post-operative convalescence, including perhaps a private nurse for a few weeks, were costly. Food, however, while still the major individual component of the budget, represented only between about a fifth to a quarter of the expenditure of the middle-class family. The higher the family income, the smaller the proportion spent on food and the more left over for elective spending. Thus, the middle classes, especially those receiving salaries of over about £500 a year, indulged in the consumption boom, which included not only houses, but motor cars, foreign holidays and other items considered 'luxuries'.

Chapter 3

Where and How They Lived

In 1934, Odette Keun, a widely travelled Dutch journalist and socialist, published a book with the title *I Discover the English.* She had little complimentary to say about housing in Britain. She had been appalled at what she called the 'dismal and dreary' slums. Even houses where well-off people lived were poorly insulated and lacked central heating. Bathrooms were freezing. There was coal smoke everywhere. The kitchens were in dark basements. The streets of foggy British cities were irregularly named and numbered and lined with dull rows of unimaginatively designed houses. To live in these houses people paid high rents. The poor suffered most; Keun gave an example of a family of seven living on unemployment benefit where the rent charged was 11/6d. for three rooms and a kitchen.

British housing was varied. The city-dwelling working class and lower middle class, who formed most of the population, usually lived in terraces, as close to their place of work as possible, without hot running water, and without electricity until the 1930s. People lived in a house or a flat, or rooms, or just one room. A flat might be purpose-built and self-contained or merely one floor of a house.

In the 1930s most people rented their homes. The owner had usually bought the house as a leasehold. This meant that it would eventually have to be returned with the land on which it stood to the freeholder or owner of the land, who was usually a large landowner or even the Church of England. As the years passed, the lease, originally issued for ninety-nine years, grew shorter and thus the house fell in value. Because the leaseholder was less willing to spend money on it, many were in bad condition. Houses rented by one tenant were often sublet into flats and rooms. The ground floor had the garden. The middle floor flat in a large house was relatively spacious. At the top of larger properties there were a couple of attics that had been intended to house the servants of the middle-class family for which the houses had originally been designed. There was only one bathroom at the most, and additional kitchen space had to be made for the multiple families that might be occupying the property. The bottom or basement rooms would probably have a coke-burning 'range' for cooking and space and water heating, but these facilities were not usually extended to the other floors.

There were still very many areas of poor-quality or 'slum' houses. Rapidly thrown up in the previous century, they were often damp. The roofs leaked because the slates and the gutters were broken. They needed new plastering and were often alive with bugs. Sometimes the floorboards had perished. They had no bathrooms. The tenants washed their clothes and themselves in a small, dank yard or perhaps a washhouse under a cold-water tap. The water closet or lavatory, used by all the inhabitants of the house, was outside, built up against the back wall. In some industrial areas of Britain, several houses might share the washing and lavatory facilities. Leeds, one of the big Yorkshire cities, was notorious for its large number of 'back-to-back' houses built close up against each other, with no backyards and with front doors opening directly from the street on to the ground-floor room. Over-occupied, sometimes with three or more people to a room, and burning coal for cooking and warmth, these badly maintained houses' areas were occupied at low rents by the poorest people.

While some municipal authorities led energetic campaigns of reform, slums were still widespread at the end of the 1930s. On 7 January 1938, for instance, the *Willesden Chronicle*, circulating in a suburb just outside the north-west London boundary, reported on a slum in a local street, Granville Road, where a Mr. and Mrs. McKay and their ten children lived in a basement with no door on the lavatory, damp walls and a hole in the ceiling. Mr. McKay was living on unemployment pay. His income probably did not allow him to pay more than the rent he was being charged, but the local newspaper considered the situation of the family intolerable and published a long letter from a reader attacking the lack of energy on the part of the local sanitary officials for not enforcing basic regulations. In Bolton, a northern town and cotton centre, which had recovered slightly from the slump, by 1937 700 of the worst properties had been demolished and some back-to-back houses had been dealt with. Yet bed bugs and insufficient ventilation were still common. The water supply was unsatisfactory, and there were not enough taps. Sometimes there was no gas supply and thus the only way to heat water was in a kettle over a coal fire. Light was provided by paraffin lamps or even in some cases candles. The water closets were in the yard, dirty, smelly, often blocked, cracked, cold and dark. The local Medical Officers of Health reported that tuberculosis and abdominal disorders were endemic in such places.

Even worse was the two-up two-down weaver's cottage shared, as his autobiography recounts, in Blackburn (Lancashire) by William Woodruff, his brother, two sisters and their parents. There was only one tap in the house, and a single gas-ring financed by a penny-in-the-slot meter. The lavatory in the yard had no flush, no light and no seat. In the summer the smell of rotting garbage was pervasive, and clouds of flies brought regular upset stomachs. Bugs, damp, cold and lack of privacy were the normal experiences of life.

Even in houses in better condition, a poor urban family might have only one or two rooms. Life was hard, especially for the wife and mother. She might not even have a kitchen but would share a gas stove and perhaps a sink on a landing with another tenant. There would be only one bathroom, which each tenant would use once a week. It might not have a hot water supply so water would have to be heated elsewhere and brought to it. Alternatively, baths could be taken at the public baths or in a portable bath in front of the fire, and successive children would have to share the water. Railway travellers would often see tin baths hanging up on the walls in back yards as the train passed behind long terraces of such houses. Margaret Powell, famous for her books about life as a servant in the first half of the twentieth century, recalled a five-floor house just off Ladbroke Grove in West London. Three families lived on each floor, each of them in one or two rooms. Because they would not cooperate to keep the common parts clean there was an appalling smell. Each two floors were provided with one small sink and a water closet.

People who were slightly better off, such as lower-middle-class clerical workers or better-paid working men in stable jobs, could take any of the abundant flats advertised in the local press at rents ranging from about a pound to 'thirty bob' or £1.10s. a week. When Esther Simons, her husband and small child moved to north-west London in 1938 they took three rooms and a kitchen with a gas cooker in a house with three floors and a basement, which had been put up in the 1880s for renting to one family with live-in servants. The house had one bathroom, where a geyser provided hot water. There was an indoor lavatory and another one in the garden up against the rear wall. The basement flat was occupied by another couple with a daughter and a teenage son. It had a kitchen range, which produced hot water for them all year round.

Later, Esther, her husband and son moved to a nearby mansion flat. Mansion flats, which builders had begun to put up for middle-class and childless couples in London in the later nineteenth century, were self-contained. This one had a porter who removed domestic refuse and took coal to the upper floors from the cellars where the tenants kept their fuel. The coal fed the very modern 'Ideal' boiler which heated the kitchen as well as a tankful of water. The 'Ideal' provided hot water in the kitchen and bathroom during the winter, but in the summer these mansion flat dwellers boiled water in kettles for their washing-up. The bathroom had a stuttering and possibly dangerous gas geyser, which had been put in as the height of modernity at the beginning of the century, and in the summer, when the boiler was not lit, provided a slow supply of hot water. However, you had to transfer the hot water from there to the washbasin, so hand and face washing, as well as shaving, tended to take place in the kitchen, where it was warm in the winter, when the bathroom was glacial. More modern kitchens and bathrooms had an 'Ascot', that is an enamelled and quite small, gas-heated gadget that provided very hot water wherever it was placed. You could have an Ascot over the kitchen sink, one over the bath and another over the washbasin. The Ascot lived up to its advertising jingle:

Happy in the morning
As the water's hot
We can bathe an army
The Ascot's done the lot

An alternative way to produce hot water, especially in the summer when the boiler was not lit, was an 'immersion' heater, which was an electric element immersed in a tank, but this was not possible to install without what was known as 'power', that is a 240-volt electric circuit. Neither the older 'mansion' flats nor the newer 'luxury' ones had central heating. In the winter, outside the warm and sometimes stiflingly hot kitchens, the flats were icy. Nevertheless, every room had a fireplace and chimney, which would have been tended probably by a resident maid when the mansion flat was first built. The maid would have slept in a tiny bedroom at the end of a long corridor. A trace of her one-time presence was the push button over the bath, by which Madam could summon the maid to bring a warmed towel. However, whatever its disadvantages, Esther and her husband, now managing a prosperous business, had a self-contained flat, with an imposing entrance and a wide and carpeted staircase, a porter, three bedrooms, a huge reception room and a bathroom just for her and her family. The rent for the former flat had been 25s. a week; for the mansion flat, it was only 5s. more.

In the high and airy North London borough of Hampstead, on 10 July 1937 the local newspaper advertised a top-floor flat of two rooms with kitchen, for £60 per year. On the first floor a 'huge' sitting room and bedroom and kitchen were for rent at £85. The 'garden' floor offered two large rooms and a kitchen for £72. The cheapest accommodation offered in the classified advertisements that week was in Adelaide Road, alongside the railway, where two attic rooms and a sink could be rented for 12/6d. a week. In his novel *London Belongs to Me* Norman Collins chooses it as a place where Doris Josser shares a couple of rooms with her friend Doreen.

Tenants would often sublet. In *London Belongs to Me*, Mrs. Vizzard, the main tenant of No. 10, Dulcimer Street, an early Victorian house in the inner London suburb of Kennington, thinks it is common to offer a room to let by putting a card in the window, so she advertises in *Dalton's Weekly*, a publication devoted to all forms of trade and private advertisements. Mrs. Josser, one of the sub-tenants, lets her daughter's room when the latter moves out. In the same novel, Mr. Puddy, the obese failed manager of a dairy, lives in the attic; Connie, the cloakroom attendant in a Soho nightclub, occupies the back room on the second floor; Mrs. Boon and her son Percy, a car mechanic, live in the room at the back of the first floor. The Jossers occupy the ground floor. Mrs. Vizzard herself, a widow, lives in the front basement. The lease on the house has only eighteen years to run before the house will have to be given up to the freeholder.

It was becoming fashionable for the well-off, especially in London, to live in modern flats, very well provided with facilities and comforts. These had spread during the 1920s. 'Court' was the favourite appellation for these elegant blocks. For young middle class couples, with their smaller families, flats were attractive because houses were becoming dearer to maintain and, perhaps more importantly, servants were increasingly difficult to find. Depending on what was offered, modern flats in blocks cost from £70 to £150 a year, including constant hot water and central heating, with a reception room, two bedrooms, kitchen and bathroom. Bigger flats cost more. One, for example, in Putney, south-west of London and attractively situated near the Thames, was offered at rents of between £285 and £350 a year. This flat was spacious, with four bedrooms, two reception rooms, two bathrooms and all modern conveniences. There was a garage, and porters always on duty, a garden and a lift. Some of these 'Courts' even had swimming pools. The ten-storey Florin Court in Central London, alias 'Whitehaven Mansions' where Agatha Christie's fictional detective Hercule Poirot lived, had a pool in the basement and a roof garden. Chiltern Court, built above the Metropolitan Railway's main station in Baker Street, had a hairdressing saloon and possessed flats varying between three and ten rooms, with rents beginning at £300 a year.

Living in flats for the middle and upper class was sufficiently new for William Heath Robinson to publish his *How to Live in a Flat* in 1936, with its amusing if supercilious text and some ingenious if unlikely space-saving inventions, and others, such as fold-down beds, rubbish chutes and many such devices which did in fact materialise later. At the same time, some people used fiery invective as they condemned flat-dwelling as leftish, foreign-like and socially undesirable. In a House of Commons debate in 1938 one member referred to 'the instinct of the English family to prefer even a very commonplace old-fashioned house to one of these modern flats in a five-storey building … We do not want our cities to become, as on the Continent, cities of flat-dwellers,' he sneered. Another speaker condemned flats as 'an abomination … never meant for human beings. Flats make Communists, while cottages make individuals and – incidentally – make good Conservatives. Any sensible Briton would sooner live in a little wooden shack of his own with a quarter of an acre, than in the finest flat or hotel'. Nevertheless, local authority or 'council' blocks of flats were widely to be seen, especially in London, where the London County Council had built large estates. Living in flats in London did not seem strange because so many generations of Londoners had lived for generations in divided houses or even purpose-built flats that private philanthropic funds such as Peabody and Rothschild had erected in the nineteenth century for the 'artisan classes' to provide better housing than the rat-ridden and damp houses where they lived.

In interwar Britain there was a great increase in publicly owned housing, particularly in Scotland where 70 per cent of the housing stock was owned by local authorities. In Bolton one-third of new houses in the 1930s had been built by the council. Most had three bedrooms, separate bathrooms, a garden, and electricity laid on. The standard for public housing was based on the Tudor-Walters report of November 1918 which recommended that houses should have a living-room, a parlour and a scullery, as well as a bathroom and three bedrooms (two of them large enough to contain two beds). There should be a larder, the absence of which had been marked in older housing. Terraces should be short and there should be only twelve houses to the acre. Building of local authority housing expanded and contracted according to how far the government was willing to provide subsidies, but of the 2.5 million houses built between the end of the Great War and 1934, local authorities built nearly one-third. The large council estates were inhabited by some of the immense numbers of almost entirely working-class people moving or being moved out of poor-quality housing in big cities such as Glasgow, London and Birmingham to new estates in rural land outside those cities. Slum-dwellers in Manchester found themselves in Wythenshawe. From an inner-London slum a family might move to a London County Council (LCC) estate in Roehampton, to the south-west of London, or to the largest of the LCC estates at Becontree, in Essex, which housed 112,000 people.

Council housing on these estates gave their inhabitants decent living conditions, but they brought their own disadvantages. Not only were the rents often too high for the budgets of the tenants, but frequently the estates were far away from where the tenants worked, requiring expenditure on fares, or long rides, perhaps on bicycles. Some men, living on the LCC estate in Becontree far out to the east in Essex, cycled as much as fifty miles a day to go and return from their work in factories along the Great West Road. Even when the Ford Motor Company opened its factory in Dagenham, it offered work only for a small proportion of the men in nearby Becontree.

Living in a house on a council estate, with its own front door, its bathroom and its electric light, and its front and rear gardens, put the working-class family in a situation a world away from one where they had lived in a couple of rooms with a shared bathroom in a Victorian property in an inner suburb, unwilling to repaint or hang new wallpaper because the house belonged to a landlord who neglected essential repairs. A modern house gave a family a wider view of the world. It also introduced middle-class practices such as the use of bathrooms, pride in gardens and scrutinising one's neighbours through the windows; and it was underpinned by ideas of respectability, hygiene and virtuous and responsible citizenship. It also encouraged men to stay at home rather than spend the evening in the pub, as well as female house pride and a concern for more efficient housekeeping. Moving to a new estate where large numbers of children were considered a sign of irresponsible parenthood made couples think seriously about adopting birth control and ensuring that their children's behaviour conformed to more middle-class standards of respecting other people's space and property. There was pressure to improve standards of dress and public behaviour, and even of the way one spoke. Indoor lavatories and bathrooms encouraged concern with hygiene and discouraged public urination and spitting. Sadly perhaps, living on the new estates probably also encouraged the chilly attitude of 'we keep ourselves to ourselves' rather than the warmth of being 'in and out of each other's houses' that was characteristic of hugger-mugger life in the inner city where it was said that doors were never locked and housewives 'popped' in and out to borrow a cup of sugar or the like. Yet class attitudes on the part of neighbouring owner-occupiers toward 'council' tenants could be haughty. In some cases, walls were put up to keep the council-house inhabitants from walking through local private estates.

There was also some tendency to scorn the behaviour of the working-class when its members were provided with decent living facilities. They were famously reputed to store coal in the bath. This was so often said that an MP, Mr. Broad, in a debate in the Commons on 22 May 1938, tried to lay it to rest, when he said:

> There has been talk about coals being kept in the bath. I know how that story began. In the East End of London, 25 years ago, some well-intentioned people built houses for the working classes and put in baths. The baths were in the scullery and had neither a water supply nor a waste pipe. The rents were very high, and the tenants found it necessary to let some of the rooms, and as in those circumstances the fixed bath was found to be more trouble than a portable bath, and as there was no adequate coal cellar, the bath was used as a coal store. That is the whole story.

Local authority properties, or simply 'council houses' came with a handbook for the tenants. The council wanted to instil a sense of pride and community. Even though the new residents might have come from the poorer suburbs of big cities and been accustomed to unhygienic habits, the new estates were to be kept orderly and the houses clean. If you couldn't meet the standards required the council would threaten you with eviction, which would be followed by rehousing you and your family in less desirable accommodation.

Between the wars, the expansion of the suburbs, particularly in London and the Home Counties, was the major feature of housing. In those years, a growing number of better-off families where the man had a stable income bought their own houses. Their somewhat higher incomes would allow them to use public transport to travel to their places of work from airy and spacious suburban districts where the roads were lined with saplings and semi-detached 'desirable residences', built by private builders, with bathrooms, hot running water, electricity and front and back gardens.

Living in the Suburbs

Between 1936 and 1939, the colossal number of 1,438,747 dwellings, mostly houses, were built in Great Britain. Some 1,067,638, or nearly three-quarters of them, were built by private enterprise, mostly in England

and Wales, and extensively in the South-East. The boom in private house construction in the 1930s changed the face of the countryside, particularly around London. It altered the patterns and the values of lower- and middle-class life for many thousands of families and allowed the better-off to live in a sort of falsely rural ambience, commuting into London daily from Kent, Surrey and most typically from the large areas of Middlesex, Hertfordshire and Buckinghamshire owned by the Metropolitan Railway Estate Company. The Railway would take you out as far as the Chiltern Hills, where the company was covering villages, estates, orchards and farms with 'avenues' and 'crescents', 'closes' and 'gardens', but never 'streets', lined with houses, each with its twee name suggestive of rural delights. Here one could live close to golf courses and tennis courts, amid woods and groves of mature trees. Perhaps the most upper-class parts of 'Metroland', as the advertisements called it, were Northwood and Moor Park, where some of the roads were so exclusive and private that they were even gated. Somewhat more modest houses were built on the Uxbridge branch of the Metropolitan Railway, where in 1934 a house cost £675. Living in such rural surroundings had the downside of a long journey to town, but a first-class season ticket from Eastcote on the Uxbridge branch to Liverpool Street Station, which brought you into the middle of the City of London, cost only £2.16s. a month. People who bought the suburban houses needed good transport into town. Sometimes builders started estates in the hopes that adequate public transport would be provided; in others, the existence of a line and a station encouraged development. So, areas where well-off London businessmen had settled even before 1914 expanded. Surbiton, Haslemere, Ashtead, Caterham, and Bromley in the south, and Pinner, Chorley Wood and Bushey in Middlesex and Hertfordshire, had convenient rail services provided one did not have to be at the office too early. The same was true of Manchester suburbs such as Didsbury, and those of Liverpool such as Southport. First-class travel was available on such lines. Brighton and London were linked by a fast Pullman service, renowned for its breakfast kippers, while the Metropolitan Line welcomed the tired businessman into its gently lit and restful bar and restaurant carriage as it left the City, drawn by magenta-coloured electric locomotives, one of which was named *Sherlock Holmes* after the fictional detective who lived in Baker Street near the Metropolitan's headquarters.

Houses were built in long lines along the arterial roads sweeping out of London, such as the Hendon Way and the Kingston Bypass. Though modern, these houses were often anchored in the past, in a sort of mock rurality, so that the owner could fantasise that he lived in the country and went up to town daily, but he was not really a city-dweller. His obsession with his garden proved that he was really a countryman at heart. At the same time, the houses were often built quite close to a high street, which would have all the necessary shops. Some houses, whose style became described as 'Stockbrokers' Tudor', were built with dark oak beams, leaded lights and multi-tinted ground-floor windows. Some semi-detached houses were provided with bow windows, gables, oak doors and porches. Developers would even add turrets to give an appearance of age and tradition. In contrast, some houses in futuristic style were built with curved 'suntrap' windows. Others had green roof tiles, giving them a 'Californian' or perhaps a 'Riviera' look. Detached, more expensive houses would be built with elegant Georgian frontages. Houses were to be individual, often with their own names, but not to stand out as too modern or vulgar. The houses of interwar suburbia aimed to be cosy and intimate, but at the same time light and individual, to look expensive but to be accessible to a wide range of pockets.

In the bathrooms of the new modern house the suite was coloured, usually green, and the piping was enclosed. Ceramic tiles shone on the walls, and the water gushed from chromium taps, and not in a trickle as it did in old houses where the pipes had furred up. Showers, however, were rare, and the bidet was not to appear until long after the Second World War, and rarely even then. There was an indoor water closet near the bedrooms on the first floor, as well as one downstairs often near the front door for the convenience of arriving visitors. Although the 1920s had seen the first low-flush suites and Bakelite rather than wooden seats, most lavatories had a high cistern, and people 'pulled the chain' and discharged a noisy rush of water into the pan. The 'toilet', no longer to be called the 'lav', would be equipped, not with newspaper as before, but with Bronco or similar rolls of specialised toilet paper, which was shiny and not really absorbent. To save space and piping, water closets were often placed in the bathroom. This may have indicated a certain relaxed attitude to privacy, but it also encouraged or reflected a more advanced view of hygiene, since it put a washbasin into proximity to the lavatory itself. Central heating was rare, so often heating was by an 'Ideal' boiler in the kitchen or a back boiler in a living room. The house would have an airing cupboard and a hot water tank and perhaps an immersion heater to provide hot water in the summer. Gas taps and electricity outlets were provided, the latter with a lighting circuit of five amps but few if any power points. The floors were of parquet, which people saw as a great improvement on the wooden boards covered with linoleum on which they had walked in older properties. The Barltrop family in fact bought a house in 1930 for £600 in Walthamstow, a north-eastern suburb of London. It had no carpets, merely boards stained a dark colour, some linoleum and the occasional rug. Another improvement was half-panelling on the walls as opposed to the heavy late Victorian textured and usually brownish-painted wall covering called 'Lincrusta' which was a permanent fixture in older houses and so strong that it could not be stripped without pulling off the plaster to which it was stuck. Some new houses would have the traditional middle- and upper-class 'tradesmen's entrance' at the side, but only the bigger ones would have a domestic servant's bedroom.

In the 1930s prices for new houses fell. In South-East England by the late 1930s prices ranged from £450 to £1,200. In the Midlands, however, a small, semi-detached bungalow could be found for £250. The statistics are amazing. By 1938, 35 per cent of private houses in Britain were no longer let to tenants but owner-occupied. Over a million families were living in houses that were being bought with the aid of loans repayable over twenty to twenty-five years, provided by building societies and secured by mortgages. In 1936 the building societies loaned £140 million at a rate of interest of 4.5 per cent compared with the £9 million they had lent in 1910.

Strangely, upper-class society, which still rented its houses, remained somewhat snobbish about taking a building society loan. The author Monica Dickens, in her *One Pair of Feet* of 1942, writing about a Hertfordshire town with a new estate, refers scornfully to 'a whole network of semi-detached paradises that you can own if you will only join the such-and-such building society'.

Buying a house required one to be able to repay roughly from about 10s. a week to about £2, although one building firm, New Ideal Homesteads, offered houses for a £5 deposit and repayment at a mere 8/1d. per week. Repayments, together with the local rates of about 4/6d. a week, were not to exceed a quarter of one's net income. Consequently, a salary of £6 a week or £300 a year would give you a comfortable margin, while £3.10s. a week or £175 per year was the minimum that would, at a squeeze, allow someone to buy a house. By the late 1930s, higher-paid skilled working men and lower-middle-class clerical workers could aspire to house ownership. To buy an average new house you would have to repay between 18s. and £1.5s. a week, so you needed a minimum net income of £4 a week. By 1939 most elementary-school teachers, senior technicians and better-paid clerical workers with salaries of between £250 and £500 a year could afford a house at the lower end of the price range, while bank officials and mid-level civil servants could manage to buy a higher-value property. 13/10d. per week would repay the loan on a £545 house. All along the Metropolitan Line to

Stanmore, which would be opened as the newly extended Bakerloo in the following year and would double the capacity of the Underground between Baker Street and Wembley Park, Laing's, major builders in the London and South-East, was building estates with houses ranging in price from £610 to £1,135. In a large display advertisement in the 7 January 1938 issue of the *Willesden Chronicle*, repayments and rates were quoted per week as £1.0.9d., £1.3.9d. or £1.12.11d. A budget for a married couple in 1938 with an income of £221 a year and buying a house for £625 with a £65 cash deposit (this was a rather optimistic sum for a £4.8s.-a-week man to save) quoted an annual repayment close on £50, including local rates. This budget was rather tight, but there were many houses that were for sale for under £625. An alternative way of looking at the economics of buying a house is that its price was often a multiple of only about two and a half years' total income. Thus, a general medical practitioner or Civil Service principal officer with £1,000 a year could buy an architect-designed detached house with rural views for a year's gross income. And higher earners had an additional advantage. The interest that they paid on their loans was an allowable expense against their income for tax purposes.

The loan was secured by a mortgage, which meant that the building society could repossess the house if the borrower defaulted on the repayments. Thus, mortgages were suitable only for those in stable jobs. For such house-purchasers, to buy rather than to rent meant that your deposit and the accumulating payments could not be recovered except by selling the house and hoping that you could realise enough by doing so to pay off what you still owed the building society. Unlike renting, you could not just move to a cheaper flat.

These hosts of new bungalows, endless rows of semis and even architect-designed detached houses were attacked for their pretentiousness and stylised triteness by, among others, George Orwell. In his *Coming Up for Air* of 1939, the hero, George Bowling, is annoyed to see his childhood village swallowed up by new houses and factories. The houses are 'Always the same, long rows of little semi-detached houses … as much alike each other as council houses and generally uglier with their stucco fronts, creosoted gates, privet hedges, green front doors'. He might have added 'their trite names'. Other problems were identified. A doctor wrote in *The Lancet* in 1938 that the new suburbs had unfortunate consequences for wives. It led to 'shallow materialism and idleness. The home is everything. She lacks external stimulus'. There was some truth in this, because traditionally, in the inner city married children had lived quite close to their parents, but in the suburbs a married daughter lacked the support of her experienced mother in housekeeping and caring for children. Apart from the loneliness of wives left at home all day awaiting the return of their husbands, there was always the worry about pay and job security. Could you keep up the mortgage repayments?

The airiness, the modern kitchens and bathrooms, the gardens and the privacy of life in the new suburbs might well not compensate for the loneliness of some, but there was a positive social side also. New residents shared in neighbourhood pursuits, played tennis and bowls, went to church and to the shiny new mock-Tudor or Georgian pub with its garden, where you could take your wife because it was not rowdy, and your children could play on the swings at the back. You could talk to your neighbour about your garden, meet him on your way to the station and have a conversation on the train to town. Of course, this assumed that your neighbour was of the same social class, but this was probable since you lived on the same estate of houses that had cost roughly the same price.

In 1934 the family of the later film historian Leslie Halliwell moved to a new semi-detached house on the hill in Bradford Road, Bolton. This was a time when terraced houses in inner Bolton still had earth closets emptied by 'night men'. Halliwell remembered how good it was to be able to have a bath at home, not at the public baths. The house was light and bright, free of the smell of burnt gas. New houses had hot water on tap; coal fires were usually restricted to the main living room, and gas and even electric heaters warmed other rooms. The kitchen was tiled and had a larder, a dresser or even a moveable 'Easiwork' cabinet for the crockery and cutlery.

The new houses and estates exuded, undoubtedly, pretentiousness and snobbery, triteness and inauthenticity, colourfully personified decades later in television characters such as Patricia Routledge's magnificent but monstrous Mrs. Hyacinth Bucket in TV's *Keeping up Appearances*, but some of the hostile comments aroused by suburban living revealed outrage that the lower class should have access to comforts and conveniences that had been reserved for the upper classes, as well as a nostalgia for Surrey, Middlesex and Hertfordshire villages and cottages, isolated and lacking though they had been in the facilities called by the developers 'mod cons', and which had now been submerged in the roads and houses of Hinchley Wood (Surrey), Kingsbury (Middlesex) and Bushey (Hertfordshire). Older residents felt nostalgic for what had gone. Mollie Hughes saw her native village of Cuffley in Hertfordshire festooned with barbed wire and notices to keep out, strung around private building sites. New houses were springing up so rapidly that after a few days' absence she would find a street of villas along a road that she had regarded as a country lane. There would be a bright red telephone box, and even a television aerial. Granted, there were more and faster trains to London, but the station staff were now 'too dignified to make jokes'. Then up would spring a row of shops, a hotel, a telephone exchange, and two or three tea shops. Sites would be marked out for a bank and a new church. The roads would be widened and speed limit warnings put up.

In Norman Collins's *London Belongs to Me* Mrs. Vizzard sits in her mid-Victorian house under 'the harsh light of the gas bracket above the mantel'. In contrast, all the new suburban residences had access to electricity. Being 'on the mains' meant that you did not need to recharge a heavy battery or accumulator to power the wireless or heat flat irons on the kitchen range (which you probably no longer had). Your carpet sweeper was an electric 'Hoover' and of course your light was electric. A rather fashionable item to own was the 'standard' lamp. This was a six-foot-high pole, on top of which was a fitment to hold a bulb, usually covered by a wide lampshade, sometimes with heavy tassels falling from it, which cast a comforting warm glow over you as you sat in a well-upholstered armchair, reading or listening to the wireless. Both the wireless and the standard lamp could be placed wherever you wanted and connected by insulated cord, called 'flex', to the electricity outlet, using an 'adaptor' that could accommodate two 'male' plugs at the same time (electricians had to be tactful when using this vocabulary in front of ladies). If you overloaded the circuit, perhaps by using an electric iron as well as something else at the same time, there might be a loud 'pop' and the 'fuse' would have to be replaced in its usually hard-to-reach cupboard. The invisible, silent power of electricity did not, as some people feared, 'leak' from the 'point', as the outlet for the current was called, but it was dangerous precisely because you could not smell it, as you could with a gas leak. It was unwise to try to install or repair the 'electric' yourself, as one amateur electrician discovers to his cost in Hilaire Belloc's famous rhyme:

> *Lord Finchley tried to mend the Electric Light*
> *Himself. It struck him dead: And serve him right!*
> *It is the business of the wealthy man*
> *To give employment to the artisan.*

The price of electricity had fallen from an earlier 6½d. per kilowatt hour to 1½d. by 1938. The Ideal Home exhibitions organised by the *Daily Mail* displayed electric cookers, refrigerators, vacuum cleaners, irons and toasters. Vacuum cleaners cost 12 guineas or £12.12s. which was three or four weeks' wages for many, or at least two weeks' for a quite well-paid man. Nevertheless, there were an estimated 2.3 million vacuum cleaners in domestic use in 1939, probably because they were given the hard sell by door-to-door salesmen and could be bought for only 3s. a week. Yet it might still be cheaper to employ a charwoman, and coal fires might work out cheaper than electricity. It was calculated that only one in 200 people used a refrigerator, compared with one in twelve in the US (where summer temperatures in many parts were consistently much higher than in Britain). Shopping in Britain was still very much a daily affair, and most people thought that a cool larder was all they needed. Milk, after all, came fresh early every morning.

Perhaps the major difference in kitchens in the new houses of the suburbs was the absence of the kitchen range and the presence of the gas cooker, a device that was common as early as 1919 as portrayed in the 1944 film *This Happy Breed* when the Gibbons family move into their terraced house and Mrs. Gibbons puts the kettle on. While films often do show a kitchen range, it was by the late 1930s being used in older houses more for space heating and hot water than for cooking, while a gas cooker, often called a 'stove', with four jets, grill and oven, was the usual means of cooking for most families. It meant faster cooking without having to keep a kitchen range clean. In Ernest Raymond's *We, the Accused,* of 1935, Mr. and Mrs. Presset, who live in an old London house, keep their range when they acquire a gas cooker.

In addition to the new cooker, the dressers for hanging cups and saucers were sometimes replaced by moveable kitchen cabinets in white or cream. The 'butler' sink gave way to the stainless-steel integrated kitchen sink unit. Yet in older properties there were still working-class families living without ovens or even ranges, who would take their Sunday joints to a local baker to be roasted in the oven for twopence. And people who lived in one or two rooms might have to share a gas stove on a landing with other tenants, like some of the inhabitants of 10 Dulcimer Street in Norman Collins's vivid *London Belongs to Me.*

As for the washing, some housewives sent it to a local laundry, and complained about missing items, lost buttons and the like. For others there was the bagwash. You took heavy white items such as sheets and pillowcases to the bagwash shop which provided a bag and returned the items still damp. The middle-class man's shirts and his detachable starched collars were washed at home or sent to a laundry. They came back in a large thick cardboard box. The usual way to do the washing at home was the copper. This was a circular metal container set in a brick structure under which a gas ring heated water. It made the scullery very steamy. Clothes had to be dried, which in damp and rainy Britain was a problem. The new suburbs were snobbish about washing hung out to dry, and in some estates, it was forbidden, or the neighbours would complain. So, the water might be squeezed out of the wet clothes with a mangle and dried on a rack consisting of a set of wooden slats fixed to the ceiling with cord, which could be raised and lowered. This had the advantage of getting the laundry out of the way, but it tended to drip. Recently washed laundry could also be dried on a clothes horse, which was a wooden frame standing in front of the 'Ideal' boiler or whatever source of heat there was. Once the clothes were sufficiently dry the new electric iron was plugged in, sometimes into the light socket in the ceiling. Then they would be kept in the airing cupboard, through which hot air from the boiler was passed.

Laundry took quite a long time and much effort. Washing machines were expensive and rare; launderettes and tumble dryers were yet unknown. Consequently, one did not change one's clothes with any great frequency, and some men wore collars that could be wiped clean daily, but only one shirt a week. Few people even in the new suburbs with their coloured bathroom suites bathed more than once a week. People marvelled at the daily shower that Americans took, as they saw at the cinema.

As for the rest of the house, Whiteley's in West London boasted in 1938 that they could furnish a small house with bed linen, curtains and carpets, as well as cutlery and crockery, for £160 or, in easy terms, with a 10-guinea deposit and twenty-four months' payments of £7, that is for £178.10s.

To move to a new house meant adopting new ideas about furniture and decoration. Many older properties were furnished and decorated in a style that went back to Edwardian or even Victorian times. The Pressets, for example, in Ernest Raymond's *We, the Accused*, live in a house with long-lace curtains in the dining-room. There is a mahogany sideboard with heavy cruets on it. The picture rail is brass and from it hang pictures of stags. The wallpaper is red, with a frieze depicting a woodland sunset repeated over and over.

The new suburbs went in for fireplaces in the 'stepped Aztec-Temple' style. Furniture was covered in a long-lasting fabric called 'uncut moquette', which was also used on seats in London Underground trains. The really fashionable item was the walnut cocktail cabinet, which people knew about because it appeared so often in films. American films often featured that acme of modernity: the white telephone, but this was rare in Britain, where many houses still had the older 'candlestick' telephone with the earpiece that was held in the hand as you spoke into the mouthpiece on the main part of the instrument.

Such was middle-class suburban life. People had to eat and to dress, however, and these matters also were often suffused with social distinctions.

Chapter 4

Eating and Dressing

'Good, Plain English Cooking'

By the late 1930s, the policy of preferential treatment for products from the Empire meant that a great proportion of British meat, dairy products, wheat, fruit and vegetables was arriving from Australia, New Zealand and all over the parts coloured red in school atlases, that is, the British Empire. In addition, food retailing was increasingly in the hands of very large firms such as Sainsbury's, the Home and Colonial, Unilever and Vestey's. Many of the items that people were buying as a normal part of their diet were factory-processed, sold in packets, cartons or tins, and described as 'instant' or 'table ready'. Growing standardisation meant that far less was being bought loose. However, there was still a lot of home delivery, but not of cooked food as would become usual in the late twentieth century. Jack and Mabel Simmonds, an elderly and housebound couple, discovered this more than fifty years later when a young couple came to visit them and suggested telephoning for a takeaway meal. Some forty-five minutes later, the doorbell rang, and Jack went to open the door. A person dressed in motorcyclist's gear was standing there, wearing a helmet that made him look like a spaceman. The spaceman declined payment for the strange-looking packets he handed over, saying that payment had already been made 'on the mobile'. The meal that the young couple had ordered and paid for using their mobile telephone turned out to consist of food that was a mixture of Middle Eastern, Chinese, Indian and Italian dishes, most of which Jack and Mabel had never seen and rarely if ever heard of.

They were bewildered. Their diet was what they had eaten ever since they had set up home fifty years earlier in the 1930s. They had hardly ever eaten out, let alone tasted any but English food. They assumed that foreign food was peculiar, over-spiced, heavy on garlic and certainly not good for you. It was noticeable that British people, unlike the French and the

Italians, had little interest in food as such, according to *The People's Food* of 1938 by Sir William Crawford, founder of a famous advertising agency. The Dutch socialist and journalist Odette Keun wrote that British food was cheap but 'indescribably horribly cooked'.

Meat and two vegetables was the norm for a main meal. A joint of beef was a favourite, but some preferred mutton or lamb. The vegetables would usually be potatoes and cabbage, brussels sprouts or cauliflower. There would be a dessert, usually called 'afters' though sometimes 'pudding' even if it was not always actually a pudding. Apple pie, apple crumble or rhubarb and custard were favourites, and that was often the only fruit that most lower- and middle-class people ate. The Johnsons, a quite well-off family in the Staffordshire Potteries district, knew nothing of avocados, corncobs, fresh peaches, or Chinese, Indian or Italian food (save Heinz tinned spaghetti). They never bought frozen food, nor did they consume salmon, except from tins. The only change from earlier years was that fruit and vegetables were more generally available all year round.

After Jack retired in the 1960s, he and his wife had their 'dinner' at one o'clock, then at six 'high tea', which was a proper meal, and a late snack at about nine that they called 'supper'. Occasionally, they had been invited to a somewhat superior 'afternoon tea' at about 4 p.m. and once or twice for 'dinner' in the evening, though this was served rather too late for their taste, and they feared that they would not be able to digest it properly before their early bedtime. The names of meals were a marker of social class. Posh people had lunch, afternoon tea and dinner, while the others had dinner, high tea and supper.

Breakfast for Jack and Mabel usually began with one of the modern cereals, such as Corn Flakes or Shredded Wheat, but sometimes they had porridge. They had a nephew at boarding school who was given hot porridge in the winter and in the summer a porridge that had been made the evening before and was served as a sort of paste with cold milk and abundant sugar. At the weekend Mabel sometimes cooked a large 'fry-up' of an egg, bacon, tomato, fried bread and baked beans from a tin. This was followed by toast and marmalade. The toaster was no more than a flat pan resting on the gas cooker jet, which burnt the bread in one part and left it untoasted in another. Jack's younger and more 'modern' sister had an electric toaster. Jack and his wife liked puddings but did not care much for fresh fruit, although the newspaper said it was good for you. When the actor James Cagney was seen to push half a grapefruit into the face of his nagging girlfriend in the American crime film *The Public Enemy* of 1931, grapefruit became fashionable for breakfast, usually in the form of tinned segments.

Jack and Mabel lived through an age when vegetarians were considered cranks, although they knew that greens, in particular, were part of a healthy diet. One of their grandchildren had told them recently that she was a vegan, but why she didn't eat eggs and butter, or drink milk was incomprehensible, for in the 1930s Jack and Mabel had been quite proud to be able to afford butter when the poor ate dripping or margarine. In J. B. Priestley's *Angel Pavement,* of 1930, Stanley Poole, the junior clerk, breakfasts economically on bread dipped in bacon fat. He drinks cocoa, which was more popular than coffee for less well-off people.

If Jack and Mabel drank anything with their meals, it would be water, or tea, though Jack had a taste for a red-coloured mixture of citrus, some other flavourings and carbonated water called Tizer, and advertised as 'Tizer the Appetizer', which he bought from the local off-licence. Other, usually older, folk bought bottled beer from the off-licence or took a jug to the pub to fetch some draught beer to drink with their dinner. The Simmondses had never drunk wine, though Jack liked an occasional glass of ale if they were on holiday in the summer in the country or by the sea. Jack remembered his father who had served in France in the Great War telling him that the 'Frenchies' drank lots of red wine. It wasn't a patch on British beer, he had assured his son.

By the 1980s Jack was obviously out of date. But when he and his wife were a young couple in the 1930s, they had eaten many things that their own parents had not known when they were young before the Great War. Basic foods had been cheap then, but they were rather limited. However, the increase in incomes and the cheapening of imports after the war encouraged people to eat a lot more eggs and dairy food, and rather less bread and potatoes.

By the late 1930s, many of the items that Mabel bought as a normal part of their diet were already prepared for cooking or merely heating up. They were sold in packets, cartons or tins. Growing standardisation meant that Mabel was buying far less loose. She bought butter in greaseproof packets, although she also liked to watch the grocer's assistant in his long white apron cut half a pound off a large chunk and pat it into shape with two little bats before deftly wrapping it up. When she and Jack had been a young couple, she used to make her own soups, as her mother had taught her to do using vegetables that could, literally, be picked up for nothing when the costermongers pushed their barrows away in the evening (not, of course that Mabel did this), but now she bought tinned soups such as Heinz's cream of tomato which she could heat up in a few minutes, as well as breakfast cereals, puddings, salmon, peas and potato crisps. Bovril and Horlicks were widely advertised as 'health foods', but they were not seen as 'cranky' or limited to the back-street shops that specialised in 'vegetarian sausages' and the like. Mabel continued to shop and chat with the grocer, the butcher, the greengrocer and the baker as she always had, but now she preferred to have her shopping delivered. Jack had arranged for a telephone to be installed so that Mabel could order items without leaving the house. A boy on a bicycle and later a man in a van would deliver most of what she wanted. By the late 1930s the milkman no longer ladled out milk from a churn into Mabel's jug but left a sealed bottle outside the door early in the morning. This was not the case everywhere, however, as the philosopher Bryan Magee remembered from his 1930s childhood in the poor London district of Hoxton. Here a Welsh dairyman kept a cow and sold milk at half a pint (about a quarter of a litre) for three farthings. One whole pint cost a penny and a farthing. However, this came to an end. The large dairy combines, United Dairies and Express Dairies, whose milk began to be delivered in 1938 in hygienically sealed bottles, bought up the small dairies and took out large display advertisements in the press, encouraging housewives to order their daily pint or quart from the milkman. In general, only the milkman and the baker delivered their products to the poorer classes, but the higher earners of the middle and upper middle classes, who lived in the suburbs, received deliveries of meat, groceries and greengrocery, and many even had fish brought regularly to the door (or in some cases the back door where the maid or the cook took in the deliveries).

In the late 1930s, only the upper classes invited guests to lunch or dinner, but Jack and Mabel and the people they knew sometimes went to tea to a relative's or friend's house on a Sunday afternoon. There you would be invited into what had been previously called the 'parlour' but was now referred to as the 'front room', or even 'inside' (perhaps because it was indeed the inside room on the ground floor). Upwardly mobile people who had bought a house in a new middle-class suburb might even call the room 'the lounge', but you would have to be as affected as Hyacinth Bucket in TV's later *Keeping Up Appearances* to call it the 'drawing room'. There, you would expect to eat fish paste, tinned salmon or tinned pilchards, perhaps on toast, as well as bread, butter and jam, and possibly two sorts of cake. The bread was always white unless you were a food faddist, in which case you would prefer brown, which many people suspected had been adulterated, perhaps with wood shavings. The Magee family, who ran a modest business, would make an effort when they invited their relations round for tea. As well as the bread, butter and jam, there would be sandwiches, cake and biscuits, and sardines on toast as well as hard-boiled eggs. You would very likely be offered tinned salmon, and the children would look forward to tinned peaches and Carnation, a brand of very sweet, evaporated milk. There would always be tea, which was made with tea leaves in a teapot or by pouring the boiling water over the leaves through a strainer. There were no teabags then. And you would be given your cup of tea in a cup and a saucer in which to rest the spoon, certainly not in a mug. The 'lady of the house', to use 1990s TV character Hyacinth Bucket's way of presenting herself, would say 'Shall I be Mother?', which meant 'Shall I pour the tea out?' She poured the tea from the teapot through a strainer so that the leaves did not end up in the cup, and there was also a little china bowl into which your hostess would pour the dregs from your cup before she refilled it. Very posh people offered you Chinese or Indian tea and invited you to choose between lemon and milk. Whether your hostess put the milk in first or after the tea had been poured depended and still does to some extent on where you lived. In Scotland and the North of England one put the milk in second, and upper-class folk did likewise in the South, but in southern England, ordinary people put a little milk in the cup first. As for sugar, it was so cheap that the average amount consumed in Britain was seventeen ounces, just over a pound or nearly half a kilogram a week, which was even more than the substantial quantities that the Victorians had consumed. This explained the bad teeth of the average Briton, especially those who were not familiar with the use of a toothbrush.

Mass factory-produced, attractively packed and heavily advertised items that catered to the British sweet tooth were widely sold in the late 1930s. You could buy bars of Cadbury's, Nestle's or Fry's chocolate not only over the counter but from automatic machines on railway station platforms. Smith's Crisps, with their convenient little blue-wrapped packet of salt that you could use or not as you pleased, was a familiar snack. Favourite prepacked and processed items by the late 1930s included breakfast cereals, such as Corn Flakes and Shredded Wheat. Since these were instant, they began to take over from porridge, until Kellogg's began to manufacture their instant Quaker Oats in their factories in Southall (Middlesex) from 1936 and Manchester from 1938. Nevertheless, by 1939, Corn Flakes and Shredded Wheat had the largest share of the breakfast cereal market.

Esther Simons didn't usually shop in the main road in the busy London district where she and her family lived or do her grocery shopping in Sainsbury's or any of the other chains, although she recalled that her own mother had been a regular customer at the Home and Colonial, a huge chain of grocers that was later absorbed by a yet larger conglomerate. Mr. Phillips, the Welsh dairyman at the bottom of the street, would send up a carton to the mansion block where Esther lived with the family's weekly groceries packed in it. She bought fresh bread every day from a shop a few yards from Phillips's, and her vegetables and fruit from Mr. Hovell, just a few yards further on, just as if she were living in 'Warmington-on-Sea', the village that, thirty years later, would be the background of another renowned TV programme, *Dad's Army*', set in September 1939 and the war years.

Tea was the national British hot drink, drunk at breakfast, in the afternoon and at 'tea-time' which might mean upper-class 'afternoon tea' or not so upper-class 'tea', eaten when the man came home from work and expected his evening meal which was called 'tea'. The popularity of tea explained the success of the song, first sung in cockney Londonese by the famous actress and singer Binnie Hale in February 1937:

I like a nice cup of tea in the morning,
For to start the day you see,
And at half-past eleven,
Well, my idea of 'eaven
Is a nice cup of tea.
I like a nice cup of tea with me' dinner
And a nice cup of tea with me' tea.
And when it's time to go to bed,
There's a lot to be said for a nice cup of tea

Coffee was much less popular, except after upper-class meals or for 'elevenses'. *Dad's Army*, which so truly represents the values and customs of the late 1930s, often has an episode set in the little tea shop – there were no specific coffee bars, just coffee stalls – which Mr. Mainwaring, the bank manager, visits every morning. While instant coffee did exist, it was hardly known in the 1930s. There was, however, a preparation known as *Camp Coffee*, a brand name that suggested that upper-class men drank it, for on its label was an officer of a Scottish regiment wearing a kilt, attended by an Indian servant who has brought him his coffee on a tray. *Camp* was a thick syrup of concentrated coffee, which you dissolved into hot milk. 'Milk and a dash (of coffee)' was available and quite popular in cafés (usually called 'caffs'). Nancy Phelan, an Australian visitor to London, noted that restaurant coffee was sometimes merely hot milk flavoured with coffee essence, or a 'mud-coloured, lukewarm beverage with floating grains'. Espresso, cappuccino and other 'foreign' (a most pejorative word) coffees were far in the future.

Francis McFarland, born in 1920, whose father was a senior postal sorter and was buying his own house in Southall (Middlesex), came home with his brother Bob every day in the 1930s from their grammar school for 'dinner', which their mother, a primary school teacher who had been obliged to resign on marriage, had shopped for and cooked that morning. Francis recalled the meal as nearly always consisting of meat and two vegetables, which would be potatoes and greens, followed by a cooked pudding, such as apple pie and custard. This was also the usual school dinner, which, by 1939, 12 per cent of children were receiving, a figure that increased vastly during the Second World War. There were also tinned foods that could be prepared for the table in a hurry, such as the well-known Heinz '57' varieties, though this number had been plucked out of the imagination of the founder of the firm. Heinz tomato ketchup joined OK sauce as the usual flavouring for bland British food. Heinz tinned (the word 'canned' was little used) baked beans and Heinz tinned cream of tomato soup, as well as Heinz tinned spaghetti and tomato sauce were on the menu in the milk bar (a snack bar with much emphasis on dairy items) that Esther Simons and her husband ran from 1938 onward.

In the late 1930s, fish and chips was the best-known takeaway and was a staple for the really poor. It was a change from bread and dripping. The chips and the mushy peas that might go with the fish provided essential vegetables. 'Fish 'n Chips', as one called the dish, was an important and sustaining part of the working-class diet until after the Second World War. It even has a serious study devoted to it (see Walton in the Bibliography). Almost every working-class district in London had a 'chippy'. Fish fryers used different mediums to fry the fish and chips. London fryers used vegetable oil; in Yorkshire dripping was the frying medium. In many parts of Lancashire, it was cottonseed oil. The dish was also popular in Scotland, where fish and chips was generally in immigrant Italian hands. In the late 1930s it was even permissible to eat fish and chips in the street, though that habit was in general considered vulgar. It was rumoured that here and there some fish fryers delivered their product to middle-class houses, but only of course when the servants had their evening off. It was not below even the highest class of reveller to finish an evening out by 'slumming' with a piece of greasy fish and some soggy chips from a newspaper and sold by a man from a sort of motorised caravan in the street. Young and wealthy revellers might then indulge in a midnight coffee from a stall. Bryan Magee recalled that you could buy chips for one penny ('a penn'orth'). Rock salmon was 2d. ('tuppence') and cod cost 3d. – 'thruppence', or in London cockney speech 'fruppence'. Haddock was dearer. The problem for this very large industry was that, unless the caterer changed his frying medium regularly, fish and chips was smelly; it was eaten in what was considered a vulgar way from old newspapers in the street and it was cheap. Esther Simons's son would later tell his shocked mother that he could buy a pennyworth of chips from a mobile 'chippy' in the street when he was evacuated to Newmarket (Suffolk) during the war. Fish and chips did indeed have a low-class taint about it. It was not only cheap but also often produced with an alarming lack of hygiene. So, by the 1930s efforts were under way to make the dish more attractive to middle-class customers. It began to appear on restaurant menus and in canteens such as at Montagu Burton's clothing factory in Leeds. Better cleanliness and hygiene reflected improvement in such standards in general. The Public Health Act of 1936 was extended in July 1938 by the Food and Drugs Act to regulate food products more closely. 'Hygiene' became a buzz word. A curious boy going to school in those days used to pass a 'Hygienic Bakery' and wonder if all the others were unhygienic. At the height of the popularity of fish and chips, there were 30,000 outlets, ranging from scruffy and smelly takeaways to Britain's most famous fish and chips restaurant, Harry Ramsden's, which had opened in Guiseley, a suburb of the Yorkshire city of Leeds. In 1931, Ramsden had moved into impressive new premises, complete with fitted carpets, oak-panelled walls and chandeliers. It was the largest fish and chip shop in the world, seating 250 people, and boasted that it entertained nearly a million customers a year.

Eating Out

In many towns and certainly in the suburbs of cities there were few and often no restaurants. Exceptionally, in Norman Collins's novel *London Belongs to Me*, Doris Josser and her friend Doreen, who have left home and live somewhat adventurously in two rooms in London's slightly foreign Swiss Cottage, are able to buy a carton of potato salad, a tin of soup and some ham in a *delicatessen* (a word so unfamiliar that it was printed in italics). If there was a restaurant near where you lived the menu was rather basic. A normal dinner in a chophouse or dining room, as the author J. B. Priestley eats in Darlington (Durham) during his tour of England, was roast mutton or beef, or boiled beef, carrots and dumplings followed by treacle pudding. On another occasion he has a meal of soup, Yorkshire pudding, roast chicken, sausages and two vegetables, followed by a pudding, cheese and biscuits and coffee. At only 2/6d. (one-eighth of a pound) he thought it good value.

However, the Victorian-style chophouses and 'dining rooms' whose style and appearance were grimly masculine, were giving way to other forms of eating out. Things were changing, and by the late 1930s many more eating places, all now quite appropriate for women, were opening. There were snack bars, milk bars, cafeterias and tearooms. In Priestley's novel *Angel Pavement*, Miss Matford, a senior secretary, has her lunch in 'a superior place, just off Cannon Street', where she treats herself to a cutlet and peas, an apple tart and cream and coffee. In contrast, Stanley Poole, the office boy, whose mother allows him a shilling a day, eats a sausage or fried liver with mashed potatoes in the Victorian Pavement Dining Rooms round the corner from the office.

All these places, except the *delicatessen*, were, of course, British. Foreign restaurants were rare. If you were adventurous you went to London's Soho district. In *Angel Pavement*, J. B. Priestley describes Norman Birtley taking Lilian Matfield to a vaguely foreign place in Soho. Priestley's description is hostile and perhaps reflects the general view of foreign eating and manners. The couple are pulled in rather than welcomed by a 'very fierce-looking, moustachioed, square-jawed Latin'. The place smells of cooking oil. The other diners look strange. The waitress has a face with 'no features'. There is an insect in the food. The wine waiter is 'an ancient gloomy foreigner'. The hostile description continues in that tone, concluded by the author telling us that 'This was a foul little place'. Priestley, nevertheless, had alternatives, also in the West End. He could have sent his characters to dine in the legendary German Schmidt's or in Bertorelli's, both in Charlotte Street, to the high-quality Italian Quo Vadis in Dean Street, or the French L'Escargot in Greek Street.

However, there were acceptable British alternatives, the best known of which were the establishments of J. Lyons and Company, known colloquially as 'Joe Lyons'. Lyons was famous for its Corner Houses, situated in the major London streets of Tottenham Court Road, Coventry Street and the Strand. Here, in luxurious surroundings, to the sound of an orchestra, you could have a variety of meals at extremely modest prices, including a four-course lunch for 1/6d. The Corner House was the place where your grandparents or your uncle and aunt took you out for a treat during the school holidays. It was the place for birthday celebrations. Ladies enjoying a day in town to shop or go to a theatre matinée would lunch in a Corner House. Couples meeting after work would have a supper in the Corner House before or after visiting a cinema. People would go up to town on a weekend afternoon and sit just inside Hyde Park, and at teatime go into Maison Lyons on the other side of Oxford Street and treat themselves to afternoon tea. In *Angel Pavement,* Turgis, the junior clerk, goes out on a Saturday night to a Corner House because young women would frequent it. It was, writes Priestley,

> a teashop that had gone mad and turned Babylonian, a white palace with ten thousand lights … acres of white napery and bewildering glittering rows of teapots … mounds of shimmering bonbons and multi-coloured Viennese pastries, the cauldrons of stewed steak, the vanloads of harlequin ices … It steamed with humanity … The atmosphere was golden, tropical.

There were several floors, with different cafés and restaurants, with varied styles of menu and price, as well as retail counters on the ground floor selling bread, cakes and confectionery. In the colossal Coventry Street Corner House in the West End of London you could have your shoes shined, your hair done and make telephone calls, aided by a girl operator. There were lifts, cloakrooms and marble-lined toilets. The teapots and milk jugs were silver-plated. Thick carpets dulled the noise so that you heard only the murmur of conversation, the occasional clink of cutlery and the elegant tones of the orchestra. The humble Turgis is greeted by a 'sleek, grave' man who enquires deferentially 'Table for one, Sir?' Turgis orders plaice and chips, tea, bread and butter and cakes. He listens to the orchestra, but, sadly, the Corner House does not live up to its reputation as a pick-up place. Another novelist of the time, Patrick Hamilton, in his *The Plains of Cement*, of 1935, describes how Mr. Eccles takes the barmaid Ella Dawson for dinner at the Corner House, 'a vast, marble, subterranean Versailles for London's hungry and teeming nondescripts', and she wonders if he is trying to seduce her.

The Corner Houses were immense; the Coventry Street one could seat 4,500 customers and the others 2,500 each. They were open all night. Coventry Street had orchestras of up to twelve musicians playing from noon to midnight. Some 1,200 staff cooked, served and washed up 60,000 meals every twenty-four hours. You were brought your order by a 'nippy', who wore a black alpaca dress with pearl buttons, a white collar and detachable cuffs with black stockings, flat, black shoes, a white apron and a cap. She carried a bill-pad and a pencil and was trained to be poised and efficient. The 7,600 nippies of 1939 were strictly supervised but well paid, with extra for working at the weekend. The hours were long and the work demanding, but so great was the pool of female labour that there was much competition for vacancies. Dozens of nippies married customers every year. For them, the luxurious and imposing décor of marble and glass of the Corner House was an improvement on working as a waitress in a chophouse or, even worse, a 'greasy spoon', where working men had their breakfast 'fry-up', in an atmosphere of cigarette smoke and over-used fat.

The Corner Houses offered a democratisation of eating out. All were welcome, though Lyons maintained a crew of brown-uniformed porters, who made sure that drunks and rowdies were excluded.

Lyons's State Café in Liverpool and the Popular Café in Manchester offered similar service. The Corner Houses set the style for restaurants in the large department stores of big cities, with their waitresses dressed as parlourmaids and meals served with a small orchestra gently tinkling or scraping in the background.

In the interwar years Lyons also ran some 250 teashops, their unmistakeable fascias painted white with J. LYONS & CO standing out in gold lettering. The teashops were standardised, with a self-service counter, along which a queue moved slowly, but faster than if you had had to wait for service. Probably its most original feature was the famous Lyons tea. This was a strong brew, and there were four teapots on the go at any one time. They stood on a small turntable. In three the tea was brewing while from the fourth the counter-hand poured out no more than four cups before moving on to the next teapot. The amount of milk in each cup was controlled as well, so that the strength and the quality of the tea was guaranteed. The tea was the last item that you collected as you moved along the counter. Then you paid a formidable lady cashier, dressed in black, picked up your tray and looked for a place at one of the tables. A Lyons teashop was noisy and did not communicate a feeling of calm like the Corner House, but it offered good value and quality. It was fast, and just right for people who wanted to have a quick meal or a snack and possibly do some shopping during their lunch hour. The age when a woman would be embarrassed to go into an eating place on her own was now well in the past. In a Lyons teashop she might even find herself sharing her table with a man.

Lyons was the best-known chain of catering establishments, but there was also the ABC, which had almost as many teashops as Joe Lyons at its peak. The ABC would serve you a three-course meal of soup, meat and two veg for 1/6. Extraordinarily, this was only a penny more than Jane Carlyle, wife of Thomas Carlyle the historian, noted a hundred years earlier in her diary that she paid for a chop and a glass of ale.

A newcomer was the milk bar. Esther Simons and her husband opened one in the London suburb where they lived, where it competed with the local Lyons teashop and the ABC, as well as a waitress-served restaurant on the upper floor of a large local department store. Milk bars were an American import, originally intended both to compete with bars that served alcohol and to encourage the consumption of milk. They were slick, shiny, multicoloured and chromium-plated, with stools against a bar as in American drugstores, on which young women perched, crossing their legs elegantly. Behind the counter were girls in crisp white, green, pink or red overalls. They served you tea, coffee, milk shakes, cold drinks and cooked snacks, such as eggs and chips, or Heinz tinned spaghetti or baked beans on toast. The milk bar sold ice-cream in cornets, between wafers, in tubs or, more impressively, in various multicoloured mixtures, additions and flavours called Sundaes served in tall glasses with extra-long spoons. London's first milk bar opened in 1935. By 1936 there were 540 and by 1938 1,475 milk bars had appeared on city streets all over Britain. Their floors were covered with different coloured tiles. The lighting was bright; they had soda-fountains and fruit juices that swirled around in a glass globe; the milk was on tap, not from bottles. It was all so snappy, so modern.

And, of course, the classier the restaurant, the better you had to dress to eat in it.

How People Dressed

A historian writing in 2010 and looking back at the 1930s observed: 'Most people nowadays cruise around looking like they've kitted themselves out in an Oxfam charity shop, but that didn't do then. You had to have smart clothes, even if you got them out once in a blue moon.' If a woman or a man cared about keeping their job they couldn't afford to dress unsuitably. The fiancé of Robert Barltrop's Aunt Hilda had a good job at Ford's in Dagenham. He wore a bowler hat and a dark overcoat. In those days you dressed *up*, not *down*. In the middle-class suburbs a woman might be doing her own housework, but if the doorbell rang, she took off her apron before opening. Nor did you want to stand out. A woman wanted to be up to date, well turned-out, but not conspicuous. It was said that a working-class girl could look like an actress, and some said a duchess, but the trained eye could tell ready-to-wear from made-to-measure clothes. And a not-so-well-off middle-class lady would often prefer to buy high-quality second-hand clothes discreetly from a magazine such as *The Lady* rather than from a chain store. In the late 1930s, clothes, especially men's, were conventional. If you wore an Aertex shirt, suede shoes or corduroy trousers you were an artist or in some ways eccentric. Nobody dressed in jeans or sports clothes, such as trainers (called sneakers in the US), which were restricted to the gymnasium and called 'plimsolls'. A low-waged man had his Sunday-best suit, which he might pawn on Monday and redeem the following Saturday. He wore old clothes for the factory or building site. Women wore aprons and, for rougher work poorer women tied sacking with string round their waists. Boys often wore short trousers until well into their teens, but adolescents aimed to dress like their mothers and fathers as soon as they could, so your first pair of long trousers was an important step in growing into an adult male. Working men did not usually wear separate stiff collars and ties, but just a scarf called a 'muffler'. Shirts with soft attached collars were only just coming in. Turgis, the clerk at £3.15s. a week in Priestley's *Angel Pavement,* buys soft-collar shirts with fashionable long points when he is courting Lena Golspie. Trousers had turn-ups and were usually made without belt loops, and with wide waists, so braces (which Americans called 'suspenders') were necessary to keep your trousers up, although you might see men labouring in the streets with broad leather belts clumsily bunching their trouser waists together. Showing your braces was 'common', even in your own garden, so men gardened in their waistcoats if they lived in the upwardly mobile suburbs. Only a few modern men wore American-style self-supporting trousers.

Working men wore heavy boots while others wore lace-up shoes, black in town and brown at weekends or in the country. Working men wore peaked cloth caps unless they rose to foreman or overseer rank, when the bowler hat indicated their status. In fact, photographs of crowds of working men taken before 1914 differ from those in the 1930s only because in the latter the men no longer have walrus moustaches. In the 1930s the fashion was to be clean-shaven or to have a very small moustache clipped short along your upper lip. A variation was the Ronald Colman moustache, worn by the film star of that name, a slightly thicker growth of hair that curved up toward the nostrils, leaving bare the centre of the upper lip. As for beards, they were eccentric, and small boys would jeer 'beaver' at hirsute men and ask them cheekily if they slept with their beards inside or outside the sheet. The greatest bearded eccentric of the age was the playwright George Bernard Shaw.

Men wore their hair short. Your mother would put a pudding bowl on your head and cut around it. Men asked the barber for a 'short back and sides'. Some working-class men wore their hair long and plastered back from their foreheads to the back of the skull with the well-known greasy white preparation called Brylcreem. Esther Simons's husband was a heavy user of Brylcreem, which caused some problems in the laundry where she sent her pillowcases.

Once you moved out of the working class and sat down at your work you wore a collar and tie, sometimes with a tiepin to hold it in place. You had to conform and dress appropriately. Professional men wore clothes that became uniforms. Doctors, for example, wore black jackets and striped trousers. Top hats were usual at the Stock Exchange. Mr. Mainwaring, the bank manager in TV's *Dad's Army*, wears a wing collar, a black jacket and striped trousers, while his chief clerk, Arthur Wilson, wears a black suit. The young clerk, Frank Pike, wears a suit but it is more like a 'lounge' suit and, while sober in colour, it is not black. Kid gloves were indispensable. As for hats, Pike wears a trilby, which men sometimes wore with the brim turned down at the back as well as the front, while his senior, Wilson, wears a homburg, made fashionable by the Foreign Secretary, the elegant Anthony Eden. The manager, Mr. Mainwaring, wears a bowler and always carries an umbrella, and a small, square-cornered case known as an 'attaché case'. Ted Josser, manager of a Co-op grocery in Norman Collins's *London Belongs to Me*, dresses formally in a bowler hat, a black jacket and striped trousers.

At the office you wore a separate collar, fixed to your shirt with a collar stud, which you would often drop as you tried to insert it into the collar while dressing. Annoyingly, the stud would roll under the bed, especially if you were in a hurry. You also wore cufflinks (cufflinks and a tiepin were frequent birthday presents for teenage boys). At the same time, younger middle-class men were adopting collar-attached shirts. Unfortunately, the collars did not have stiffeners and stuck up untidily or were too long and covered your tie. The zip (a short form of the American 'zipper') had been introduced into the backs of women's dresses, making the lady's maid unnecessary, but men resisted its use in their trouser flies. What if the zip broke or got stuck? You wore a dark suit, as did all middle- and upper-class men not only at the office but also for visiting and most other activities. If you could afford it, you would have your suit personally tailored for you in London's Savile Row, and it would have the various extras that you wanted, such as extra pockets in the front and a particular number of buttons on the cuffs. Otherwise, you could buy a high-class suit at Austin Reed's or go somewhat down-market and order your suit from Montagu Burton or the Fifty-Shilling Tailor. The branch manager would take a variety of your measurements, send them off to a factory and make whatever adjustments were needed when you collected the suit a few weeks later. Burton's prices began at 55s. By 1939 there were 565 Burton shops. Bryan Magee, whose father was a men's outfitter, recalled that made-to-measure suits were usual for the lower middle class, such as shopkeepers and publicans. And, in the days before central heating, cloth was much heavier.

Nevertheless, in 1931 Lady Troubridge, observing contemporary manners, was noting that latitude had 'crept in' since the Great War. Lounge suits were now allowed, even though they had to be sober in colour. A new men's shop in London, Simpson's in Piccadilly, had a snack bar and, in 1936, it demonstrated television and displayed an aeroplane on the top floor, plus appropriate items for the sporting gentleman such as guns and fishing tackle. Simpson's sold more relaxed male clothing: soft collars and plus fours for wearing other than while playing golf, as well as self-supporting trousers. All the same, you were expected to wear white tie and tails at upper-middle-class events such as balls and dinner parties, though you might get away with a dinner jacket and a bow tie. This had to be properly tied. John Betjeman, later Poet Laureate, wore a made-up bow tie, which he kept flicking, to the intense annoyance of his future mother-in law, Lady Penelope, wife of Field Marshal Sir Philip Chetwode.

While on Sunday the working-class man might put on his best suit, by the late 1930s in the suburbs you would wear a sports jacket, made of worsted or tweed, perhaps with leather-covered buttons and a slit in the back, which made it look like a hacking jacket and as if you had recently got down from your horse, particularly if you also wore cavalry twill trousers.

Schoolmasters who had begun their careers before 1914 wore wing collars until well after the Second World War. The next generation wore suits, but the younger men who were in their twenties in the 1930s wore sports jackets and grey flannels, as does assistant master Norman Sandys in Ernest Raymond's *We, the Accused* of 1935. He also wears brown brogues. Some men might even dare to wear crepe soles, which in the thirties were known as 'beetle-crushers' or, rudely, 'brothel-creepers'. Bill, the medical student, in *London Belongs to Me*, wears a sports jacket and grey flannels, but he is a medical student and thus his informality is tolerated. So was not wearing a tie, or even wearing a roll-neck pullover, as some university lecturers did. E. M. Delafield, whose *Diary of a Provincial Lady* tellingly reflects the author's opinions, comments that, at a literary event in London, some young men were in flannel shirts without ties, though most were in evening dress. In the 1930s some men wore two-toned shoes, commonly called 'co-respondent shoes' because wearing them was thought to indicate that you were the sort of man (otherwise known from upper-class school slang as a 'bounder' or 'cad' until the Prince of Wales adopted the two-toned mode) who seduced other men's wives and ended up scandalously in the divorce court. In one description of a Lyons's Corner House, the band wears light blue pinstripe, ginger shoes and trilby hats. The servant girl Margaret Powell sees the band as 'flashy', which would seem to be an understatement. Percy Boon, the garage mechanic in Norman Collins's novel *London Belongs to Me*, wears a purple suit to go out, and has a light check suit also. However, for his criminal activities he wears blue pinstripe. Half of London wears blue pinstripe, he tells himself, so his clothes won't make him identifiable.

When a working-class man went to bed, he might well sleep in his long pants and vest, but middle- and upper-class men wore pyjamas. These were usually striped, although the films were making mono-coloured American-style pyjamas more familiar. Men's pyjama trousers were not elasticised around the waist; the waistband accommodated a braided cotton cord, which was tied in a bow to hold the trousers up. The problem was that the cord sometimes disappeared into the waistband and female skills were required to tease it out with a pin. The cinema also showed women in pyjamas in the bedroom, though most women wore nightgowns, known colloquially as 'nighties'. Women's pyjamas, very wide and floppy in the leg, called 'beach' pyjamas, became fashionable for daring formal wear in the 1930s. However, photographs show that most people remained fully dressed while on the beach.

Another model for both younger men and most women was the styles worn by royalty. Queen Elizabeth, who came to the throne in December 1936, was widely admired for her clothes, while Edward, Prince of Wales until January 1935 and then Edward VIII until he abdicated in December 1936 and became Duke of Windsor, was renowned for his hatlessness, socks with coloured diamond patterns, and for wearing pullovers in fancy or Fair Isle pattern rather than a waistcoat. This 'modern' way of dressing infuriated his father, George V, whose only eccentricity was to tell his valet to put the crease down the sides of his trousers rather than the front.

Men had to wear a tie. This could be a badge of class, especially if it indicated the school you had attended or the regiment in which you had been an officer. Nobody of the middle or upper class went tieless except perhaps on the beach, and then men who were wearing collar-attached shirts folded the collars over the back of the collars of their jackets. Ties were compulsory in schools, often even for girls, as were the hated girls' hats and the boys' school caps, often of hideously unmatched colours and which had extra touches to indicate your status in the school or how good you were at games. Blazers for both sexes or a light dress or gymslip for girls were worn in the summer, and grey trousers or a grey suit for the boys in all seasons. School uniforms were an opportunity for headmasters and headmistresses to indulge their obsessions about 'their' school and how much better it was than the others and how the pupils could be easily identified in public. Uniforms were also a rich source of income for the shops where they had to be bought because the more individual a school uniform was, the fewer shops would agree to stock it, with the consequent mark-up in price.

As for underwear, long, older-fashioned women's knickers were elasticised around the legs as well as the waist, so it is strange that men's underpants were either buttoned or, awkwardly, fitted with loops through which you passed your braces before securing them to the buttons that were sewn around the waist of your trousers. If you needed to lower your trousers during the day it would be unwise to undo your front braces because they would leap upward pulled by the rear braces, and if you were wearing a pullover a major process of undressing would have to follow. A wiser procedure was to take your pullover off over your head first and then pull your braces off your shoulders without undoing the buttons.

Women's clothes in the late 1930s were more dignified in some ways than the boyish look and short skirts of the 'flapper' age of the 1920s. Skirts were longer, cut on the bias, tight and smooth so that the female form was more emphasised. You could display the slimness of your body as well as your curves. Evening dresses often revealed your entire back, and you wore cheeky or sporty little hats and frilly dresses.

Statistically, you were now as likely to buy your clothes in a department store as have them made by a dressmaker. Mrs. Josser in Collins's novel *London Belongs to Me* buys a blue dress at Bourne & Hollingsworth in London's Oxford Street before she meets her prospective in-laws. It cost £3.3s., which was close to a normal weekly wage. A hat cost her 10/6d. more and gloves 4/11d., so the outfit set her back a sizeable £3.18.5d.

Women were beginning to be seen in trousers, called 'slacks', but the garment was high fashion and not daily or work wear as it would become during the Second World War. Women's underwear was becoming ever lighter (the word 'scanties' was sometimes used) and often limited to 'camiknickers', a combination of a bodice and knickers, with a tailored slip. Underwear for women of all social classes became cheaper with the introduction of crêpe de chine, artificial silk, Celanese and rayon, together with mass factory production methods. Plain white tended to be replaced by pastel or pink. With the brassiere, usually called a 'bra', which was coming into use among younger woman, discreet padding was now built into your underwear, and nobody would know. While massive whaleboned corsets were still worn, especially by older and larger ladies, newer girdles or corselettes, which combined the bra and the corset in one garment, were on sale. In 1935 the pantie girdle came in. It had no seams or bones and so could be worn under a tight dress without displaying unsightly signs of its presence. You held up your stockings, a garment which you always wore, summer and winter, made of silk if you could afford them, with a suspender belt (garter belt in the US) or with clips fixed to your girdle or elasticised 'roll-on'. Barbara Pym, the novelist, describes her underwear as blue Celanese 'trollies' (knickers), a pink suspender belt and a pink vest. Both men and women wore 'combinations', especially in the winter, which combined – hence the name – an upper and a lower garment and were often made of wool. British houses were notoriously badly heated, and combinations were an alternative to various forms of thick underwear. A famous item, into which young girls were forced like a straitjacket, was the 'liberty bodice', so-called because it freed children from restrictive corsets. 'All it did,' writes Margaret Powell, 'was to suppress the flesh and make it flat.'

Women's hair was no longer cropped as in the 'flapper' age but longer, curved round the neck or rolled into a ribbon shape around the head. In late 1938 hairdressers introduced the 'pageboy' look in which your hair fell straight to the shoulder and curved inwards at the ends. You had to wear a hat for most events, and middle-class women were always hatted in public. It could be a pillbox with a tantalising veil, a beret that you hoped made you look French or a large confection leaving your face in full view.

As for winter wear, few worried about cruelty to animals in the fur coat industry, and many women wore a fox stole slung over their shoulders with its head, paws and claws on display. A fur coat of mink, Persian lamb or even sable was what you really wanted and one of the ultimate indications of your husband's or lover's wealth and power. And you might aim to show your own power by wearing aggressively high-heeled shoes. These, with quite a tight skirt, made you walk along with fast little steps and a wriggle that many men found sexy. So, you had to tread the line between elegant and common with some care. Plucking the eyebrows until you looked permanently astonished was the fashion, much copied from the young film star Marlene Dietrich, who displayed a cold or even cruel look. Rather riskily, you might dye your hair platinum blonde to look like another star, Jean Harlow, for Hollywood rather than Paris was now the style to imitate. Delicate nail-varnishing (bright red was vulgar) had come in, while lipstick, powder and paint were no longer restricted to women of doubtful morals, or actresses, and young women often applied it in public. Makeup had even spread to suburban housewives. Things were changing. In 1934 Cole Porter had written the lyrics, 'In olden days a glimpse of stocking was looked on as something shocking, but now, God knows, anything goes.' London was more advanced than the provinces. When Mrs. Delafield wears a new lipstick, her husband objects. 'He should go to London,' she confides to her diary. When she goes to the capital, she has her eyebrows plucked and buys face cream, rouge, powder and lipstick, wondering what her husband will say when she returns. Inevitably, some women overdid it. John Osborne, the 'kitchen-sink' playwright, describes his mother's use of cosmetics:

> Her lips were covered in some sticky slime … which she bought at Woolworth's. She had a cream base … covered with a powder, which she showered off in little avalanches when she leant forward … lots of rouge … and an overgenerous dab of 'Californian Poppy' perfume, known to schoolboys as *fleur des dustbins*.

People rarely bathed more than once a week, so advertisements warned you, menacingly and coyly at the same time, against 'B.O', or 'body odour'. You were encouraged to use Lifebuoy, a bright red soap, which got up your nose and made you sneeze. Even worse was 'mouth odour' ('what your best friend wouldn't tell you,' wrote the copywriter), which was to be combatted with Macleans' toothpaste ('Did you Maclean your teeth today?' was the advertising slogan)

Observers of change would have had much to note. Nevertheless, despite the newness of the way women were dressing, for working-class women and others of a certain age, underwear was still a vest, long knickers, a coarse petticoat and cotton stockings held up with garters. The grandmother of the distinguished British social historian Harold Perkin still wore split drawers tied around her waist with a ribbon. On the cusp of the second major international war of the century, some elderly women were still dressing in the style and perhaps even in the same clothes that they had worn in 1918, at the end of the Great War, as Katie Johnson's character Mrs. Wilberforce does as late as 1955 in the film *The Lady-Killers*.

John Osborne's grandmother dressed in the 1930s as she had thirty years before, in a long skirt and a straw hat, covering swept-up hair. She smelled of lavender water and mothballs and wore a brooch to close her high-collared blouse.

The real change, nylon, and then terylene, was to come later. On 15 March 1939 Samuel Courtauld announced the patenting of nylon, to be made in the United Kingdom by Courtauld's and ICI, but it would be as yet too expensive to compete with rayon, the artificial fibre of the late 1930s.

Chapter 5

Health and Education

The statistics showed that by the late 1930s immense progress had been made in public health since the start of the century. In particular, infant mortality, which in 1900 had seen 142 deaths per 1,000 live births, had been reduced to 55 per 1,000 by 1938. Thus, the chances of your baby dying before it was a year old had fallen by about two-thirds. It was no longer necessary to keep producing children in case they died before reaching the age when they would have begun to contribute to the family expenses. For this reason, though for many others also, the birth rate fell from 24.6 per 1,000 of the population just before the First World War to 15.5 in 1938. Not all was rosy, however. Figures for deaths in childbirth and of low expectation of life were still disturbingly high in poverty-stricken areas of industrial and urban Britain. In rural areas also health was particularly poor, not only because of low wages and the scarcity of medical assistance, but also because rural housing was often damp. Bronchitis, rheumatism and tuberculosis were frequent. The depressed regions and poorer families continued to see their babies die, the worst case being, as might be expected, the town of Jarrow where unemployment was so heavy. In 1935, infant mortality in Jarrow reached the appalling figure of 114 per 1,000 live births.

Most women relied on a midwife, perhaps even an untrained one, and gave birth at home. Through much pressure, among others by Lucy Baldwin, wife of the prime minister until 1935, pain relief using gas and air machines was more and more widely provided in the latter 1930s. By this time also it was common for pregnant women and new mothers to attend one of the 3,500 maternity and child welfare centres open in 1938. The pregnant woman or new mother might be able to get advice from the health visitor or district nurse. The situation was getting better. Sulphonamide drugs began to be used in maternity wards. Furthermore, new legislation required all births to be attended by trained midwives from July 1937. This would be financed nationally at a cost of £500,000 a year.

Recent experiments had shown that a small amount of extra food during pregnancy also reduced maternal mortality substantially. An immediate result was that by 1938 fewer than 4 in 1,000 mothers died in childbirth. While this figure showed a great improvement, seventy years later death in childbirth would have fallen to the minute proportion of about 1 in 10,000.

In addition, by the end of the 1930s people were living longer. Average expectation of life in 1900 had been 58.7 years for men and 62.9 for women. The Depression had the effect of lowering these figures, but by the end of the 1930s the average age at death had risen to 64. In Norman Collins's novel *London Belongs to Me*, it is significant that Mrs. Vizzard says that she expects to have died by the age of 64 and so does not try to extend the lease on her house.

Legislation in the 1930s brought improvements for people in general. For instance, the Public Health Act of 1936 required doctors to notify the local authority of any cases of serious infectious diseases and introduced powers of compulsory disinfection and quarantine. The Factory Act of 1937 forced employers to provide hygienic and appropriate lavatories, and the Food and Drugs Act of 1938 enforced quality standards for food, drugs, medical devices and cosmetics.

Better food, better housing and public sanitation in cities, as well as widespread immunisation against smallpox, were to a considerable extent responsible for the better health and longer lives of most people in British cities during the late 1930s. Medical inspections, free milk and free dinners for some children were now part of the education service.

There had been great progress in medicine and surgery, but medicine was still impotent to cure serious disease. Most deaths among younger people were caused by tuberculosis. Among those over about 50 cancer was the largest cause of death. Diphtheria was common until mass immunisation came after 1940. It caused an annual average of 1,800 child deaths. The Lancashire cotton town of Bolton suffered an outbreak of diphtheria in 1937 with twenty-three deaths. Tuberculosis was widely recognised and treated in sanatoria but in Bolton you caught it from the damp air in cotton mills, and often it was dismissed as 'chestiness'. In that town, where the disease ought to have attracted concentrated medical treatment, there was only an under-resourced isolation hospital.

In comparison with medicine in the late twentieth and the twenty-first centuries, this backwardness stands out. In the 1930s there were no vaccines to protect against poliomyelitis or hepatitis B. Transplant surgery was unknown, as were inhalants for asthmatics, or dialysis machines to do the job of failed kidneys. There were few defences against heart problems: no statins, ace inhibitors or beta blockers. Techniques such as scanning, angioplasty, endoscopy, modern colonoscopy and 'keyhole' surgery were many years in the future. Helicobacter pylori was unknown as a cause of duodenal ulcers. Laser eye surgery as used to remove cataracts was not developed, and anaesthesia was provided with ether through a mask, without the pre-operation injection of drugs to induce unconsciousness. The dangers of smoking cigarettes were hardly recognised. Public concern with men's health and fitness had arisen when a great number of the volunteers presenting themselves for service in the South African War at the beginning of the century had been rejected through unfitness. However, this did not change greatly, for only one-third of the conscripts of 1917–18 were found fit enough to be soldiers, and another third were stated, in the words of Prime Minister David Lloyd George, to be 'almost physical wrecks'. But after the improvements in health policy and treatment in the interwar years, 70 per cent of the conscripts for the Second World War would be found fit for service.

What remedies were available? A person who looks at newspapers from the late 1930s is struck by the number of advertisements for patent medicines compared with what may be claimed in an advert today. We no longer read about 'night starvation', which you could relieve with Horlicks. 'Inner cleanliness', meaning regular emptying of the bowels, was promised by patent medicines such as Ex-Lax chocolate, California Syrup of Figs, castor oil, Bile Beans, Eno's Fruit Salts and even Corn Flakes and Shredded Wheat. Constipation was caused largely by an absence of fibre in the diet and was widely feared. 'Have you done your duty?' was the euphemistic way for boarding-school matrons and hospital sisters to enquire whether you had, as is said today inelegantly but without being thought vulgar, 'done a poo'. 'Shit' was absolutely unmentionable and 'crap' was hardly known. 'Mummy, I want to do some duty,' wails young Dudley in Ernest Raymond's novel *The Kilburn Tale*.

John Boyd Orr's famous 1937 report on the relation between diet and health calculated that half the British population did not earn enough to be able to buy an adequately healthy diet and that 30 per cent lived on a diet that was insufficient. The poor consumed low amounts of milk, eggs, fruit, vegetables, meat and fish. Even the somewhat less poor and particularly the old, with low incomes, suffered poor health. Too many people lived on what in the twenty-first century would be called 'junk' food. The results were rickets, dental caries, tuberculosis and anaemia, accompanied by constipation and gynaecological difficulties.

The public was advised to consume foods that were said to have health values. On railway station platforms very large and permanent metal plates told your mother that 'anaemic girls need Virol'. Presumably they were hinting that adolescent females needed to make up for their loss of blood during menstruation. In his novel *At the Chime of a City Clock*, D. J. Taylor guyed the advertisements for health tonics, writing, 'Susie was one of those bright, bouncy creatures of the kind you see in adverts, hiking all day on a slab of Vitamalt.' One famous slogan was 'Phyllossan fortifies the over-forties'. Everybody knew the remedies for headache, such as Aspro, the commercial name for aspirin, and Milk of Magnesia and similar alkaline products for bad digestions and the very common duodenal ulcer. Vicks VapoRub and Vapex for colds contained camphor and menthol. Mr. Josser in Norman Collins's *London Belongs to Me* tries to keep coughs and colds away by wearing a pad stuffed with medicated cottonwool called Thermogene over his chest. For those who could afford it, sun-worship and various forms of expensive dieting were thought to be cure-alls. Antibiotics were not yet generally available, so stinging iodine was put on cuts. When Esther Simons's son fell over regularly in the playground of his preparatory school, he skinned his knees badly. The school was well run and staffed by a matron who would apply a 'kaolin poultice' which had to be as hot as possible and had the effect of drawing out the pus. When young Robert Barltrop had whooping cough, his mother gave him ipecacuanha root, although a popular remedy for whooping cough was to take the child to where roads were under repair and let him or her breathe in the fumes of the tar.

Of course, patent medicines would often work, but there were others that were fraudulent. In June 1938 one Sunday newspaper was advertising remedies that claimed to be able to cure epilepsy, heart disease, varicose veins, piles, eczema and rheumatism, and one single drug that was effective against hay fever, asthma, malaria, influenza, insomnia and 'most forms of pain'. Even effective patent medicines ignored serious causes of symptoms and dissuaded sufferers from seeking proper medical advice and investigation. But was this easily available? What could doctors really do, and what were hospitals like?

Am I Covered?

The National Insurance Act of 1911 insured low-paid manual workers and others against unemployment and sickness. They paid for it with a weekly 4d. stamp, to which the employer contributed 3d. and the State, that is general taxation, added 2d. They could consult the 'panel' doctor and be prescribed free medicine. Wives were not covered except for giving birth, when a grant of £1.10s. would pay for the midwife. The result was that women neglected their health. By the 1930s the earnings limit for protection by National Insurance had risen to £250, by when some 20 million men were covered. Wives and self-employed men were not covered, so they had to pay the doctor. It cost 3/6d. a time, so you tried home remedies first. The working-class district of Walthamstow in north-east London featured a 'quack doctor', who held forth to a crowd and gave advice on diet. He wore a white coat, and his wife was dressed as a nurse. His stall in the market was covered with flasks and test tubes. He talked about his 'surgery', and he performed one or two tricks to sell his 'medicines'.

People with higher incomes paid for themselves, although there were many 'Friendly Societies' that, in return for contributions, insured you privately. An important one was the Hospital Savings Association. The doctors needed the fees of these private patients because half their income came from them. Many practices would be found to be in debt when the National Health Service arrived in 1948.

'Sick clubs' needed as many members as they could get, so the *Willesden Chronicle* of 7 January 1938 carried an advertisement for such a club that for 8d, a week would provide benefits for six months. Esther Simons contributed 8d. a week to a Friendly Society where she lived in East London. Benefits of various sums were granted. Among them sickness pay (for thirteen weeks), a consultation with a physician, spectacles, a part of hospital costs, together with costs for transport to hospital and to a convalescent home, ending with costs for a tombstone. Esther Simons gave birth and underwent a serious operation, both in hospital. Possibly, she contributed to the Hospital Savings Association. Perhaps she also benefitted from living in London where hospital provision was better. In the same year her mother died in her sleep at the early age of 53. The death certificate stated that she had died from chronic bronchitis and emphysema leading to heart failure. The strain of poverty probably had a significant effect.

As for hospitals, these were still largely seen as charitable foundations for the poor. Bolton's Royal Infirmary relied on fees from those patients who could afford to pay, and on charity. Hospitals employed a 'lady almoner' whose task was to assess whether and how much patients should be asked to pay for their treatment. Local people were loyal to their hospital. In the last two weeks of 1937 Willesden General Hospital recorded ninety contributions, ranging from 10/6d. to £10. People gave gifts in kind, including books, postage stamps, fruit and groceries. Alexandra Rose Day, on 23 June, was dedicated to hospital collections. On that day in 1937

£765.12.1d. was collected for hospitals in Hampstead, a generally wealthy London borough. Rich industrialists, such as Lord Nuffield, leader of the motor industry, would in due course provide iron lungs for every hospital in the country.

Many hospitals were small and, while often popular, lacked important facilities. Hornsey General, in North London, reported in September 1937 having admitted only nine patients in the previous week, performed twenty-two X-rays, and had treated twelve 'casualties' (Accident and Emergency today). It specialised in therapeutic massage and ultraviolet ray treatment, with which it had treated 300 patients, probably several at a time. The much larger Hampstead General Hospital, in a neighbouring area, reported 125 occupied beds and 1,586 attendances at its Outpatients Department and at Casualty. Its theatres had carried out forty-nine operations.

There were significant developments in medicine. Radiotherapy was rapidly developing. Transfusion with bottled blood advanced the progress of surgery. It had been introduced during the Spanish Civil War of 1936–39, where taking the blood to the wounded at front-line casualty centres saved many lives. A new drug called M & B, after May & Baker, the firm that first made it, was used to treat pneumococcal meningitis, middle ear diseases following measles, and scarlet fever. Bill, the medical student in Collins's *London Belongs to Me*, remarks on the efficacy of M & B. The drug had been used for the first time in 1938 to treat pneumonia and later saved the life of Winston Churchill. It would in time be superseded by penicillin.

Ordinary people's medical treatment depended to a considerable extent on the consciences of local practitioners. Many were clearly devoted, treating their 'panel' patients with as much care as they did their paying patients. Others gave more time to their private patients, who came into the surgery, which was usually the doctor's house, by the front door, while the 'panel' patients came to the back door. The system was widely felt to need reform. One of the most popular novels of the time, with sixteen impressions between July 1938 and June 1939, was A. J. Cronin's *The Citadel*. The author, a doctor himself, describes a mining company in Wales that employs three doctors. The company deducts money from wages and pays the doctors according to how many men sign up with each of them. The doctors devote themselves to their paying patients and employ ill-paid junior assistants to see the miners. The practices do not have proper facilities for diagnosis and classify high temperatures as 'pyrexia of unknown origin', without seeking further explanation. The new doctor, who is the mouthpiece of the author, discovers that he has an outbreak of typhoid fever on his hands, in an area devoid of a hospital or an isolation ward. The local Medical Officer of Health is idle, so the new doctor investigates and discovers that a local sewer is broken and is leaking into the wells. The novel was a bestseller and was made into a successful film and played an important part in advancing the case for a national health service, free to all.

Middle-class people and the wealthy went for their operations to 'nursing homes', as they were known. These were equivalent to private hospitals today. If you were ill you would stay at home, the doctor would visit, and you would engage a private nurse. When the diarist of E. M. Delafield's *Diary of a Provincial Lady*, caught measles, a serious disease that affected her eyes, she convalesces by the sea with a nurse in attendance.

Surveys done during the Second World War showed what a crazy patchwork the system was. By the outbreak of war, still only half of the population was covered by sickness insurance. The introduction of the National Health Service in 1948 revealed how much the population had been neglected previously. However, the greatest victims of the general neglect of ill health were working-class wives. They had no access to free treatment except when giving birth. It was calculated that over one-third of a survey of 1,250 working-class wives had 'indifferent' health, and a quarter of the wives suffered conditions that were described as 'grave'. The most frequent ailments of working-class wives, worn down as they were by pregnancies, lack of time to rest, poor diets and generally inconvenient and insanitary housing, were found to be anaemia, headaches, constipation, rheumatism, various gynaecological ailments including prolapses, as well as bad teeth, varicose veins, leg ulcers and phlebitis. They had very little access to oculists or dentists.

If you had difficulty seeing the newspaper or a library book you could buy a pair of spectacles 'off the shelf' for 6d. from Woolworth's. You tried on a pair and then another and tested yourself against a few lines on a card. That would do if both your eyes needed the same lens, but not if you had a condition that demanded a prescription.

As for your teeth, the availability of free dentistry from 1948 revealed a mass of untreated dental disease. British teeth were characterised by widespread decay, pyorrhoea and sepsis. This also had consequences for the digestion. In the days when you had to pay for a session in the dentist's chair, you might well decide to have all your teeth taken out. At least this would free you from the toothache that you would suffer as your teeth steadily rotted. A set of false teeth was sometimes a present for one's twenty-first birthday. In working-class areas, few adults had all their natural teeth, and most had at least partial dentures.

People who were mentally unstable were met with extreme prejudice and were looked down upon in society for being born the way they were. They were treated in grim asylums, or not at all. While the Mental Health Act of 1930 did make a start, psychiatric care in the 1930s was still very limited. There was essentially no treatment for schizophrenic patients, for example. Psychiatrists attempted to treat their symptoms by prescribing drugs such as sedatives, which suppressed the patient's nervous system, and trying a few different mind-body therapies. Treatment for psychiatric disorders could be harsh, including insulin shock therapy, electro-convulsive therapy and lobotomy. This was a form of brain surgery that might reduce mental agitation, but it often left the patient passive and apathetic.

People read about the arrival in Britain, on 6 June 1938, and saw it on the cinema newsreels, of the Viennese psychiatrist and analyst Sigmund Freud, in flight from the Nazis who had taken over Austria. Freud died on 23 September 1939, but his daughter Anna continued his work as a child psychiatrist, founding a centre for mental health in later years.

Most people had to see the doctor, take medicine or go to a hospital at some time or other, but everybody had had experience of school, in their own lives and later in the lives of their children.

Education

Following the Education Act of 1870, by 1881 elementary education was both compulsory and free for all. By the 1930s compulsory education for all children was seen as vital in a world of growing civic-mindedness, aspiration, consumption and technical advances.

In 1918, the school-leaving age was fixed at 14, so that anyone born after 1905 now had the benefit of thirteen years of education between the ages of 5 and 14. All those under 60 had enjoyed at least some years of basic education.

Millions of people who in June 1945 would vote for the Labour Party's policy of major social change had been schooled in the interwar years. After the war, the planned but long-deferred raising of the school-leaving age to 15 and the introduction of secondary education for all between the ages of 11 and 15 would be seen to benefit everyone, except possibly the employers of cheap and young labour.

The education system of the 1930s was like a pyramid, with the point representing the very small number of university students. At the bottom were close on four-fifths of the nation's children, for whom education was just the elementary school. You probably attended one of the great three-storey or even larger buildings erected since 1870, with their rows of two-seater desks on a stepped floor, rising toward the back of the classroom so that back-row pupils could see the blackboard and hear the teacher. Some were ill ventilated, heated by black stoves in each room, grim looking, and already declared unsuitable, while others were warm, with immense radiators, large windows and ample playground areas. Esther Simons's son attended secondary school in an ancient elementary school building, condemned in 1937, which had one semi-underground playground and another unsafely sited on the roof, and appallingly unwelcoming lavatories and washing facilities, though it was well ventilated and heated. Bryan Magee reminds his readers that, as trains run through the inner suburbs of London (and it must have been the same in other cities of Britain), one sees

> Huge buildings in three unusually high storeys … they all have the same windowed classrooms, the same parquet-floored classrooms and assembly halls, the same asphalt playgrounds with pitches for games marked out in white, the same external colour schemes on their facades. In one of them you could be anywhere in Edwardian London, the desks, the smell of chalk, the bell, the huge radiators …

Rather earlier, Arthur Conan Doyle had put the following lyrical words into the mouth of his famous detective, Sherlock Holmes. The schools were '[brick] islands in a lead-coloured sea. Lighthouses, beacons for the future … to civilise and socialise with values of morality, civic behaviour and work discipline'.

As for nursery education, in 1939 there were only 103 funded nursery schools. Lucky parents found nursery places for only 6,000 3- and 4-year-old children. However, the Infants' divisions of some elementary schools admitted children under 5. Four-year-old Paul Vaughan's mother took him with her when she walked with his elder brother to school. When Paul learned that he couldn't stay at school with his brother, he wept, and the teacher said he could stay.

Pike's Lane elementary school in Bolton, closely examined by social observers in 1937, had been built in 1875. It accommodated over 700 children between the ages of 5 and 14. It housed 300 infants, 200 juniors and over 200 seniors. Despite progress in reducing class sizes, more than one-third of children in 1938 elementary schools were being taught in classes of over forty, sitting in tightly packed rows with two children at a desk that would probably have been one of the original ones of the late nineteenth century, now splintered and carved with old pupils' names. Classes with children of different ages were still usual, especially in rural areas. In such conditions, and despite numerous recommendations for more child-centred teaching, most children's experience was lecturing by the teacher and use of the blackboard (a practice known as 'chalk and talk').

At Pike's Lane, after morning assembly and prayers, the first lesson was Scripture, followed by 'sums', that is arithmetic (fractions, decimals and long division). Then came a brief 'playtime'. The children had to learn to spell twenty words a week and write them out fifty times if they failed to do so. Neat handwriting was an important skill that might help you get a job in an office. The classroom had a stock of steel-nibbed pens that were chewed down to the ends. The desks had porcelain inkwells that were filled from a metal and white-enamelled jug in which, as many older people remember, blocks of solidified ink were dissolved. The job of filling the inkwells was a privilege granted to the 'ink monitor'. In later times, autobiographers were to remember different aspects of their elementary school experience. The later philosopher Bryan Magee remembered only the chanting of the multiplication tables round the class, terminating with the triumphant shout of 'twelve twelves are one hundred and forty-four'. In the private preparatory school that Esther Simons's son attended, there was always one boy who would get seven times six wrong, and he would get a whack with the ruler on his hand. You expected this. In some schools there was also a great deal of caning, mostly on the hand, as Robert Barltrop noticed, but he contrasts it with another school where he went. Here, the cane stayed in the cupboard. Hitting children, in any case, was common, and few thought that there was anything wrong with a cuff round the ear. Indeed, in middle-class homes formal spanking and even beating were accepted.

Learning by rote or repetition was often scorned by progressive educationists, but Bryan Magee insists that without constant repetition he would not have learned the tables. He probably learnt the imperial weights and measures in the same way. These were the mysterious 'rod, pole and perch', which were terms used by different professions for the same length, and thus of no use to most people. You learned that twelve inches was a foot and three feet made a yard. Twenty-two yards was a chain, which was the length of a cricket pitch; ten chains were a furlong (used only in horse racing), which was thus 220 yards or one-eighth of a mile. Obviously, you had to learn pounds, shillings and pence, and how to add them up, dividing the pennies by twelve and the shillings by twenty. Sixteen ounces made a pound in weight, so you soon learned that a 'quarter' of sweets meant four ounces. You were weighed in stones, which had fourteen pounds each, so if an American film referred to a person weighing so many pounds you had to divide the amount by fourteen to produce a meaningful weight in British terms. In school athletics you ran the quarter mile, which was known as the 440 yards, and the half mile or 880 yards, so you knew that there were 1,760 yards in a mile. You were not going to come across decimal lengths and weights, so few people could think in decimal terms, although decimal arithmetic was taught. If more science had been taught in elementary schools the situation would have been different, but lack of equipment and probably teachers meant that science tended to be limited to botany, which was useful if you lived in a house with a garden. Even the grotesque school proprietor Squeers, in Charles Dickens's novel *Nicholas Nickleby* of a century earlier, taught botany, although his knowledge did not extend to spelling the word, which he wrote as 'bottinney'.

Music required only a piano and someone who knew how to play it, or often just a teacher who could sing. Long after leaving school, you remembered the songs, among them 'Wher'er You Walk', 'D'ye Ken John Peel', 'There Is a Tavern in the Town', 'Early One Morning', 'Sweet Lass of Richmond Hill, 'John Brown's Body', and 'Kemp Town Races'. Much time also was spent on English literature, read aloud around the class or by the teacher: Lamb's *Tales of Shakespeare*, *Robinson Crusoe*, *Uncle Tom's Cabin*, *Pickwick Papers* and *The Scarlet Pimpernel* were favourites. Esther Simons remembered being introduced to Chaucer. She could also recite Portia's speech about the quality of mercy from *The Merchant of Venice.* Her younger brother proudly recited Wordsworth's poem *Daffodils* to his grandchildren. Her son heard about Captain Marryat's *Mr. Midshipman Easy* from a teacher and asked the librarian in the local public library to get it for him.

Most parents approved of the values taught in school, such as cleanliness and good manners, honesty, refined language and sexual modesty. Teachers laid stress on middle-class standards of pronunciation. London children were taught to eradicate their cockney pronunciation by reciting 'How Now, Brown Cow', reflecting the view of the playwright George Bernard Shaw in his Edwardian play *Pygmalion*, staged again in 1938, that if you pronounced 'properly' you could advance socially. So, dropped 'aitches' and glottal stops such as 'bread and bu'er' were discouraged. In Bryan Magee's London school, the children were made to say the upper-class 'craws' instead of 'cross' and to pronounce 'often' as 'orphan'. But it didn't work, remembers Magee. In London's Hoxton district, he wrote later, correcting children's speech was like trying to bail out the Atlantic with a teaspoon. At Pike's Lane School in Bolton, the children scorned the teaching of 'swanky accents and talk'.

Esther Simons, her sister and her younger brother were bright children who won prizes and certificates which they treasured. They recalled their schooldays in the 1920s with pleasurable nostalgia, and resented being, in their words, 'dragged out' of school on their fourteenth birthdays because the family needed the few shillings they could bring in from a job. At least Esther and her sister were not kept at home by their mother to do housework or care for younger children. Furthermore, in some areas parents kept the children away from school to earn some money. This, however, had to be hidden from the 'truant officer', a man feared in the district, who would energetically seek out the absentees.

To be taken out of school at the first possible date was particularly resented in later life when some boys and girls felt that they had been prevented from progressing sufficiently to take and perhaps pass the 'scholarship', which might have opened the path for them to secondary education. In other cases, they were grateful for the sacrifice of their parents. Will Green, who later married Esther Simons's sister, went to a grammar school even though his mother, a restaurant cook, had been abandoned by her husband. Nevertheless, many children such as the anonymous 'Mary Smith' in A. P. Jethcott's study conducted in 1941–42, who 'passed the scholarship', did not take it up because her father was unemployed, and their parents could not afford the expense or forego their daughter's earnings. There were also cultural reasons for not taking up places in the grammar school. William Woodruff's sister, who came top in the entire county of Lancashire in the scholarship examination, could not go to the grammar school in Preston because her father refused to see the value of education for girls. On the other hand, the parents of Harold Perkin, later a distinguished academic, were given a generous sum for sports clothes and school uniform by the Labour council of Stoke-on-Trent.

Robert Barltrop's teachers in the Infants' department of his north-east London school were all women, but when he went up to the Juniors, they were mostly men, many of whom had gone through the Great War while others were approaching the end of their careers. The women teachers were either very young women or older unmarried women. Women had to resign on marriage. If a teacher was a 'Mrs.', it usually meant that she was either a supply teacher or a widow, often because of the war. The 'feminisation' of elementary education would be a post-1945 phenomenon.

Secondary School

One of the major areas of discussion was the change in what was taught to older children, meaning from about 11 upward. In areas that had the resources to do so, particularly the relatively wealthy and progressive London County Council, the senior boys and girls in the elementary school could follow a more advanced course with specialised teachers for individual subjects. Secondary education in a different school, at least for the 9 per cent or so of children who were judged able to profit from it, was beginning in London even before 1914 in fifty 'central' schools. These offered three years of secondary education. In 1935 about 120 out of every 1,000 children passed into secondary schools. One historian of education writes, referring to London, that 'amid the harshness of the interwar years examples can be found in the very poorest areas of children who were taught to swim, acted in Shakespeare plays or learnt the violin'. A well-run central school could give children up to four years of solid and stimulating education. Great progress was made in the interwar years, so that by the late 1930s an average of a quarter of children moved to secondary education. London had eighty-seven central schools and most elementary schools had senior departments, called 'higher tops'. Esther Simons's younger brother went to a London elementary school. When he left in 1929, probably to go for a year to a central school, the headmaster wrote on the certificate pasted into his prize book that he was 'top of the class'. Nevertheless, he ended up in a tailor's workshop and, though he became a skilled craftsman, never fulfilled his intellectual potential.

The figures for 1938 showed that slightly over one-third of children aged over 14 were still receiving full-time education, but only for a year or so. Only 4 per cent of 16-year-olds, and only 2 per cent of 18-year-olds were still in full-time education. If you were from a working-class family, you had only a one in ten chance of getting the full benefits of secondary education. As the Second World War began, your access to secondary schooling and even more to higher education was still a function of your social class and your parents' income, but not your ability.

Even though there was some secondary education provided, there was also considerable opposition to children staying at school after they turned 14. It came from industry and elsewhere, which thought that most elementary school children could not assimilate post-elementary education nor benefit from it. Despite reports that said that all children should have some sort of secondary education, by 1938 progress was still slow. It was calculated that some 600,000 children were still in entirely unreorganised schools. 1 September 1939 was the date on which the Education Act of 1936 had stated that the school-leaving age was to be raised to 15, but that was the day when Germany invaded Poland, so Britain had other preoccupations. The school-leaving age would have to remain at 14 until after the war.

Grammar Schools

Of the few who enjoyed secondary education, only an even smaller number found their way to the grammar school, sometimes called 'county high school'. The grammar school was the avenue that led to obtaining the School Certificate, and the higher-rated 'matric' qualification. In their turn, these examination certificates led to the white-collar job in commerce, to the civil service, to one of the professions or even the university.

By the late 1930s some 14 per cent of 11-year-old elementary school children 'passed the scholarship' and obtained a free place at a grammar school and sometimes a small grant for uniform. However, in England and Wales if your father was a professional or managerial man you were four times as likely to go to a grammar school than if he was a skilled manual worker and five times more likely than if your father was an unskilled manual worker. In the grammar school, probably for the first time, working-class or lower-middle-class boys or girls met their middle-class fellows who had attended private preparatory schools, whose parents spoke differently, were professionals, and might even own a car. Some pupils entered the grammar school by an examination set by the school itself, basically in English and arithmetic, and then there were the fee-paying pupils, for whom entry was relatively easy. A well-run grammar school would try to iron out these social differences by an elaborate uniform, a school tie, a blazer, and particularly a school cap with a badge. Richmal Crompton's William is pictured on the dustcover of that popular series wearing a garishly coloured cap. Esther Simons's son wore a cap in two clashing colours, reversed on the peak. For the grammar school that Robert Barltrop attended, short grey trousers and knee-high black socks with a red edge round their tops were required, as well as sports and gym kit. All this could be bought from only one local stockist and cost a hefty sum. Many parents of able children could not afford to pay for the uniform. Other parents made great sacrifices because they were extremely proud that their child was going to learn Latin (which they thought an essential part of a doctor's education because he scribbled his prescriptions in a few Latin words), that the school had extensive playing fields, was divided into houses like the Greyfriars of the Billy Bunter Stories, and had prefects and a head boy or girl. At Robert Barltrop's London grammar school they even used Latin words such as '*Cave*' ('Look out!). Cheating was 'cribbing', and the Head was known as the 'Beak'. The masters and, in the girls' schools, mistresses – not just 'teachers' – wore gowns, though rarely mortar boards, and spoke 'posh' like the doctor and the vicar. They all had university degrees, indicated by letters after their names, sometimes with 'Oxon' or 'Cantab' in brackets and the word 'hons.', indicating that their degree was of a higher status than the mere 'pass' degree that was often taken at Oxbridge.

In the grammar school there was a library and a huge assembly hall. The 11-year-old would look with awe at the honours board, which listed the pupils who had achieved entrance to universities, and the long lists of ex-pupils who had been killed in the Great War. The grammar school had excellent facilities, science laboratories, sports fields, and a gymnasium with a PT or 'gym' teacher who had a special qualification in the subject.

The point of a grammar school was to push its pupils to the highest academic achievement possible. Some pupils, perhaps the majority, would leave without much examination success, but at least they would go into an office, not a factory or workshop. Those with examination success would frequently go into a solicitor's or an accountant's practice. Will Green obtained employment with a firm of estate agents. Francis McFarland passed the qualifying test for entry into the clerical grade of the Civil Service. This meant that he was put on a salary scale with guaranteed annual increases and the chance of ascending to a higher grade and could look forward to retirement at 60 with a pension. It was not to be sneered at when office jobs were not all that easy to obtain. But examinations were the gateway to everything. As the head of Will Green's grammar school wrote in the school magazine: 'The highest education available is now open to all suitable boys, merely by passing the appropriate qualifying examinations.' This was the assumption and the ambition of the growing number of grammar schools all over the country, and perhaps the beginning of what has come to be called the 'meritocracy', or rule by those who deserve to do so because they have passed examinations.

However, to pass the School Certificate, known as 'General Schools', was not enough. For this you needed merely to have passes in five subjects. The important achievement was to 'get Matric'. This meant securing five passes, all at the same time, in English language, English literature, maths, a foreign language, and Latin or a science, and with 10 per cent marks more than the mere pass. 'Matric' was short for 'matriculation' which meant exemption from a university entrance examination, but it had come to mean a leaving certificate of higher value than the General School Certificate.

The grammar school was indeed an academic forcing house, but it did not neglect games. Here, its imitation of the fee-paying 'public school' was obvious. The heroes of the grammar school were the sports captains. Not just cricket and football were played, but also the upper-class rugby. Masters were sometimes appointed because, in addition to their formal qualifications, they could coach games. In some grammar schools, there were cadet corps, whose members clattered up and down stairs in their army boots, irritating those masters who had pacifist views. Grammar schools also encouraged out-of-school intellectual activity, with debating societies and chess clubs, which teachers were expected to support.

Private Schools

Pupils whose parents paid fees to get them into the grammar school had probably previously attended private schools but had not been able to pass the Common Entrance examinations of some great independent grammar schools or even the so-called public schools. Alternatively, there was no shortage of other private schools. All told, there were 82,000 recognised private schools in 1930. Middle-class parents would send a child to one of them that took young children, in the hopes not only that their offspring would mix with better-spoken or often cleaner classmates, but that they might get a free place at a grammar school or at least get into one even if the parents had to pay.

Preparatory or 'prep' schools prepared children for more exclusive schools, to which they went at the age of 13. These were clearly middle- and upper-class institutions. In the 1948 film *The Guinea Pig*, Richard Attenborough plays the part of Jack Read, a bright lower-class boy who is, in effect, the 'guinea pig', allowed as an experiment into the upper-class Saintbury school. Another one is Mark Linley in the Billy Bunter books. Mark is a very unlikely ex-factory hand who has gained admission to Greyfriars School because he is very bright. When the boys go on strike, they make him their form master.

When private-school boys reached the age of 18 they would go on to university or move smoothly into some upper-middle-class business or financial occupation with the aid of their father's connections.

Some girls went to one of the institutions operated by the Girls' Public Day School Trust, which had high academic as well as social standards. Parents, however, were in general unwilling to spend money on their daughters' education. Few girls remained in school after they reached 16.

Public Schools

The most wealthy and influential sent their sons to one of the great 'public' schools such as Eton, Harrow, Winchester, Wellington, Rugby, Westminster, Haileybury, Charterhouse and Shrewsbury. In 1939, out of 830 bishops, judges, magistrates, senior civil servants in Britain and India, governors of Dominions, bank directors, railways and the like, three-quarters had been educated in public schools. In these schools, Classics dominated the curriculum and games the social side.

Adult Education

For the determined, there were ways of continuing your education. William Woodruff enrolled at evening classes, progressing to the Workers' Educational Organisation and at 19 to the Oxford Catholic Workers' College, which led him to a distinguished academic career. He was one of the 6,000 in adult education apart from the 13,000 in teacher training colleges and the 50,000 at universities in 1938. The ladder was very steep, however. In the late 1930s only one-fifth of university students had begun their education in an elementary school. An infinitesimally small number had working-class backgrounds. The bald fact was that only 2 per cent of British 19-year-olds were receiving any form of full-time education. This was the smallest proportion of any advanced country in Europe.

There was, however, another route into the middle class from the elementary school. The local press carried quite large advertisements for business 'colleges' such as Pitman's and Clark's. 'If you want your daughter to obtain a well-paid post,' announced the advertisement, the business college was the place to go. Clark's College taught business skills and prepared teenagers for the Civil Service. Gregg's was another such institution. Its advertisements boasted high pass rates in the examinations of the Royal Society of Arts and in placing its students in jobs paying up to £2.10s. a week, which was the usual rate in London for a junior typist. Shorthand and typing skills would get a girl out of the factory and into the office, with all that meant in terms of better pay and rising status by adopting middle-class dress, speech and manners.

While in general, education consisted largely of rote learning, with some relaxation in music and art, several teachers and educational theorists were familiar with progressive theories and tried to base their teaching on creativity and on child-centred and self-directed learning. This was resisted, particularly in the grammar school, but the new ideas were slowly gaining ground in the Infants and Juniors divisions of the elementary school. As one historian writes: 'Classrooms gay with children's own paintings, equipped with weighing scales, water-measuring jugs, modelling clay, building bricks, Wendy houses, toyshops … first began to be seen and then to be widely copied …'

The overall value of education was deference to the authority of teachers and to people of a higher class. Girls were expected to be ladylike, and boys were punished for using foul language. Teachers emphasised the value of thrift and hygiene, particularly in areas where money was short and hygienic habits were scarce. In the 1930s schools stressed moral standards and character training, often above the general level of the district. Patriotism was underlined. Physical education was called 'drill' in the preparatory school that Esther Simons's son attended, and it took the form of rhythmic arm swinging, marching in step and marking time. When he himself taught in a grammar school long after the Second World War, on 11 November, the anniversary of Armistice Day in 1918, each class, accompanied by its begowned form master, marched past the school's war memorial, turning their heads to it in salute.

Chapter 6

The Other Half of the Population

What Should Women Be and Do?

As millions of men were demobilised in 1918–19, after the end of the Great War, the multitudes of women who had replaced them at work during the conflict were dismissed. This process went on during the 1920s and speeded up as the Great Depression began to bite in the early thirties. Jobs should be kept for family men, it was argued. Resentment against working women became marked. As a result, few middle-class women had entered the professions by the late 1930s. Only a minute number retained their civil service administrative grade posts. The BBC, a new structure and institution, which had employed married women when it was inaugurated in 1923 and had placed women in important posts, became steadily more male-dominated.

The most desirable image of a woman was that of a housewife and mother, not a career woman. Social pressure encouraged a woman's housewifely role. Her 'career', it was often stated, should be marriage. Schoolgirls were expected to and did help their mothers in domestic chores. In London County Council schools in the mid-1930s older girls spent two afternoons every week in the domestic science class, in preparation for their lives as wives and mothers. Those working-class women who did remain in traditional female employment, such as in the cotton industry, were poorly paid. The alternative was paid domestic work, shop work, or very unskilled tasks. For the middle-class unmarried woman there were two major professions: nursing and teaching.

Nursing was pre-eminently a female profession. The hours were long, the pay poor and the discipline strict. School teaching was the other main female professional occupation, but it was shared with men. The female teacher, however, was paid less than the male, receiving an average of £254 a year, compared with a man's £334. It was argued that a woman had only herself to maintain while a man had responsibility for a family. Some women did however have family responsibilities, and some men did not. The proper way to give family men more, it was argued and much later accepted, was by tax relief for his wife and children.

Such are the usual generalisations. Nevertheless, there seems to have been another side to the position of working women in late 1930s Britain. In fact, British women comprised nearly 30 per cent of the labour force, the same as before 1914. In some fields, such as secretarial and other office work, opportunities opened up, as they did in the relatively light and clean assembly work available in new factories. And, while it is true that the professions were male-dominated, this is not to say that no women held professional posts. By 1935, there were 116 female solicitors and 79 barristers. In medicine, the 477 female general practitioners of 1914 had become 2,800 by 1931, although this was still such a small proportion of the profession that a female doctor would be referred to as 'the lady doctor'. In his novel *London Belongs to Me,* Norman Collins's Mr. Josser refuses to allow a female doctor to examine him, but the author clearly portrays this as out-of-date prejudice. Some professions were aggressively masculine, which was the point of the film in which 'Mrs Pym of Scotland Yard', the title and the main character of the film of 1939, solves crimes over the heads of hostile senior police officers. The attitudes toward women who aimed to fill male roles were thus on the road to change.

For the time being, however, women who worked in male-dominated professions or were prominent in public life were seen as exceptional and there were few of them. Most women in the late 1930s lived in another world from the one that their great-granddaughters would know ninety years later. Few women in the 1930s had had opportunities for more than elementary education; they were paid less than men if they did work, and most had only marriage, children and domesticity to look forward to. But how most women felt about their role is difficult to judge. Memoirs of professionally successful women often complain about their unfair struggles in early life, but not every married woman who did not work outside the home felt that hers was an inferior situation. She was proud to be called 'Mrs.' and to change her surname on marriage. It meant that a man had chosen her to run his house and bear his children. If addressed as 'Miss' she would bristle and retort 'Mrs, if you don't mind!' She was now no longer under her own parents' authority and in her new role she often handled the weekly income, decided how the house was to be run, the meals, the children's upbringing and even where the family went on holiday. The husband who lived 'under

Above: A family in the 1930s.

Right: A school prize.

Bear Street Sunshine Milk Bar, Leicester Square.

London buses.

Right: Camp Coffee advertisement with an imperial tone.

Below: Capstan cigarettes advertisement.

Chamberlain and Hitler at Bad Godesberg, September 1938.

A day at the beach, mid-1930s. (Chris Cocks)

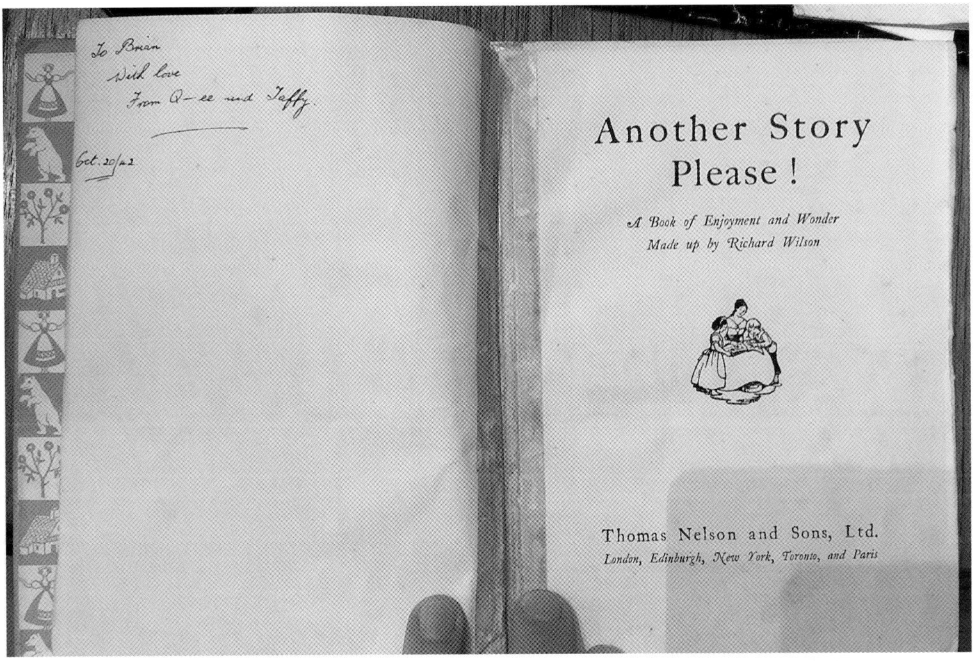

Above: Children's literature.
(Courtesy Christopher Masters)

Right: Cigarette card for Ogden's cigarettes, themed British costume series.

Gaumont State Cinema, Kilburn, after it closed down.

The Grange Cinema.

A 1930s classroom, British Schools Museum, Hitchin. (Paul Shreeve, Creative Commons 2.0)

DORKING, SURREY.

RESIDENTIAL PROPERTIES

in and on the outskirts of this favourite old-fashioned Town, between the North Downs and Leith Hill, near open Commons and a wonderful variety of well-wooded undulating country available by a network of foot and bridle paths, near two Golf Courses, 24 miles from London (Electric Trains).

All are on sand soil, from 230 to 350 feet above sea level.

TO BE SOLD BY AUCTION,

At the RED LION HOTEL, DORKING,
On MONDAY, OCTOBER 12th, 1936,
at 4 p.m.

WITH VACANT POSSESSION.

"NEW CLAN," HARROW ROAD, WEST.

6 Bed, Dressing, Bath and 2 Sitting Rooms ; Lounge Hall ; Attractive Garden and Orchard ; Total area 2R. 20P.
Exceptionally well built. ... ... Freehold.
Upset price £1,200 (Half cost).

In conjunction with Messrs. WALTER HALL & SONS, 1, York Street, Baker Street, W.1.
Solicitors : Messrs. SMALLPEICE & MERRIMAN, Guildford.

"GLORY VIEW," TOWER HILL.

3 Bed, Bath and 2 Sitting Rooms. Built 1907 and well fitted. Freehold. Upset price £550. For investment or occupation.
Solicitors : Messrs. HART, SCALES & HODGES, Dorking.

Houses for sale on auction, 1936.

Jarrow Marchers, October 1936.

Lifebuoy soap advertisement, 1929. (*Daily Mail Yearbook*)

Above: Maison Lyons Corner House, Marble Arch, London W.1.

Right: Metro-Land brochure – price 2d.

Nurses, with gasmasks, 1939. (Wellcome)

The Odean Theatre, Morecambe, 1937 – architect Harry Weedon's impression.

How to put on a baby's gas helmet, hints for mothers.

Billy Bunter and *The Magnet*.

Right: Queen Elizabeth. (Wikicommons)

Below: A London trolleybus pulls out of the London Transport depot, Carshalton. (UK Photo and Social History Archive)

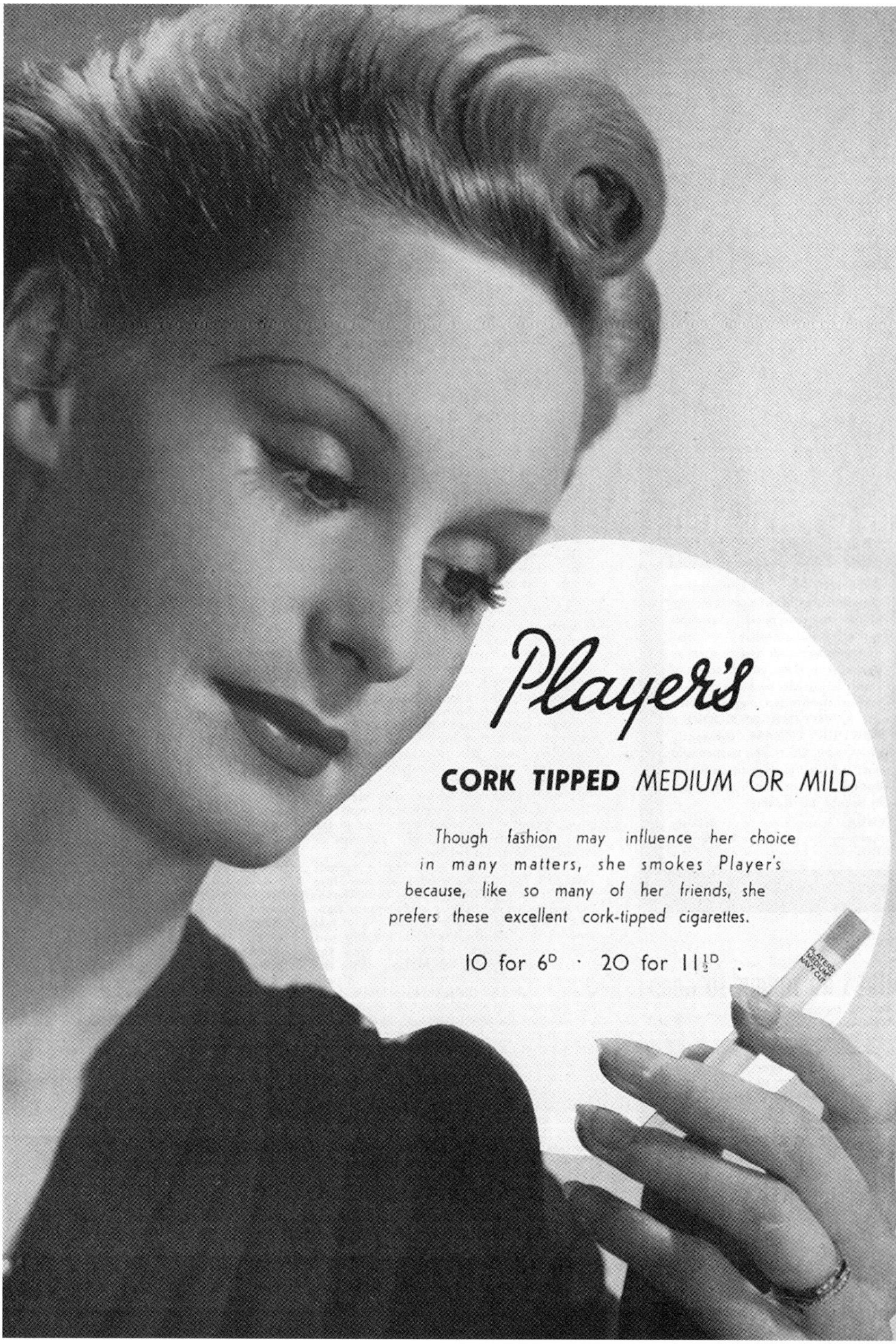

Player's cigarettes aiming at the women's market.

his wife's thumb', as the expression had it, was not rare. As the earlier music hall song went:

> *They hadn't been married for a month or more*
> *When underneath her thumb goes Jim ...*

Furthermore, the situation was on its way to change. Single women did seek work, unless they came from upper middle-class families, who thought that a girl was better off knowing only appropriate feminine skills, such as how to arrange flowers and handle the servants. Working-class girls had no choice. They had to get jobs, if only to support their parents and younger siblings. There were growing opportunities for them in shop work, particularly the large chains and department stores, and in offices. Even factory work was becoming cleaner and attracting better-educated girls. Jerry White, describing what was known as 'the worst street' in North London, reported that by the later 1930s, if local girls were neatly dressed and well spoken, carefully made up and coiffured, they could get jobs in fashionable ladies' dress shops and as cinema usherettes.

Yet this was not to say that these young and often self-assured women were approved of by the older generation. Agatha Christie, in her *The Case of the Middle-Aged Wife*, of 1934, records Mrs. Packington referring to her husband's typist as 'A made-up little minx, all lipstick and silk stockings and curls'.

How much and how skilfully a woman used cosmetics was a dividing line between respectability and commonness. As lipstick, powder and paint, not to speak of rouge, nail polish and the permanent wave, became indispensable, so cosmetics, which had been considered immoral or vulgar before 1914, were now just a part of how a woman, at least a young one, presented herself, and perhaps even if she was a middle-aged housewife. Ernest Raymond, in *The Kilburn Tale*, tells the reader that Mildred Rostrum is experimenting with cosmetics, at the same time as her daughter Brenda paints her fingernails. Brenda's aunt reproves her. Lipstick is bad enough, she says. Another novel of the period, Norman Collins's *London Belongs to Me*, describes Connie, the ageing ex-actress and nightclub cloakroom attendant, as applying 'eye-black' 'shamelessly', meaning probably that she overuses it. But Connie knows about eyeshadow because she was an actress and she still works in an atmosphere that is disreputable and louche, so it is normal for her to apply cosmetics generously.

Single women did indeed have greater career opportunities than married ones, but middle-class married women either happily gave up their careers or did not have much education, except perhaps of the genteel, undemanding sort approved of by society that would qualify a young woman for a little pleasant office work until marriage took her off to the new semi in the suburbs or the airy local authority estate. Here, if the husband's income allowed, she might have a charwoman for the heavier work. However, by the later 1930s, adverts showed the lady of the house cheerfully and deftly handling the new vacuum cleaner herself. Servants were getting harder to find because by then opportunities for less well-educated and less well-off women were greater. So, although the groceries, meat, bread and milk would still be delivered, the new middle-class housewife would have to cook and perhaps clean the house herself.

Married women who went out to work were rare. Esther Simons's elder sister-in-law stopped work when she married. She shopped in a leisurely manner every morning, exchanging pleasantries with the shopkeepers. She cleaned her house once a week, cooked an evening meal, and sometimes went up to London's West End to see a play in the afternoon. There was no question of her taking paid employment, although she was childless. Esther herself also gave up work on marriage and childbirth, but she took a job again when her husband lost his employment. Her younger sister, already occupying a senior office position, continued to work after marriage, which shows that her employer took a more modern position on married women working in his firm. She thus provided herself and her husband with a comfortable joint income, but they did not consider children an immediate requirement. Those three women, married respectively in 1927, 1933 and 1936, reflected the change in the expectations of married women over about a decade.

Changes in what women expected and what was being proposed to them were echoed and encouraged by the popular press. While the daily newspapers did allow space for hostile views about 'modern women', particularly if they smoked or applied cosmetics in public, they also celebrated female achievements and welcomed new opportunities for women. The *Daily Express* and the *Daily Mirror*, which had the largest circulations, challenged the equation of 'femininity' with domesticity. They offered their female readers a broader set of interests, at the same time as they strove to attract the working women who read the papers to think about matters other than finding a husband and starting a family. Mr. Smeeth, in J. B. Priestley's novel *Angel Pavement*, reads the paper on the tram on his way home, and is struck by how many stories are angled toward women. There were a lot of these that his wife would like to read, he thinks.

At the same time, in the latter 1930s you could see more and more pictures of attractive women in the newspapers, and read journalistic pieces about them, so while the newspapers reflected the growing assertion of women's independence and equality, they also underlined women as objects to be judged based on their physical appearance. Journalism and advertising emphasised cosmetics, slimming and 'sex appeal'. This last term had occasionally been used earlier but seems to have become frequent in the late 1930s. Women were now being put on view in the press for their clothes, hair, and figures. They were pictured in bathing costumes, lingerie and new fashions. Some women might object to this, but most probably looked forward to being able to imitate the 'new woman'. To be slim became essential, as was to maintain a youthful appearance. 'Keep Young and Beautiful' was a very popular song performed by Eddie Cantor and a chorus in the 1933 film *Roman Scandals*. It got straight to the point:

> *Keep young and beautiful*
> *It's your duty to be beautiful*
> *Keep young and beautiful*
> *If you want to be loved*

Was the instruction to keep 'young and beautiful' ironic? It did not seem so. Far from resenting such impertinent instructions with their implied threat of losing a man's love, women actively followed the cult of slimming or losing weight by dieting. Slimming attracted much advertising and information about female 'vital statistics', an expression that had been used to refer to the birth and death rates of a nation, but which was now commonly used to describe the bust, waist and hip measurements of film stars and other women on public view. If legs were less displayed than in the short skirts of the 1920s, they were certainly suggested by the bias cut of new fashions, which had the effect of making dresses cling to the body. Backs and arms were on view more. Women were also encouraged to engage in healthy physical activity. Hiking and cycling in shorts were favourite weekend pastimes of both sexes. Sunbathing in the new open air pools or lidos encouraged the search for suntans and the urge to have a shapely body to display. While J. B. Priestley's often-quoted statement (in his *English Journey,*) that factory girls looked like actresses was an exaggeration, it did mark the tentative beginning of classlessness in single young women with good jobs and money to spend.

Keeping fit by walking, sunbathing and dieting became an obsession, to the extent that women's smoking, while much scorned as unfeminine by older people, was excused on the grounds that it limited the appetite. Smoking, however, would probably not have been approved in the influential

Women's League for Health and Beauty, which had 166,000 members by 1939. The League produced immense public displays of rhythmic movements performed by skimpily clad women in London's Albert Hall and other centres all over Britain. At its peak of success 5,000 women assembled at Wembley Stadium in May 1937 to celebrate the Coronation of George VI and Queen Elizabeth.

The Women's League for Health and Beauty was founded by Mollie Stack and continued by her daughter, Prunella, who was described as radiant, strapping and 'Nordic'. This was a code word, replaced by 'Aryan' in Nazi Germany, for the ideal racial type. There was something Fascist-like about hundreds of healthy-looking women performing rhythmic but unsexy movements in skimpy but not particularly exciting garments. Indeed, the Women's League for Health and Beauty thought in eugenicist terms and saw women as 'natural race builders'. The aim was to promote 'racial health' through physical exercise. The leaders of the movement worried, as did many others, about the 'future of the race'.

Perhaps the most famous individualistic women were the aviatrixes, the pioneer female aviators, among them Amy Johnson, the first British woman to fly solo to Australia, in May 1930, and the American Amelia Earhart, who flew the Atlantic in 1932. They were the really emancipated women who did what only men had been thought capable of achieving. Yet Amy Johnson could not obtain regular employment flying until war came. American films made the emancipated career girl a familiar figure in 1930s Britain. The American actress Joan Crawford and her like were tough and aggressive as well as sexy. Sexy wisecracking was the characteristic of the notorious Mae West. In the film *We're No Angels*, a man boasts, 'I've done things and been places' to which Mae West retorts in her exaggeratedly sexy voice, 'I've done places and been things.' Claudette Colbert, acting in sophisticated comedies, and Rosalind Russell, playing a fast-talking newspaper reporter, offered models of women of independent mind and manner.

Yet, despite the encouragement seemingly given by the newspapers to young women to follow their ambitions, the 'agony aunts' who became a feature, particularly of the women's magazines that sprang up in large numbers in the late 1930s, considered themselves obliged to maintain accepted standards of how women should live their lives. One young husband of 1936 whose wife wanted him to help keep their flat clean was supported by an agony aunt in no uncertain terms: 'Your wife has no right to expect help from you at all … I could plan her day for her, leaving her with plenty of leisure to spend with you in the evening.' But that particular wife did not go out to work, so it does not seem likely that she would expect her husband to help to clean their small flat. So, was the reply provoked by a real question?

How women behaved was, however, a serious issue, and linked to widespread and profound anxiety about changes in morals and values. The major event in the common memory was the Russian Revolution, with its confiscation of property and the murder of the Russian Royal Family only twenty years earlier. Myth had it that Soviet women had been declared 'public property'. Even if this was probably judged by many as an unfounded scare story, it was known that in the Soviet Union religious marriage had been abolished and divorce was easily granted. It was normal in Communist Russia for women to work; abortion was permitted and provided. More recently, in the Spanish Civil War, which had begun in July 1936, reporters had described trouser-clad women soldiers among the militias fighting against General Franco's military insurgents. Spanish couples on the Republican side could now marry informally and a female Spanish minister of health had introduced abortion on demand. Fear of violent and profound change in society was widespread in many other parts of Europe. While in Italy and Germany such worry had led to the rise of Fascism and Nazism, with their doctrine that the proper place for women was in the background – the Nazi slogan was 'Children, Church and Kitchen' – in Britain unease about rapid change in society lay behind the essential conservatism of the electorate, which voted overwhelmingly in 1935 for the Conservative Party. Even the concerns of the British Left about the neglect of women's health, deaths in childbirth, infantile mortality rates and a population that was not increasing its young people at an appropriate rate, drove eugenicist thought, according to which only the 'better strains of the race' should be encouraged. This lay behind the opposition to family allowances for an 'inferior' class that some people thought produced too many children, in contrast to their approval of a more responsible class that should be encouraged to have more children. Fears were expressed about depopulation and the physical deterioration of 'the race'. However, in Britain this went only as far as some official discussion about voluntary sterilisation, always hedged about by ifs and buts.

Sex and Birth Control

Of course, women's health was important, and the health of mothers even more so because it affected their children. The least well cared-for mothers were usually the poorest and the most ignorant. Their lack of education, in the sexual sense, could be defined as their ignorance about copulation and pregnancy, or rather their unawareness that the two need not necessarily be linked.

If in the twenty-first century, sex is related to love, desire and pleasure, a century ago it was associated primarily with marriage and pregnancy. In the 1930s the great pioneer of family limitation was Marie Stopes. Her clinics gave advice and provided contraceptive equipment. Her book *Married Love* advocated what became known as 'companionate marriage', which meant a sexual relation between spouses that did not necessarily lead to pregnancy, and which therefore would relax the wife's apprehension and the husband's frustration. The fact that it was usually called at the time 'birth control', was itself an indication that the point of it was to reduce the excessive numbers of pregnancies undergone by some women. The entire question was fraught with embarrassment and prejudice. When Miss Pankerton, a feminist and Oxford graduate, talks to Robert, the husband of E. M. Delafield's anonymous author of the *Diary of a Provincial Lady*, about 'companionate marriage', which might be a euphemism for birth control, she receives no reply, for Robert, a model for husbands of the time, cannot bear anything out of the ordinary, that is anything, says the author, that might make him think.

The birth rate of 24 per 1,000 in 1914 fell to 18.3 per 1,000 in the 1920s and to 14.8 in the following decade. By then, the average number of children per family was two, which was one reason for the popularity of George VI's family of two daughters. In 1939 England and Wales had 2 million fewer children under 14 than in 1900. The new suburbs seemed to be full of one-child families. Esther Simons had one child; her elder brother and younger sister had none. The fall in the numbers of births reflected the increase in the use of methods of preventing conception. The ideal was already present as early as 1924 when a popular song included the following lines:

Just Molly and me,
And baby makes three.
We're happy in my blue heaven

Marie Stopes's 1918 book *Married Love* had sold a million copies by 1939. Her *Wise Parenthood* of the same year went through ten editions. These popular and easily read publications would be found beside tens of thousands of marital beds. Probably millions of men had been introduced to the condom during the Great War, when it was still seen more as protection against sexually transmitted disease than a contraceptive. Stopes recommended rather less convenient methods, but ones that were under a woman's control, such as the cervical cap, although this had to be fitted. Nevertheless, in the 1930s it was mostly the husband who took responsibility for contraception. It was seen as the duty of a responsible man. Women were embarrassed and reluctant to buy appliances and they sometimes judged themselves as immodest for visiting a Stopes clinic.

Prenatal clinics were being opened, for local authorities had been encouraged by the 1918 Maternity and Child Welfare Act to spend money on care for mothers and babies. By 1937 54 per cent of new mothers were attending such clinics. Free milk was being distributed and the proportion of births in hospital had increased substantially. Reflecting the fear of depopulation, in 1936 Neville Chamberlain, Chancellor of the Exchequer, increased the tax allowance for the second and subsequent children. Thus, birth was encouraged but birth control was not, and despite some pressure from women's groups, all that was permitted in the publicly funded clinics in the early part of the thirties was to provide contraceptive information if pregnancy for the woman in question would be dangerous.

Yet, despite widespread ignorance, which was added to religious hostility, to doctors' unwillingness to give advice and to fears of depopulation, in 1930 the British Medical Association accepted that its members might provide contraceptive advice if wives were in physical danger from pregnancy. Catholic authorities remained hostile, but the Church of England, having condemned birth control at the 1908 and 1920 Lambeth Conferences, gave its approval for birth control in some circumstances at the 1930 meeting. By the later 1930s, also, married women were receiving contraceptive advice from some doctors at local authority clinics, although there was of course no question of advising single women. Birth control gradually began to be termed, more positively, 'family planning', and the Family Planning Association was formed in 1939. Nevertheless, hostility to providing contraceptive advice continued. Pharmacists might even refuse to sell contraceptives to women whose married status they doubted. Some feminist groups even hesitated about providing birth control information on the grounds that this would remove the need for men to have to be 'trained' by their wives not to demand intercourse. By the end of the 1930s contraceptive knowledge had reached the lower middle class, but for the less well-educated as late as 1939 the small and limited family was still the rarity. The socialist economist and historian G. D. H. Cole wrote, tongue in cheek, the following rhyme, to be sung to the tune of a Christmas carol, a fact that many would have thought close on blasphemous:

The middle classes, me and you,
Already know a thing or two,
But the poor, they breed like rabbits,
They have the most distressing habits.

Using contraception was neither easy, cheap nor convenient. The simplest form of reliable protection, the condom, was crude and needed to be lubricated. It prevented spontaneity and men feared losing erection if they used one. In the mid-1930s the London Rubber Company was still producing only about 2 million condoms a year compared with 100 million thirty years later. The insertion of a contraceptive sponge by the woman was clumsy and hardly practical in the overcrowded dwellings of the poor. The cervical caps and other devices that Marie Stopes offered were difficult for a woman to fit herself. They were used only by small numbers of women who overcame the feeling of immodesty aroused by the need for sexual intercourse to be anticipated. Douching of course required a bathroom and preferably a bidet, an object that seems in Britain to have been regarded as 'Continental' and even sinful. The commonest method of contraception in early twentieth-century Britain was withdrawal of the man before he ejaculated, known as *coitus interruptus*, a technique that created apprehension in both sexual partners, and which often did not work and led to 'accidents'. A much later investigation, based on a wide study of surviving and, by then elderly, spouses, suggests that over half of 1930s couples used withdrawal or the condom while smaller numbers used pessaries, caps and diaphragms, and a large number simply abstained from sex over long periods. All the sample, however, claimed to exercise some form of control. The fall in conceptions and the birth rate was undeniable. Some knowledge about 'safe periods' in the female cycle may have been possessed, though in her well-known autobiography the ex-domestic servant Margaret Powell recalls that 'We didn't chat about those sort [*sic*] of things' and 'Nobody told me about the 'safe' period.' Margaret Powell did, nevertheless, graduate to using a cervical cap, which she found unattractive and uncomfortable, and she remembered that you had to keep returning to the clinic for it to be refitted. You also had to wear it all the time, because 'you never knew when your husband wanted sex'. Couples, she repeated, didn't discuss sex. 'It just happened.'

The level of ignorance was high. Professor Harold Perkin's autobiography tells of a woman who had been taught to introduce the 'Dutch Cap' every time she and her husband made love, but who thought that this was unnecessary if they did so when he came home during the day for his dinner. Rennie MacAndrew, writing 'for adults only' in the late 1930s, complained that girls had been kept ignorant, told merely to avoid males, and that sex was a taboo subject. 'Fortunately,' he wrote, 'sex education has now improved a little.' His books were published by a firm with an address in London's Charing Cross Road, which was where the 'rubber' shops were centred. These sold contraceptives and books that discussed sex. MacAndrew's book was highly popular and was being sold as late as 1961, by which time it had reached its fifteenth impression. Marriage manuals were increasingly frank in their explanations of sexual behaviour. An English translation of the Dutch gynaecologist van der Velde's *Ideal Marriage* was published in 1926. It remained one of the best-known works on its subject for several decades and was reprinted countless times. Nevertheless, anything other than 'natural' or 'spontaneous' lovemaking was thought by many to be artificial, immodest, unnatural and sinful.

Sex was not commonly discussed in the 1930s, even between spouses. Parents of adolescents had been brought up in the Edwardian age, often in extreme ignorance of sex. They had resisted their children receiving sexual information. Young people seeking enlightenment were faced with a wall of silence. Unlike in the twenty-first century, 'menstruation', 'masturbation', 'vagina', 'penis' and 'clitoris' were words that journalists and novelists just did not use. At another level, the comedians of the age had to be masters of allusion, and their jokes about sex sound crude and unamusing to the modern ear. People of the 1930s would be amazed at the lack of verbal restraint in the twenty-first century, when 'normal' and 'nice' people speak openly of sex. In the 1930s one simply did not refer, at least in public and in the presence of the opposite sex, to such matters. Of course, sex before marriage or infidelity within marriage was by no means unknown, but it was discussed in an undertone. A child who revealed some illicitly acquired knowledge was hushed. Little Brian Magee, born in 1930, was forbidden to enter his parents' bedroom, let alone jump into their bed. He never saw his parents unclothed. Even if a girl had gleaned some knowledge from other girls, it was the ideal not to know, to claim innocence. In Ernest Raymond's novel *The Kilburn Tale*, Brenda Rostrum tells her father that she is not pregnant, but it would have been far beyond the bounds of propriety for her to tell him how she knows, and, although she might have done so to her mother, the novelist would not have dreamed of reproducing the exchange in his text. Better-educated women probably did know more, but their knowledge would still be theoretical. While there was ample and often favourable portrayals of 'modern', adventurous and independent female living, sexual equality and freedom were not encouraged. At most, such behaviour was seen as eccentric. While women's magazines might give some carefully expressed advice on sex in marriage, the press kept off the subject, which was still hedged about with embarrassment and prohibition. Nevertheless, the end of the 1930s saw the emergence of a portrayal of sexiness in a very discreet way, and for the benefit of probably quite worldly men, in the magazines *Men Only* and *Lilliput*. The latter, costing a pricey sixpence, first appeared in a glossy format in 1937. Its nudes were artistic rather than provocative. The famous *Daily Mirror* character 'Jane' appeared first as early as 1932 in her underwear as a cartoon, but she didn't strip completely until the Second World War. 'Jane' was a drawing rather than a photograph. She wasn't provocative, however, and was comic more than anything else.

Sex was thought to be and often referred to as 'dirty'. Men, of course, knew the coarse words. They learnt them from older boys, but they were rarely used outside a specific and aggressive male situation. To use such sexually associated words as expletives was rare and disapproved of, especially in the presence of women. Women themselves thought it proper to deny their own interest in sex. The portrayal of Yorkshire wives of an earlier generation in the late-twentieth-century TV series *Last of the Summer Wine* illustrates this vividly. The women are proud to have kept their husbands at arm's length. The 'proper' attitude was that, for a wife, sex was what she had to put up with. Thus, contraception was not much talked about either, except in whispers between women. It might even be seen as interfering with the naturalness of conjugal relations. For some wives, male abstention might even be seen as a loving act, protecting them against unwanted pregnancies.

It would be unwise to apply twenty-first-century attitudes toward sex to the way that pre-1939 couples saw their relationship. There were loving partnerships even without what today would be considered mutually satisfying sexual intercourse. In the 1930s there was a slow advance in the direction of companionate marriage and in seeing sex as an expression of love between married partners, which could be advanced by wise birth control practice and greater equality between husband and wife, even though at the same time sex remained a taboo subject, to be discussed if at all in whispers. Inhibition, ignorance and consequent distress were slowly giving way before frankness, knowledge and pleasure, but Alex Comfort's famous book *The Joy of Sex* was still far in the future.

Abortion

Since contraception was hard to access and not very easy to use, abortion, sometimes provided by a helpful neighbour and at others self-administered with heavy doses of laxatives or various other methods, was frequent, and death or sterility were not rarely the result. In 1937 between 44,000 and 60,000 abortions were estimated to be performed annually, and some 10,000 women died. There was, however, an Abortion Law Reform Association, which campaigned to make abortion legal, safe and freely available. Pressure led to the establishment in 1937 of the Birkett Committee, whose purpose was

> To inquire into the prevalence of abortion, and the present law relating thereto, and to consider what steps can be taken by more effective enforcement of the law or otherwise to secure the reduction of maternal mortality and morbidity arising from this cause.

One famous case was heard in court while the Birkett Committee was sitting and reflected the changing view. Aleck Bourne, consultant obstetrical surgeon at St. Mary's Hospital in London, terminated the pregnancy of a girl aged 14 who had been raped. He wanted to test the law on therapeutic abortion, so he informed the authorities of his act and was duly prosecuted. His defence was based on the grounds that it was already legal to abort a pregnancy if the mother's life was in danger. Here, he claimed, it was the psychological health of a young girl that was imperilled. Bourne was acquitted by a jury that was nudged into the verdict by the judge. However, while the Birkett Committee heard a great deal of evidence, most of which recommended better contraceptive education, it also recognised that most of the pregnant women who aborted their foetuses did so because their family income and circumstances were simply insufficient to be able to feed another child. Nevertheless, all that the Birkett Committee did was to underline that abortion was legal if pregnancy was likely to 'endanger her [the mother's] life or seriously endanger her health'. Consequently, it recommended giving a certain margin of discretion to doctors to perform abortions without being accused of acting illegally. Little really changed.

Companionate Marriage

Marie Stopes's campaign saw marriage and conception as a patriotic duty and birth control as a method, not of reducing the population, but on the contrary of decreasing the reproduction of its 'least fit' elements. However, the growing popularity of the condom encouraged the attitude of 'companionate marriage', and thus of a slow change in the relations between husbands and wives. Such a change, which was becoming evident in the late 1930s, could be described as emerging among a generation of young marrieds who linked birth control with the beginning of seeing sex as an aspect of egalitarian marriage and a pleasurable act for both partners, rather than a husband's right whether it resulted in his wife's pregnancy.

Pre-Marital Sex

As for engaged couples, pre-marital sex was not uncommon and could not be concealed if it led to pregnancy. Official figures as early as 1904 had suggested that about a fifth of all first births had resulted from conception before the parents had married. The figure was much greater by 1938, when the Registrar-General estimated that 30 per cent of mothers had conceived their firstborn child before marriage. Marriages may have been arranged once the woman was pregnant, but it was more likely that, with a marriage date fixed, females were less resistant to male demands. Virginity of brides was important, but sexual activity between fiancés was looked on with a certain tolerance.

Free Love

Only a small percentage of births was to unmarried mothers. These were the 'illegitimate' children, commonly referred to as 'bastards' who had been 'born out of wedlock'. Pregnant single girls were often sent away to special institutions, sometimes run by the Salvation Army, and many of them harshly disciplinarian, to give birth without their neighbours or their parents' friends knowing. Some girls were effectively imprisoned under the Mental Deficiency Act of 1913. Only well into the twenty-first century did some of these single mothers, now elderly, succeed in tracing their children, who had been either adopted or taken into orphanages. More fortunate girls brought their babies back into the family where they might be passed off as a late and unexpected child born to the pregnant girl's mother.

So, was there free and enjoyable sex between unmarried men and women? The 1930s saw young people enjoying holidays in Blackpool, as well as Brighton, Scarborough and particularly at Billy Butlin's new holiday camps with their mixed bathing, beauty competitions, sunbathing and dancing. Despite these acquiring the reputation of havens for sexual licence, observers concluded that what was known as 'knee-tremblers' or heavy petting was more usual than actual intercourse.

The extent of free love, or sexual activity between the unmarried in the later 1930s, is difficult to gauge because it was concealed. Unmarried couples did not live together openly. Even though there may have many unmarried couples who did live together, perhaps because one of the two could not obtain a divorce from a living spouse, such pairs tended to refer to themselves as 'Mr. and Mrs.'. Smart circles and West End plays might chatter about sex, but girls were lectured to be 'firm' and resist men's demands. Unmarried women who surrendered their virginity were unlikely to admit it. Opportunities in any case were difficult. Young people were heavily policed. Francis McFarland attended a mixed grammar school in the early 1930s. He could not recall any sexual activity between the adolescent boys and girls. Organisations such as the Church Lads' Brigade, the YMCA, the Scouts and the Girl Guides reflected the intense anxiety about the moral condition of the young, who had to be diverted from the calls of their bodies. Sex, and its preliminary activities, such as flirting, kissing, petting and so on were seen by many as sinful, and by most as undesirable. At Oxford, Barbara Pym, the later novelist, recalled that undergraduates could be sent down for kissing in public. Nevertheless, she recalled, heavy petting or 'snogging' was common enough, and might even lead to mutual orgasm. Sexual intercourse, however, before marriage was unusual even for well-educated girls up at Oxford. Rennie MacAndrew, a 'modern' writer of books that spoke openly about sexual matters, saw no harm in a man caressing a woman intimately and the resultant mutual orgasm, but not many would have agreed with him. Perhaps the most extreme and revolutionary views were expressed by the feminist, socialist and free love advocate Stella Browne, who in her own evidence to the Birkett Committee on Abortion, spoke against the social pressures faced by men and women and stated her opinion boldly:

> I do not think that to refrain from sexual intercourse out of fear, whether fear of the unknown, fear of venereal disease, fear of a baby, fear of ridicule, or fear of damages in the Divorce Court,

> or anything like that, is in any way a virtue. I think that sexual intercourse between those who love each other and understand each other is the most beautiful and valuable thing in life.

A liberated world such as Stella Browne dreamed of would have required full knowledge by young men and women about contraception. Yet a large proportion of both sexes was ignorant of almost everything to do with sex. Even the manuals of the 1930s were written for married couples and, although often assiduously read by the unmarried, they avoided describing the fundamental mechanics of lovemaking.

However, sex between the unmarried and as a natural and indeed healthy recreation was very slowly coming to be accepted. Sexuality according to this view should be rational and humane, not directed or restricted by religious teaching. Moreover, it should be egalitarian. The sexual revolution that flowered in the 1960s had its roots in the late 1930s.

Sex in Fiction

Mention of sex between the unmarried in fiction might include a statement made by Mr. Golspie in J. B. Priestley's *Angel Pavement* of 1930. What does the author expect his readers to think when Golspie says he is looking forward to spending time in London where the girls are 'a bit stiff perhaps, though not as stiff as they used to be'? In fact, how reliable are the accounts in fiction in general? When Orwell's George Bowling has sexual intercourse with Elsie Waters for the first time, he is a virgin, though she is not. Is this what a reader of the book published in 1939 might have expected of an event set in 1912, that is, that a virginal man was likely to achieve a sexual relation only with an already experienced woman? And what were the readers of Orwell's *Keep the Aspidistra Flying* of 1935 meant to think when they read about Gordon Comstock nagging his girlfriend Rosemary Waterlow for sex, even though he is too careless to equip himself with a condom. When Gordon presses Rosemary to allow him to make love to her (or 'sleep with her', which was the accepted euphemism), and Comstock's friend Philip Ravelston is depicted as making love to his own girlfriend, is this to be assumed as likely enough for Orwell and Gollancz, his publisher, to think the subject appropriate for a novel? Rosemary rejects Gordon's advances because he has forgotten to acquire a condom, but he defends himself on the grounds that 'you don't think that I go in for that sort of thing, do you?'

He selfishly tells Rosemary that she must 'take her chance' (of getting pregnant). Earlier in the novel Gordon makes disparaging remarks about 'French letters', as condoms were called, and he associates them with free abortion clinics as examples of deplorable change. Gordon's views on sexual relations are portrayed by Orwell as decidedly backward-looking. But Comstock is sufficiently self-aware to admit to himself that he only pretended to be shocked that Rosemary, though a virgin, had taken it for granted that he would provide himself with a condom before they made love. In any case, neither of the lovers enjoys the essential privacy for sex. She lives in a ladies' hostel, while he has an inquisitive landlady. To find privacy the author must put Gordon into a slum rooming-house where the landlady doesn't interfere. In the latter 1930s there were few but nevertheless a growing number of places where the young could have the necessary privacy, such as the car and, for the well-off, the roadhouse, an institution as famous for illicit sex as the American motel. However, until the early 1950s girls at Cambridge colleges had to move their beds into the corridor when a man was visiting.

Keep the Aspidistra Flying ends in kind of a redemptive act. Rosemary gives herself to Gordon out of absolute love in the grimy surroundings of his Lambeth room. When she learns she is pregnant she tells him that she will do whatever he wants, either seek an abortion or return to her parents with the resultant disgrace. Gordon abandons his principles, re-enters the money economy that he despises, and returns to his job composing advertisements. The couple marry and settle down to domesticity in a flat. So, in the end, the reader can relax.

Adultery and Divorce

The anxieties caused by adultery were made sharply poignant in the film *Brief Encounter*. Although made in 1946, this famous film, starring Celia Johnson and Trevor Howard, was based on Noël Coward's 1936 play *Still Life*. Both Alex Harvey and Laura Jessop, the leading characters in the film, are married with children. They are fiercely attracted to each other, but she suffers an intense sense of guilt. They do not manage to consummate their desire because they are interrupted by the untimely arrival of Alex Harvey's friend, who expresses his disgust at what the lovers would have done had he not returned to his flat unexpectedly. Given that both Alex and Laura are married and have children, the contemporary audience was unlikely to have had much sympathy for them, although such seems to be the intention of the film. In fact, most spectators would have felt a sense of relief, for they were not being required to sympathise for what they had been schooled to believe was sinful.

Upper-class adultery, however, was not rare. The Hon. Mrs. Brian Guinness, sister of the Hitler-obsessed Unity Mitford, was living openly with the British Fascist leader Oswald Mosley. Senior politicians and their spouses, including David Lloyd George, Duff Cooper, the Marchioness of Londonderry and Ramsay MacDonald, had lovers and mistresses. Dorothy Macmillan, wife of a future prime minister, was conducting a long affair with the MP Robert Boothby. So long as the matter was kept out of the press and the divorce court, upper-class 'carrying on' was tolerated. But there was a limit. Edward VIII, king since January 1936, though yet uncrowned, had had affairs with married women, which were seen merely as 'a young man sowing his wild oats', but to marry a divorced woman who had two living husbands and convert her into the queen of England was out of the question. So, the American Wallis Simpson, whom he had determined to marry, could not be accepted, nor could Edward be king and Head of the Anglican Church and be married to Wallis at the same time. He had to abdicate and be replaced by the ideal family. Fortunately, one was there already: his brother and sister-in-law the Duke and Duchess of York, and their two daughters, whose popularity soared.

Divorce in Britain was no mere formality. To have been divorced, especially if you had been the guilty party or the co-respondent, bore a moral stigma. People who had been involved in a divorce found they had to change their names and move away. Nor was divorce an easy matter in the 1930s. The only sure route was the adultery of one of the spouses. Only in 1937 was desertion for over three years introduced as a justification. If both spouses had been unfaithful, it was assumed that they had colluded, and divorce would be refused. There had to have been a matrimonial offence by one party. Judges were concerned to maintain the principle that marriage was for life even if the spouses lived apart. The standard process was for the husband to allow his wife to divorce him, even if she was the unfaithful partner, because this was seen as the chivalrous thing to do. So, aided by a helpful solicitor, the husband arranged, for a fee, to be seen in bed with a woman, often in the somewhat raffish seaside resort of Brighton, in a hotel where the chambermaid acted as witness to his infidelity. The whole business of divorce was satirised by the barrister, independent MP and humourist A. P. Herbert in his comic novel *Holy Deadlock*. Here, the innocent husband feels that he cannot divorce his wife because, if she is described in court as an adulteress, her lover and future husband, who works at the BBC, will lose his post because he is the 'co-respondent'. The BBC, headed by the puritanical Lord Reith, cannot allow itself to be associated with him. Furthermore, the petitioner, usually the wife, must be instructed privately by her solicitor that, when the judge asks her if she wants her adulterous husband back, she must not say that she does, because in that case the judge, whose principle is to preserve a marriage even if it is unhappy, will deny the petition.

Homosexuals

The Sunday newspaper *News of the World*, which combined moral outrage with titillation, scoured the local papers for police accounts of homosexual behaviour. Being homosexual was not illegal, but scandalous homosexual acts were prosecuted. Public lavatories in some areas were well known for 'cottaging', while it was not unknown for better-off homosexuals to use the modern roadhouses for assignations. Certain public figures made little attempt to disguise their sexual interest, among them in particular the famous song composer and playwright Noël Coward. The musician Ivor Novello, the actor John Gielgud, the poet W. H. Auden, the novelist Christopher Isherwood and others were well known for their preference. While discreet homosexual lives were left undisturbed, public complaints brought a heavy-handed police presence into an area of open homosexual activity. Epping Forest, for example, not far from the heavily populated suburbs of East London, was a known meeting place for homosexuals. Under some public pressure, at times the police carried out raids in London's Hyde Park. Some tendency toward more open homosexual behaviour in the late 1930s attracted increased police activity, and prosecutions followed. But the police did not raid Lyons's Corner House in the Strand, which was notoriously known as the 'Lily Pond' and a meeting place for homosexuals. Identifiable homosexuals were a common sight in London's West End. Nevertheless, magistrates tended to dismiss cases where the police had behaved as agents provocateurs. The real danger for homosexuals in important positions was blackmail. Some married and distinguished men were ruined when their proclivity was revealed. Homosexual behaviour was well publicised in the public-school novel. Reformers of the law wrote earnest articles about it. Yet at the same time it was still often spoken of as an aberration, a phase in adolescence, and even a psychological disease. For most people, homosexuality was simply incomprehensible.

Sex, then, was slowly approaching the time when it would cease to be discussed in whispers, but it would take a major war and some fifteen years of change to reach the moment of liberation marked by the legal decision that in 1960 allowed the unexpurgated paperback publication in Britain of D. H. Lawrence's *Lady Chatterley's Lover* and a decade later the appearance of Alex Comfort's famous sex manual, significantly titled *The Joy of Sex*.

Chapter 7

What's on at the Pictures?

As working hours decreased and wages rose, so the demand for opportunity for leisure increased. By the late 1930s many of the prerequisites for a modern leisure industry were already present: Britain had a very large urban market, big business was taking an interest in the profits to be made from leisure and public transport was better organised and available. Lastly, new technologies were coming on stream. One of them was the moving picture, to which had been added speech in 1929 and technicolor in 1935. Now the cinema was on the brink of substantial expansion.

Before the Second World War people didn't talk much about 'films'. They said 'pictures'. You went to the 'pictures' at the 'picture house', or the 'picture palace'. You rarely called it the 'cinema'. Going to the pictures was the most widespread of British leisure activities. It attracted two-thirds of all expenditure on entertainment in the years just before the Second World War and would go on to reach its peak of popularity round about 1950. Britain had 5,000 cinemas by 1939. About 19 million people went to the pictures at least once a week, and some went many times. In their early married life, Jack and Mabel Simmonds, whom we met in Chapter 4, often visited a cinema three times a week.

Going to the pictures was a rite, as was the daily visit to the public house for some men. Surveys in Liverpool and York revealed that about half the population went to the pictures at least once a week. You went, perhaps having chosen the cinema whose programme of films you wanted to see, but often, rather like television viewing half a century later, you picked any programme that seemed interesting, perhaps just on the basis of the 'stills' or photographs of scenes in the films. These were enclosed in windows on the external walls of the picture house. In addition, the local paper carried notices of what was on at the cinemas in the area, and often reviewed the films. Shops sometimes put a board outside with a film poster displayed on it. There was a flood of films available, so much so that some picture houses changed their programmes as many as three times a week. As Robert Barltrop writes in his memoir of life in Walthamstow, in North London, in the 1930s, 'after the latest Will Hay comedy or *The Hurricane* at the Granada, or *Captains Courageous* at the Dominion, it was possible to go the Queen's on a Sunday evening and see *Sanders of the River*, which you had missed a year or two ago'.

Cinema performances were continuous. You didn't necessarily aim to get to the cinema at the beginning of the main feature, or, as it was called, 'the big picture'. People would go into the cinema during the film and stay until the film came around again. 'This is where I came in,' you thought, and you left or perhaps stayed on to watch the rest of the film again. You might be in the cinema for as long as three hours, for cinemas always showed two films, and often a third, shorter one, such as a Mickey Mouse, Popeye or Donald Duck cartoon. And in addition, there were three different newsreels, according to the cinema you went to, of about fifteen minutes each, and sometimes an interval for advertisements. Big cinemas often put on a short organ concert also.

Before 1914 the pictures had been a mostly lower-class form of entertainment, and the buildings themselves tended to be either temporary, or unattractive and in some cases so rundown and dirty that they were known as 'fleapits'. Sometimes the picture, or 'bioscope', was a one-reel projected in the local music hall as one of the attractions. By the late 1930s many picture houses were showing their age. Their projection equipment was out of date and unreliable, and their seating decrepit. The 'Bijou' picture house, colloquially referred to as the 'fleapit', which is the subject of the film *The Smallest Show on Earth*, with a young Peter Sellers and Margaret Rutherford, made in 1957, typifies this. However, as bigger and more luxurious cinemas opened in the new suburbs in the 1930s, and with the coming of 'talkies' and later technicolor, the pictures steadily attracted the middle class. In consequence, the ticket prices reflected the feeling that the social classes should be kept separate. Seats cost less toward the front and were dearer in the circle. Yet the cinema never became so expensive as to dissuade even the poorest, because prices were kept down during the day, when for the unemployed the pictures offered both entertainment and warmth. One survey discovered that 80 per cent of young unemployed people went to the pictures at least once a week. The magnificent Gaumont State in Kilburn, which opened in late 1937, offered seats for the afternoon performance (called 'matinée' as in the theatres) for 6d. and 9d. in the stalls, and a shilling in the huge circle, but many picture houses kept admission prices as low as

3d. and admissions for a penny were not unknown. A calculation in 1934 concluded that 43 per cent of admissions to the pictures cost 6d, the same price as a pint of beer, or less, and most of the rest between 7d. and 10d. For the young, who went more than the elderly, the pictures offered cheap entertainment. The Saturday morning film shows for children could cost as little as 2d., while Brian Magee remembered that silent pictures were still being shown in the thirties for a penny in mission halls in poor districts.

Marketing investigations showed that the cinema tended to be more attractive to women, offering an afternoon's entertainment for a woman with grown-up children who had time on her hands. A woman who would be chary of going into a pub on her own or even with female friends thought nothing of going to the pictures by herself. Laura Jessop, in the famous film *Brief Encounter*, has a regular weekly custom of going into the nearby town to change her library book, have lunch, go to the pictures and get back in time for when her husband returns from work.

Cinemas were everywhere. In Bolton, the Mass Observation investigators of 1937 noted that the city's 180,000 inhabitants were served by forty-seven picture houses, many of which were very close to each other. The average entrance charge was 6d. In highly urbanised Britain, probably most people could walk to at least one cinema. In the heavily populated London district where Esther Simons and her family lived, they could walk in a few minutes to the Kilburn Picture Palace, the Maida Vale Picture Palace, the Grange, the Gaumont State and the Envoy, and there were many more cinemas in the adjoining areas of Willesden, Harlesden, Cricklewood and almost everywhere around. In 1935, the County of London accommodated 258 picture houses.

Super-Cinemas

The interwar years witnessed the building of many palatial, exotic or modernistic cinemas. Some were built in a sort of 'Hollywood-Arabian Nights' style; others like Renaissance palaces, Egyptian temples, and one, in Southall (Middlesex), with a tiled exterior with a red pagoda roof and dragons. Others were ultra-modern in architectural design, with huge, futuristic external walls. In the 1920s the most modern picture houses had tended to be in London's West End, but not exclusively so. The Grange, in Kilburn, on a corner and surmounted by a large cupola, opened in 1914 with over 2,000 seats, a tearoom and accommodation for social events. The Maida Vale Picture Palace, only a short bus ride down the road, had opened in 1913. It had two copper domes at either end of the building, which stretched lengthwise just off the main road. The Lido in the developing north-west London suburb of Golders Green opened in 1928 with nearly 2,000 seats and parking for a hundred cars. It was the first London cinema equipped for talking pictures.

The cinemas of the late 1930s were much better equipped than before. Rather than mere spaces for showing films, their promoters aimed at creating entertainment centres to which people would flock because they were welcoming in general. Outside London, Bolton saw the formal opening, with a municipal band and speeches by local worthies, of the Art Deco Odeon in 1937. It had 2,534 seats and a café. Its opening big picture was *Dark Journey*, a spy film set during the Great War with the stunningly beautiful Vivien Leigh and Conrad Veid, the saturnine German actor and refugee from the Nazis.

The new super-cinemas were often built in the poorest and dreariest parts of big cities. In London, Commercial Road in Whitechapel had the Troxy, while the Trocadero, copying the name of a famous restaurant and entertainment centre in Piccadilly Circus, was in the rather rough South London district called the Elephant and Castle. Towering, both physically and in its magnificence, over all the new luxury cinemas of the 1930s was the Gaumont State, in the north-west London suburb of Kilburn. The ceremonial opening of the State on 20 December 1937 was itself filmed by the Gaumont-British newsreel. Over the next two or three years, competition from the State probably brought about the demise of several of the smaller picture houses in Kilburn. It outshone anything that had been built before. It could seat 2,648 spectators in the stalls and 1,356 in the balcony, a total of 4,004. Its tower, in cream and black, imitating the Empire State building in New York, still soars over the busy district, although the State has not functioned as a cinema for many years.

The State had a wide, palatial entrance with a huge chandelier modelled on one in Buckingham Palace, and deep pile carpets. Two curving staircases with white marble banisters took you up to the circle. Like the others of its kind, the State was a 'super-cinema', but it was also a theatre equipped for live performances on a full-size stage, with twenty dressing-rooms and an orchestra pit. Its restaurant served afternoon tea, which you could have brought to you on a tray at your seat. The manager, elegant in evening dress, welcomed the patrons, as the filmgoers were called. The State's toilets had marble urinals for gentlemen, and mirrors and Lloyd Loom chairs, shaded lamps and pink decor for the ladies. It had a huge Wurlitzer organ, which rose from under the floor and revolved. This was a spectacular object, shaped like a jelly mould. Its panels were illuminated from within by constantly changing colours, and the organist, clad in a white dinner-jacket, played popular music such as 'In a Persian Market' or 'Coronation Scot'. The Gaumont State also had a large restaurant and halls for weddings and similar celebrations.

Going to the pictures in one of these new cinemas would take you away from your small flat or room in a gloomy house, possibly still lit by gas, with its peeling wallpaper, shared bathroom, and old and worn, perhaps Victorian, furniture. You would enter a world of gilded palaces, top-class hotels and Hollywood mansions with swimming pools and luxury bathrooms. The new cinema was a fantasy place with a name to match, and its role was to take you out of your humdrum life and into a fairy tale world, for at least a few hours. In Norman Collins's novel *London Belongs to Me*, Doris Josser and Percy Boon leave their multi-occupied, unmodernised Victorian house, and visit the newly opened Toledo Cinema (a Spanish-sounding name suggested drama, heat and steamy romance). They marvel at the soft carpeting, the fountain in the forecourt, the organ as it rose from the floor, and the deep padded seats, into which they sink as they watch the picture and eat ice-cream from a tub with small, flat, wooden spatulas, not in a cornet or wafer which would have got all over their hands and fallen on their clothes.

The names of cinemas were indeed intended to suggest both luxury and fantasy. You came off the grimy street with its lorries, buses or clanging trams into a cinema with an exotic or grandiose name such as Odeon, State, Ritz, Regal, Ambassador, Rio, Savoy, Granada, Alhambra, Plaza, Empire, Majestic, or Palace. You were, at least temporarily, wafted out of the dullness of your monotonous daily life, rather as you would be if you went for a meal at a Lyon's Corner house, and for a slightly lower price. Cinema tickets, even in the brand-new and luxurious Kilburn Gaumont State in the evening, cost only 9d. at the front of the stalls, a shilling in the middle and 1/6 at the back. Circle seats were charged at 2/6d. and a luxury 3/6d. in the front balcony. The State, in addition, gave you excellent value. You saw a 'big' picture as well as a second, perhaps shorter and older, film, together with a variety show lasting up to an hour. Joss Ackland, later a well-known actor, recalled from his childhood that at the State you could also see a ventriloquist, high wire acts, high-kicking chorus girls and a singer. The State's programme for the week beginning Monday, 24 January 1938 (there was a special programme on Sundays) was *Kid Galahad*, with Edward G. Robinson, Humphrey Bogart and Bette Davis, who were leading Hollywood stars, and *Action for Slander*, with the well-known British actors Clive Brook and Ann Todd. The variety show included the piano duo Rawicz and Landauer, a singer, acrobats and a juggler.

As you settled into your comfortable seat, in the warm darkness, and the thick curtains slowly opened over the screen, the certificate of the British Board of Film Censors appeared at once and remained there for a moment. This stated that the film had been given its certificate by the Board. It was either a 'U' (meaning 'Universal'), or an 'A' (standing for 'Adult'). Children were allowed freely into a 'U' picture and looked forward to a programme where both films had 'U' certificates, meaning that they did not have to persuade a parent to take them or, as was often the case, to ask an unknown adult to 'take me in, please'. There was a formal notice pasted to the window of the kiosk where tickets were sold proclaiming that the adult had to be a 'bona fide' relative or guardian of the child, but not much notice was taken of that.

In the films themselves there were platinum blondes, sultry brunettes, heroes, nightclubs, rolls of dollar bills, Arabian Nights, cowboys, and film stars of unutterable glamour, doing extraordinary things in large American cars, planes and luxury trains, and, in musicals, breaking into song and dance. You fantasised that you were Shirley Temple, the most popular child star ever, Fred Astaire, the great dancer, and his partner Ginger Rogers, a handsome actor such as Clark Gable, Robert Taylor, Cary Grant or Gary Cooper; perhaps an actor who played violent criminals like James Cagney, or one of the great British stars such as Robert Donat, Leslie Howard, Charles Laughton, Ralph Richardson and, as the decade ended, the incomparable Laurence Olivier. Among the female stars there were Greta Garbo, Marlene Dietrich, Joan Crawford, Hedy Lamarr, Bette Davis, Rosalind Russell, Carole Lombard, Katharine Hepburn and many others. Women imitated their clothes and hairstyles, envied their makeup and avidly followed their activities, marriages and love affairs as recounted in film magazines such as *Picturegoer*. For young people at least, film stars offered models of behaviour. An example of this appeared in the TV programme *Dad's Army*, televised from 1968 and set in early Second World War Britain. Private Frank Pike, who is about 18, is allowed to hold the Home Guard unit's one Tommy gun. He swivels it around, yelling 'duh-duh-duh-duh' and 'take that!' as he imitates the snarling American gangsters portrayed by George Raft, James Cagney and Edward G. Robinson, whom he would have seen at the local picture houses.

Films were British or American, but you could see foreign-language films in the 'art' houses, such as the Academy in London's Oxford Street and the Cameo-Poly in Upper Regent Street, where the presence of a commissionaire parading up and down outside dressed as a gendarme added to the excited feeling of Frenchness that you would feel as you took your seat. Smoking was allowed in cinemas, so you might go so far as to provide yourself with a 'Gauloise' cigarette to enhance the fantasy.

Mabel and Jack Simmonds had eclectic tastes, and would give any film a go, but Esther Simons's husband liked big musical films, which were in general the most popular. He watched Fred Astaire and Ginger Rogers as they danced in the Busby Berkeley musicals, among them the famous *Forty-Second Street* of 1933, *Top Hat* of 1935 and *Follow the Fleet* of 1936. In 1936 *Rose Marie* was the biggest musical hit, about a romance between a Canadian 'Mountie' and an opera singer. It starred Nelson Eddy and Jeanette MacDonald, who made several films of the same genre together. Esther Simons herself had a particular dislike of seeing men dancing in top hats and tails, and preferred sophisticated comedies with handsome American actors such as Clark Gable in *It Happened One Night* of 1934 and Cary Grant, who was the leading man in two of Mae West's pictures. Neither Esther nor her husband thought very much of the poor-quality British films that were made to satisfy the requirements of the Act of 1927 which insisted that a substantial proportion of films shown should be British and were soon dubbed 'quota quickies'. In fact, British pictures were often disliked because they were cliché-ridden, stagey and either obsessed with the romantic past or the current minor problems of well-off people who wore evening dress, said things like 'By Jove' and spoke with exaggerated 'cut-glass' accents, while working-class people were portrayed as comic, often by actors who couldn't actually imitate the London cockney or other regional lower-class accents. In British crime films the police inspectors tended to speak in authoritarian upper-class accents even though they were promoted from ordinary police constables who spoke in tones typical of the working class from which they were usually recruited. The settings were dull and British emotional restraint as portrayed in films was seen as artificial. British filmgoers almost always said, when asked, that they preferred American pictures. These were classless, tough and dynamic, slick and polished, fast-moving and technically perfect. In addition, the star system of the large Hollywood studios created immediate recognition by filmgoers of the big stars' names, which enhanced the reputation of the films. Men liked the tough-guy actors in American Westerns and crime films. For women, American films signified glamour, romance, a world of stylish clothes, high-quality cosmetics, modern kitchens, big luxury cars with white steering wheels that the women drove themselves, and the physical luxury of well-heated or air-conditioned homes.

However, British films improved markedly in the second half of the decade of the 1930s, especially with the arrival of directors and producers, of whom the most famous were the Korda brothers, from Continental Europe, and actors taking refuge from the Nazis, such as Anton Walbrook, Anton Diffring and Herbert Lom. You could go to the pictures and see one or more of the highly successful series of biographies and historical dramas, such as *The Iron Duke*, about the Duke of Wellington, *Catherine the Great* in 1934 with Greta Garbo, *Fire Over England* in 1937, Alexander Korda's *The Private Life of Henry VIII*, with Charles Laughton, and two pictures about Queen Victoria (Herbert Wilcox's *Victoria the Great* of 1937 with Anna Neagle and Anton Walbrook, as well as his documentary-style *Sixty Glorious Years* of 1938). Very popular imperialist, adventure and war films included *Mutiny on the Bounty* in 1936 and *Lives of a Bengal Lancer* and *Sanders of the River* of 1935, *Elephant Boy* of 1937, *The Drum* of 1938 and *The Four Feathers* of 1939.

Such films, watched by millions of British people, but looked at from nearly a century later, seem to have assumed unquestioningly the rightness and power of British institutions and of British foreign and domestic policies. The male heroes, such as Robert Donat and Leslie Howard, personified chivalrous and gentlemanly behaviour and British patriotic values. As glamour figures they portrayed romantic rather than earthy love interest. British actresses for their part were either approachable ('Just like us', people used to say), like Gracie Fields, innocent and virtuous though very pretty like Jessie Matthews, or quintessentially English ladies, like Anna Neagle, with a genteel and non-threatening allure, in contrast to the dynamic, warmer, sexier but perhaps somewhat more striking American stars such as Katharine Hepburn, Joan Crawford and Claudette Colbert, who added her French accent to her American brightness. The later British pictures of the thirties were well made and created an attractive alternative to American crime, musical and Wild West subjects. American cinema, however, probably reflecting the context of the New Deal of President Roosevelt, began to produce films that questioned society as it was. It was in the thirties that American crime films began to reflect social concern, with *Little Caesar* of 1931, with Edward G. Robinson, and the exceptional social criticism of *I Was a Fugitive from a Chain Gang*, with Paul Muni, and *Each Dawn I Die* of 1939 with James Cagney and George Raft. British filmmaking, however, was not directed to any of the burning questions of the day, such as the effect of unemployment on the lives of ordinary people, or the poor level of social welfare. It had nothing to say about police corruption, and no desire to criticise the Church of England, the monarchy or the judicial system. The British Board of Film Censors strove to exclude political comment or social issues from the screen. The censors rejected a proposal to make a film of Walter Greenwood's novel *Love on the Dole*. The censors liked to see film narratives that showed reform, but none might portray revolution. *The Scarlet Pimpernel* of 1934 in which the British nobleman, Sir Percy Blakeney, alias 'the Scarlet Pimpernel', played by Leslie Howard, rescues innocent victims of the French Revolution, depicted revolution as brutal and chaotic, even had it been necessary in eighteenth-century France. This was also the tone of the 1935 film of Dickens's novel *A Tale of Two Cities*, where Ronald Colman plays the part of the hero Sydney Carton. Moreover, the British censors sought to maintain traditional views of gender, work and the nation. These films reassured people about pre-1914 values of masculinity, valour and honour.

The spectators welcomed films demonstrating class harmony or at least the acceptance of the status quo, and particularly pictures that approved and glorified the Empire and British history. Even light-hearted and comic pictures, starring the extremely popular George Formby and Gracie Fields, both with homely northern accents, reflected cheerfulness despite the persistent unemployment in the north of the country. Gracie Fields' films, for example, *Sing as We Go* of 1934 and *Keep Smiling* of 1938, portrayed the working class, but in a way that approved society as it was constructed at the time. In *Sing as We Go* the cotton mill is miraculously reopened and the workers return to the looms, while in *Keep Smiling* the owner of the shipyard responds to Gracie's petition and reopens the yard just as national rearmament begins.

The censors, presumably following national policy, insisted that no portrayal of Left versus Right or Rich versus Poor was to be encouraged. Political and religious controversy were to be avoided. Furthermore, no form of sexual irregularity was to appear in a film. Middle-class standards were to be imposed. All vulgar words were deleted from scripts, including words such as 'nuts', 'bum', 'lousy', 'gigolo', 'belly', strumpet', 'harlot', 'bitch', 'bastard', 'bloody' and many more. Scenes of women undressing and any mention of birth control or abortion were forbidden. So, George Formby's pictures, like Donald McGill's vulgar seaside postcards, acted as the escape valve. The background to McGill's as well as Formby's sexy innuendoes was marriage, not lust and promiscuity. American crime films, for their part, were subject to the Hay's Code of 1934, which banned profanity, nudity, graphic violence and rape.

Comic films were a way of conveying some social issues. Laurel and Hardy and Abbott and Costello in America complemented the different type of clowning of British Will Hay, and both were highly popular in Britain. Statistically, in fact, more comedies than any other genre were screened in Britain, though crime – never of course to be glamourised and always punished – and musicals followed close behind. There was no real or authentic portrayal of the working class, nothing like the 'kitchen-sink' dramas of the 1950s. Only toward the end of the 1930s were British films made with some social content, and with suggestions that not all was well in British society. As an example, the film of *The Citadel*, A. J. Cronin's very popular novel criticising the lack of proper medical care, opened in 1938. The same author's *The Stars Look Down*, about a mining disaster, filmed before the war, opened in January 1940.

It was considered important also that a film should not wound the susceptibilities of another country. Thus, Alfred Hitchcock's *The Lady Vanishes* of 1938 suggested nefarious activities of a Nazi sort in a fictional European country, but without mentioning Nazi Germany. Several explicitly anti-Nazi films were proposed but the censors advised against making them. A similar fate met a proposal to make a film about Lawrence of Arabia, for fear of wounding Turkish feelings. However, Hitchcock's *Secret Agent* of 1936, an anti-German film about the Great War, was made. A film about the trial and execution of Nurse Edith Cavell by the German army in Brussels in the Great War was also made in 1939, though it was not released until after the Second World War had begun.

1939 was probably the best year for films before the war. People flocked to see *The Wizard of Oz*, with Judy Garland, following the previous year's full-length Walt Disney animation *Snow White and the Seven Dwarfs*. which 28 million cinemagoers saw. The long, technicolor *Gone with the Wind* of 1939 became a landmark in people's memories. Few would forget the gentlemanly Ashley Wilkes, played by Leslie Howard, who marries Olivia de Havilland's frail Melanie Hamilton. He is contrasted with the tough egoist Rhett Butler, played by Clark Gable, while weak Melanie is matched against the manipulative and strong Scarlett O'Hara, played by Vivien Leigh.

In the 1930s, 'going to the pictures' could, if you wanted, mean going only to any of a vast number of undemanding crime, comedy, Westerns and other films of greater or lesser value. Nevertheless, films of works of literature and cultural interest expanded the wealth of what was available at the pictures. Publishers' advertisements proclaiming 'You've seen the film, now read the book' were displayed near cinemas to people who had been introduced at the pictures to Dickens' *David Copperfield*, Tolstoy's *Anna Karenina*, Buchan's *The Thirty-Nine Steps*, Shaw's *Pygmalion*, Baroness

Orczy's *The Scarlet Pimpernel*, Conrad's *Sabotage*, Rider Haggard's *King Solomon's Mines*, Alexandre Dumas's *The Count of Monte Cristo* and Hugo's *Les Misérables*, all to be watched for a few pence or at most a couple of shillings in Britain's thousands of picture houses.

Apart from the films themselves, seeing one of the various brief newsreels was an important part of the visit to the pictures, so much so that, by 1936, there were eighteen specialised 'News Theatres' in London and others in important British cities where you could see extended versions of filmed events. The short newsreels shown in each film performance at the pictures played a significant part in forming people's views about what was going on. Politicians spoke briefly before the film cameras, and you were shown brief shots of what was happening abroad, though often the spoken commentaries were flippant. The newsreels also tended to encourage British insularity by reporting violent events in foreign countries in a way that contrasted them with Britain as a country of stability and peaceful progress. Without being censored, the newsreels did withhold certain items of information. For instance, the British public response to the Spanish Civil War of 1936–39 was basically humanitarian and stressed that Britain should not become militarily involved. Coverage by the newsreels was superficial and there was a tendency to report on Spain with remarks of 'The Romantic Sunny South and Land of Tomorrow is now riven and despoiled by war' kind, uttered in the breathless and high-pitched tones of the commentators of the time. However, as bombing became more intense in Spain, at least one of the newsreels, *Movietone News*, featured the famous racing driver Sir Malcolm Campbell warning that Britain should introduce Air Raid Precautions or ARP, and telling the audience that he was constructing an air raid shelter in his garden.

For ordinary people, the pictures were a cheap treat as well as a dark and warm place to sit and perhaps 'canoodle' (that is, pet or snog) with your girl- or boyfriend. Sometimes, recalled a cinema manager of the time, there was more sexual activity going on among the audience in the back row than on the screen. The pictures were seen as welcoming and safe, so much so that at the Troxy in Commercial Road in London's East End, the front rows were reserved for nursing mothers. During the school holidays leaving a child in the cinema was considered a safe thing to do while its mother got on with her daily tasks.

Going to the pictures for couples in the late 1930s was a weekly and often a more frequent habit. The colourfully uniformed commissionaire or the dinner-jacketed manager at the door of the palatial new super-cinema, the glass-enclosed box office and the counter from which you could buy sweets and ice-cream, the uniformed ushers and usherettes with their torches showing you to your seats that you could reach only by many 'sorry's and 'excuse me's', the girl with the tray of ice-cream and fruit juice that you drank with a straw, the swish of the heavy curtains as the lights went down, the momentary glimpse of the British Board of Film Censors' certificate, followed at once by the logo and crashing introductory music of the film-producing company, the films themselves, the trailers for 'All Next Week' and 'Next Sunday For One Day Only', the newsreel, and everything else that the pictures gave you by the late 1930s, all these things were part of the regular background of daily life for millions of British people in the years just before the Second World War. The pictures were part of people's lives, although they played less to reality and more to their wishes and their fantasies and escapism, their attitudes and fears, and perhaps also to those of national policies and propaganda. The evening ended with the national anthem, and although you might rush and try to get out before its solemn tones echoed, most people stayed and even stood to attention. The pictures were a huge part of mass British culture and immensely influential.

This caused some disquiet. J. B. Priestley's Mr. Smeeth, in his 1930 novel *Angel Pavement*, grumbles about young people's obsession with the pictures: 'The bit [of sense] they leave school with is knocked out of them by pictures nowadays. They think about pictures – movies and talkies – from morning till night. They're getting jazzed out of their little heads.' Something quite similar would be said later about television and later still about social media and was to some considerable extent true.

Music Hall and Theatre

The darkness and the large screens meant that you watched the action on the cinema screen 'from inside', as if you were actually there and not, as in the live theatre, from outside, through a proscenium arch. Yet the huge tide of the pictures did not mean that more traditional ways of watching other people acting parts in a story or doing things to amuse the audience had ebbed away. Although the cinema was particularly the centre of female interest, the middle-aged, the elderly, and men in general often found the music hall more attractive. Many London suburbs and other towns still had their local 'Empires', 'Hippodromes' and 'Alhambras', opened in the eighties or nineties of the previous century, and they continued the music hall tradition of variety acts and

Christmas pantomimes. Seaside resorts such as Blackpool, Scarborough and Brighton maintained music hall theatres on their piers for the tens of thousands of summer day trippers and holidaymakers. A survey of London in 1934 reported that despite the spread of the cinema there were still five music halls operating in the capital and six more in the suburbs (though the number had fallen since the forty that had been open in 1912). Esther Simons and her husband ran a milk bar that advertised the local music hall, called the Kilburn Empire, so they were given a couple of free tickets every week. They rarely went, however, because cinema was more to their taste, though they took their young son to the pantomime at Christmas. Seats at the Kilburn Empire cost from 4d. in the gallery to 2/6 in the stalls. The programme was a variety of acts. After the overture from the band in the orchestra pit, out would dance a line of high-kicking chorus girls. Then there was perhaps a high wire act, a dancer, a comedian, a classical pianist, probably a serious singer, and other 'turns'. The real attraction was the 'top of the bill', a comedian or other entertainer of national fame. But the music halls were beginning to lose out to the luxurious new cinemas and the big bands that could be heard on the wireless. Music halls, in competition as they were with the cinema, began to overdo sexual innuendo and vulgarity and a few daringly offered the audience nude poses. This was the speciality of London's Windmill Theatre, just off Piccadilly Circus, in what might have been an attempt to imitate the Moulin Rouge in Paris, except that in London nudes were forbidden to move. So long as the nudes didn't move, the Lord Chamberlain, who was the theatre censor, permitted them. After all, nobody objected to unclothed statues. Stories abounded about groups of adolescents who released mice onto the stage, with the resulting panic and running around of the nude females, desperately covering themselves.

London's West End was full of theatres, but the typical play of the time was about upper- or middle-class people, with servants tripping on and off the stage, and a young man jumping through the French windows calling out in a high-pitched voice 'Anyone for tennis?' Comedies, especially those by Noël Coward, who portrayed the decadence of smart society, and light musical plays were the mainstay of the London theatre companies. One of Noël Coward's most popular songs was 'Mad Dogs and Englishmen Go Out in the Midday Sun', an early satire on colonial attitudes and behaviour. Another 1930s favourite by Coward was 'Don't Put Your Daughter on the Stage, Mrs. Worthington', reputedly as Coward's response to a lady of that name who nagged Coward to find a part for her daughter. 'Smart', if superficial, comment on sexual matters became acceptable so long as it took place in stagey upper-class voices, and provided all came right in the end. The highly popular and undemanding musicals were often written by Ivor Novello, who composed emotional songs that became famous for years. One of them, 'We'll Gather Lilacs in the Spring Again', was to be heard everywhere. The most successful musical of the time was *Me and My Girl*, in which the widely fashionable song and dance 'the Lambeth Walk' was introduced. Others, among them *The Maid of the Mountains*, *The Desert Song* and *the Vagabond King*, were very popular, being performed both in London theatres and by amateur or repertory companies up and down Britain.

The theatre was a middle-class institution and, except in middle-class and mainly London society, was not a dominant part of living in late 1930s Britain. Neither its content nor its very high cost, relative to the cinema, attracted manual workers or lower-middle-class clerical employees. In the late 1930s theatre seats, whether in the stalls or the uncomfortable upper gallery, known as 'the gods', were notoriously expensive. Outside London, even large cities had only a few live theatres, which hosted travelling repertory companies. One estimate in late 1935 concluded that only 150 theatres remained in Britain out of 450 twenty years earlier, and that the national audience for theatre had declined from 3 million to 1 million weekly (compared with close on 20 million for the cinema). Half the theatre audience was in the capital.

The BBC

By the mid-1930s, radio, usually called 'wireless', was well established. Wireless sets were still expensive. Esther Simons's husband bought one for £9, which was well over two weeks' wages for most working men. There was also a 10s. annual licence to pay. It might have been thought that, given the cost, only middle-class homes would have owned sets. However, prices went down rapidly, so much so that the *Willesden Chronicle* of 7 January 1938 was advertising wireless sets at prices from 59/6d. (just under £3) to 9 guineas or £9.9/-. Consequently, by that year 72 per cent of British households had a wireless licence and were listening (people often said 'listening in') to sets that were now easy to switch on and to tune. This figure was an average, nevertheless and, although in London and the Midlands almost all households had a wireless, the numbers were far fewer in Scotland and Wales. Even if you had a set, only 65 per cent of British homes had mains electricity, so large numbers of listeners were obliged to use accumulators, which were very heavy batteries that had to be taken into special shops to be recharged.

Consequently, the wireless, whose broadcasts were governed by the puritanical Lord Reith, Director-General of the British Broadcasting Corporation, or BBC, was an item that held pride of place in the 'front room'. Esther Simons's family listened to the wireless in the kitchen, especially during their evening meal, where there was a speaker connected to the wireless set itself, which was in the infrequently used 'front room'. Their wireless was tuned permanently into one programme. This was the BBC's National programme, whose offerings were slightly less concentrated on classical music, drama and serious talks than the London Regional station, and thus more to the taste of less well-educated folk. The BBC announcers, who, at the insistence of Lord Reith, wore dinner jackets even though they could not be seen by the listeners, spoke in what was known, and often attacked, as 'BBC English', which sounded only slightly less affectedly superior than stage speech. Its tones were dull, staid and even sensed as hostile by many people. On the positive side, however, the authoritarian tones of the announcers meant that the listeners considered it a reliable source of information. Apart from the news broadcasts, the BBC's major contribution was to make classical music much more widely available. It had its own Symphony Orchestra, conducted by Sir Adrian Boult. Through the BBC anyone who had access to a wireless could get to know drama, opera, symphonies and chamber music, and every year the BBC broadcast the Promenade Concerts or 'Proms' from the Queen's Hall in London.

Possibly wireless's major contribution was as a unifying national force. Families listened together to the news bulletins. People would gather around the wireless set, perhaps in a neighbour's house, to listen in awed silence to the royal message on Christmas Day ever since George V's gruff voice came over the airwaves in 1932 saying, in words written for him by the author Rudyard Kipling, 'Through one of the marvels of modern science, I am enabled, this Christmas Day, to speak to all my peoples throughout the Empire …' All could 'listen in' to the Oxford and Cambridge Boat Race as it took place on the Thames, the Cup Final from Wembley Stadium, and the Grand National steeplechase from Aintree, near Liverpool. All could be present in spirit, remembering their dead relatives, as the king and the leaders of the nation laid their wreaths at the Cenotaph on Remembrance Sunday only a score of years after the end of the Great War. And millions heard what was the most important national message of the decade, before the prime minister announced on 3 September 1939 that Britain was at war with Germany. This was the king's abdication speech, made at 9 p.m. on

11 December 1936. One of Edward VIII's phrases has been repeated by the media many times since:

> 'But you must believe me when I tell you that I have found it impossible to carry the heavy burden of responsibility and to discharge my duties as King as I [Edward laid heavy stress on the 'I'] would wish to do without the help and support of the woman I love.'

And, in case the BBC ever took itself too solemnly, many millions would not forget the obviously drunk ex-naval officer and now wireless commentator, Tommy Woodroofe, on 20 May 1937, trying in a rambling way to describe the Spithead naval review. He kept saying 'the Fleet's lit up'. He meant that the ships were illuminated but actually it was he who was 'lit up'. He had indulged in too many drinks in the wardroom of his old ship and in the end became comically incoherent.

'We Are the Ovaltineys'

However, many listeners preferred the commercial Radio Luxembourg. The cheerful and informal matiness and the hard-sell advertising of this station contrasted with what many people thought were the intentional long silences between the end of a piece of music on the BBC and the announcer saying in his distant, cold tone 'You have just heard …'. On Radio Luxembourg you could hear the 'Ovaltineys' with their theme tune 'We are the Ovaltineys, little girls and boys', a programme which claimed to have an audience of over 1.2 million, all listening to and, it was hoped, going to buy the malted milk drink Ovaltine. Another similar hot drink, Horlicks, was supposed to satisfy the invented problem of 'night starvation' and consequent daytime weariness. On Sunday evenings, remembered Robert Barltrop, instead of the solemnity of the BBC, he looked forward to the Rinso Music Hall, and for years after he remembered the jingle:

> *It's amazing what Rinso can do,*
> *Just an hour and your whole wash is through.*
> *I'm really not joking – Ten minutes for soaking.*
> *Remember, for boiling, just two.*

In the winter, test cricket match commentaries were relayed from Australia, introduced by the jingle for De Reske cigarettes: 'Mine's a Minor, the best cigarette you can possibly get.'

Comedy, Music and Song

By the end of the 1930s, however, the BBC's programmes began to be less starchy, and to consider that they had a duty to amuse as well as to educate, not just the children, for *Children's Hour* was as old as the BBC itself, but their millions of adult listeners. Now the Corporation began to introduce light comedy and drama. There were interviews with personalities who were featured in *In Town Tonight*, a programme signalled by the noise of traffic, brought to a sudden end by a policeman's stentorian bellow of 'STOP!' Then the announcer intoned, 'Once again we stop the mighty roar of London's traffic, to bring you [followed by the name of some important person who would be interviewed].' There was also comedy to be enjoyed. Laughter would now be permitted. You would look forward to *Monday Night at Seven*, which was later moved to 8 p.m., and the to-and-fro comic dialogue in *Band Waggon* between Arthur Askey and Dickie Murdoch, and from July 1939 onward, the famous *It's That Man Again* or ITMA. 'That Man' was Tommy Handley, who sparred verbally with other characters whose names and catchphrases always brought a laugh. 'Mrs. Mop' was the charwoman who asked, 'Can I do you now, sir?'; 'Colonel Chinstrap' regularly misunderstood what Handley was saying and assumed he was being invited for a drink. 'Don't mind if I do,' he would say in a ponderous military voice. 'Mona Lot', nicknamed 'the lugubrious laundress', would whine, 'It's being so cheerful that keeps me going.' But comedy was as far as the BBC went. There were no serials on the wireless featuring working-class people and certainly no regional accents to be heard among the principal announcers.

While classical music was still very frequently broadcast, you could now hear many orchestras playing light music, with well-known American songs such as Cole Porter's 'Night and Day, 'I Get a Kick Out of You', 'I've Got You Under My Skin', or Jerome Kern's 'Smoke Gets in Your Eyes'.

Songs were extremely popular in general. You heard them on the wireless and then bought the sheet music. Robert Barltrop remembered that even schoolboys swapped the sheets. Many people knew how to play them on the piano and they sang them, sometimes in the pub but also at home. Dancing lessons on the wireless were all the rage. They often took place during the BBC's late-night (10.30 to midnight) dance music programmes, featuring the better-known bands from Monday to Saturday, though never on Sunday, which the BBC took very seriously. Dance music was broadcast from big hotels, nightclubs and restaurants. Schoolboys, recalled Robert Barltrop in his autobiography, knew all about the big bands of the time. There was Henry Hall, who led the BBC's own dance orchestra, and whose signature tune 'Here's to the Next Time' was one of the best-known contemporary melodies. Jack Payne, Jack Hylton, Bert Ambrose, Roy Scott, Harry Roy and several other big bands could be heard every night. Every Sunday the *News of the World*, which sold millions of copies, published a popular song with words and music. The big bands were often accompanied by a singer. One of the best known was Al Bowlly, who sang in what later seemed a rather effeminate and high-pitched voice. Nevertheless, he received huge volumes of fan mail, although no singer was as popular as the American Bing Crosby, who both sang and appeared in films.

The wireless broadcasts of dance music were extremely popular. Pushing back the carpet in your new suburban semi and dancing in the evening to the music on the wireless was a pleasant pastime for a couple. They might even invite their neighbours or family members to come and dance to the music put out by the radiogram. This, their treasured possession, was a large piece of veneered furniture concealing a radio and a gramophone. It played discs, called 'records', turning at 72 revolutions a minute, a speed that made the expensive automatic changer a desirable if not a must-have, especially if you wanted to listen to classical music

Television

After many years of experiments, television broadcasts began in late 1936. On 12 May 1937, the first outside event, the coronation of George VI, was shown on TV. By 1938, two hours daily of television programmes and more on Saturdays were going out from the studios at Alexandra Palace in North London. At 3 p.m. there was *Health and Beauty* followed by a comic cartoon, then a few minutes of skating. Once a day there was *Movietone News*, which you might have already seen at the pictures, then at 3.45 an intermission during which jazz was played. The transmissions ceased until 9 p.m., when there was a play. Television developed rapidly and was soon broadcasting cabaret and variety, scenes from theatre shows and topical programmes with invited guests. Television was very new, and there were only about 30,000 sets in use by the time war came and the service was completely shut down. Prices came down rapidly once the service began but a set still cost about £30 in 1939, which was beyond most people's reach. To have a television set marked you out as wealthy and eager to obtain new technical products, and you were expected to invite people to your house to 'view' outside events such as the Oxford and Cambridge Boat Race, the Football Cup Final at Wembley Stadium, the Trooping of the Colour on Horse Guards Parade, the tennis tournament at Wimbledon or the Test Match at Lord's Cricket Ground.

A Nice, Quiet Game

The wireless and the radiogram began to take the place of the ubiquitous piano and sheet music, although children were still much encouraged to learn to play an instrument. Nevertheless, cards were very popular. Some preferred pontoon, while bridge was a middle-class favourite for both sexes. Among old amusements that became very popular again in the 1930s was the jigsaw puzzle. Esther Simons employed a nanny for her son when family finances forced her to go back to work, and he would always remember the two jigsaw puzzles she brought with her. When completed, they displayed the newly built Cunard liners *Queen Elizabeth* and *Queen Mary*. But perhaps the most exciting of new games was Monopoly, which you played with dice and by moving tokens around a board marked with the names of streets. The aim was to achieve 'monopoly'. You were issued with a set amount of mock money at the beginning of the game. You used it to 'buy' valuable real estate and to bankrupt the other players by charging them high rents if the luck of the dice landed them on your expensive properties.

The cinema, the theatre and most of the other diversions of the late 1930s required you, however, to go out, or to watch or listen to what other people chose for you and when they wanted you to consume it. Reading, however, was much more within your own control.

Chapter 8

Reading

As you sit in a carriage on the London Underground in the twenty-first century and watch people, what strikes you is that most of them are staring at their smartphones. In the years just before the Second World War, in contrast, almost every traveller on the London 'Tube', in the bus and local trains would be reading a newspaper. Since almost all newspapers were broadsheets, people were invisible behind rows and rows of the *Daily Telegraph*, which was the place to search for office jobs, and the popular *Daily Express*, *Daily Mail* and *Daily Mirror*. The left-wing dailies were the *News Chronicle*, the Labour Party's *Daily Herald* and the Communist *Daily Worker*. As you went home in the evening, you would probably buy one, two or even three newspapers – after all, they only cost a penny each – from a newspaper seller who was shouting '*Star*, *News*, *Standard!*'

Provincial capitals had their own daily papers, of which the *Liverpool Echo* had the widest circulation of just under a quarter of a million, but several had closed in the face of competition from the big London dailies, brought overnight by express trains. Local evening papers, however, were widely read in Newcastle, Bristol, Manchester, Leeds, Birmingham and other big cities.

More than 10.5 million copies of the London newspapers were bought daily, and 13.5 million on Sunday. Two-thirds of the population read at least one newspaper every day, while three out of four people read a Sunday paper. They would buy the paper at the station bookstall on their way to work, or it would have been delivered in the early morning to their home by a paperboy from the local newsagents. It was quite usual for two papers of different styles to be taken (you 'took' a newspaper). In many households a local newspaper would also arrive once a week, carrying a great deal of material of local interest, particularly advertising, details of local films or council politics and costing perhaps a few pence compared with the penny of the national daily that you took. There were also three influential weekly

Catholic newspapers, as well as the Anglo-Catholic *Church Times* and the *Church of England Newspaper*.

On Sunday, almost everybody read a newspaper, and many took several. The *News of the World*, the *Sunday People*, the *Sunday Express* and the *Sunday Dispatch* sold about 8 million copies between them. If you went into a newsagent's shop you might see, spread out, not only these favourites, but also *Reynold's News*, the *Sunday Graphic*, the *Sunday Pictorial*, the *Sunday Referee*, the highbrow *Sunday Times* and *The Observer*. Many families took several.

Robert Barltrop recalled that in his adolescence various papers were delivered to his family home. His parents took the modern, although Conservative, *Daily Mail*, and his father liked a weekly sports paper called *Topical Times*. His mother did competitions from several papers, especially if there was a chance of a prize. They also read the *Walthamstow Guardian* and laughed when the paper reported pompously that Sir Oswald Mosley, the leader of British Fascism in the 1930s, had addressed a meeting, when they knew that he had spoken from a hayloft in a stable. Barlthrop liked the *Daily Sketch*, which was well illustrated and seemed to be written for modern, young people like him. Esther Simons's family liked the *Daily Express*. It was very keen on preferential trade deals with the Dominions, which Esther's husband favoured. Her son liked the famous Rupert Bear serial. In fact, cartoons and serials were often what people turned to first. The *Daily Express* had one about a married couple called the Gambols. The *Daily Mail*'s Teddy Tail and the *Daily Mirror*'s Pip, Squeak and Wilfred became legendary.

By the late 1930s individual newspapers were employing desperate measures to persuade people to change their daily paper, including virtually 'giveaway' offers of encyclopaedias or tea sets. The *Daily Herald*, for example, offered its new subscribers sixteen volumes of Charles Dickens's novels for a mere 11s., to be paid in easy instalments.

The press was using large headlines, well-set-out print and high-quality photojournalism. It employed female journalists and published material of interest to women. Its sports coverage was wide. At this time, in the *Daily Mirror* in particular, illustrations became a bigger part of the newspaper and headlines were more prominent. It went downmarket, appealing to the working rather than the lower middle class. It published glamour pictures and reported divorce cases in a bright and daring, though not sniggering or tittering, style. It had plenty of comic strips, including the inimitable 'Jane' who lost her clothes regularly. By 1939, the popular press had developed its appeal to a mass market, concerning itself with people's domestic anxieties, and giving ample space to readers' letters and women's concerns. From the political point of view, the press was overwhelmingly Conservative. Progressive thought attacked it for its Tory bias, its encouragement of consumerism and its acceptance of society as it was.

Books and Libraries

The range of reading in the late 1930s was vast, as was the reading public at all levels. While the wireless was a rival to reading, television was not yet sufficiently widespread to offer a challenge. In fact, rather than hamper reading, the cinema and the wireless seem to have encouraged it. The novel, the novelette and the comic were ubiquitous and almost as easily available as the newspaper. As for statistics, the 9,000 new titles that had appeared annually before 1914 had expanded to 14,000 by 1939. In particular, the tide of new fiction, both for adults and children, was swelling. From the 1930s new genres came into the fiction market, among them American Crime, to be added to British Crime, Romance and the very popular Westerns. According to George Orwell, down-and-outs seemed to read nothing but books about Buffalo Bill. Tramps even exchanged them in their lodging houses. Most people, who had little leisure and had left school at 14, read more and more popular, or 'lowbrow', that is relatively accessible, material. At the same time, cheap reprints of more demanding classic novels became more easily available and more attractively produced.

Books, however, cost more to buy than a seat in the cheap and warm cinema. You could of course borrow some reading matter from a library. But this meant that working-class readers who had been educated only up to the age of 14 had to venture into the possibly forbidding and middle-class atmosphere of the public library, where the books were not always on the open shelves. You might have to select them from a catalogue or ask the teacher-like librarian for a book on a particular subject. For some people, the public library was merely the place where you could search for a job in the newspapers which were fixed to sloping wooden panels against the wall and which you had to consult standing up. For others, the newspapers were of interest only for details of horseracing and betting, and it was not unknown for librarians to dissuade readers from consulting the papers for this purpose by blacking out the relevant columns. And for many, the public library was just a place to keep warm. But, even so, the economic depression of the 1930s created a rise in book borrowing and, for many, the library was a place of delight. South Wales miners' libraries were a striking example of this. The Miners' Institute in Tredegar was outstanding.

It spent £300 a year and was justly proud of its stock of 20,000 books for a population of only 10,000.

In time, open access to the shelves replaced asking the librarian to fetch a book for you and card catalogues succeeded the out-of-date printed or even handwritten lists of holdings. One boy, growing up in the mid-1930s, always remembered hearing a woman sitting behind him in a bus say to her companion: 'I do like library books.' Of course, she meant that she liked novels, which she borrowed from the library. At the same time, the increase in reading among working-class people created some anxiety. Public librarians tried to restrict their stock, avoiding 'light' fiction. Paul Johnson recalls that his uncle became Chief Librarian at Eastbourne and strove to keep D. H. Lawrence – hardly 'light' fiction – off the shelves.

The 1920s had seen an increase of 84 per cent in book-borrowing from public libraries. By the end of the 1930s the number of issues had climbed to an annual 247.3 million. This represented six items for every person in the population, which means that many borrowed far more. Esther Simons must have been one of them, for, although her husband was not a reader of anything but the newspaper, she borrowed several novels a week. She read them while she was preparing meals and, propping them up against the bottle of OK Sauce, she sped through them while she was eating. She claimed that the doctor had told her to read during meals, which was considered ill-mannered, because it would make her eat more slowly and ease her indigestion. Remarkably, despite the general cutbacks in funding, local councils increased their spending on public libraries by 45 per cent between 1933 and 1939. Grand, new and handsome central public libraries were opened in many towns, including Manchester, Sheffield and Birkenhead.

Even so, too much of the stock was old and insufficient. What was more, there was a long-existing middle-class worry that books which the lower classes borrowed free of charge could carry infectious disease. Indeed, public library books carried a warning that they were not to be returned to the library if there had been a case of infectious disease in the borrower's household but should be handed in to the sanitation department of the local council for disinfection. One result of this was the popularity of various sorts of private libraries.

Paying to Borrow a Book

The middle and upper classes of British society were used to paying to borrow books. W. H. Smith's ran libraries in many of their 460 branches, as did Boot's the Chemist (in the film *Brief Encounter* Laura Jessop changes her library book at Boot's when she goes into town once a week). Harrod's, the huge store in London's Knightsbridge, also hosted a library. These libraries offered a more elegant and informal space and a wider selection of romantic, escapist, crime and adventure novels than the public library. The ancestor of them all was Mudie's, established in 1842. Mudie's had branches in the City, the West End and Kensington. Its catalogue contained a massive 1,282 pages. The subscription included the cost of sending books to any part of the United Kingdom. For an extra subscription, you could have a monthly supply of books sent abroad to a relative.

Although many middle-class readers shunned the public library because they were fearful of picking up infections, the lower classes, in their turn, were wary of the public library. They found dealing with the middle-class librarians forbidding and felt uneasy in the silence that was imposed. In general they did not find the stock of books very stimulating. As a result, 'twopenny libraries' (because you could borrow a book for twopence a week) sprang up everywhere to serve their needs. A new novel that was in high demand could pay for itself in less than a year. In a new part of Stoneleigh (Surrey), a twopenny library was buying a hundred new books a month in 1935. Sub-post offices ran lending libraries, and some enterprising people took packs of books around the new housing estates on their bicycles to lend to housebound housewives. George Orwell describes a twopenny library in his *Keep the Aspidistra Flying*. Mr. Cheeseman keeps it in the working-class district of Lambeth, in South London. Orwell's disapproval is patent:

> This was one of those cheap, arid, evil little libraries ('mushroom libraries', they are called) which are springing up all over London and are deliberately aimed at the uneducated. In libraries like these there is not a single book that is ever mentioned in the reviews or that any civilised person has ever heard of. The books are published by special low-class firms and turned out by wretched hacks at the rate of four a year, as mechanically as sausages and with much less skill. In effect they are merely fourpenny novelettes disguised as novels, and they only cost the library-proprietor one and eightpence a volume. Mr Cheeseman explained that he had not ordered the books yet. He spoke of 'ordering the books' as one might speak of ordering a ton of coals. He was going to start with five hundred assorted titles, he said. The shelves were already marked off into sections – 'Sex', 'Crime', 'Wild West', and so forth.

According to Orwell, who seems to have visited a particularly low quality of library, Mr. Cheeseman lent the books at 2d. a time. If each one cost him 1/8d., it would be paid for in ten loans. The books were arranged by type, rather than titles or authors. You could choose 'Sex', 'Crime' and 'Wild West' among others. That Mr. Cheeseman labelled his Romance section 'Sex', seems, however, unlikely, and Orwell's condemnation seems not only exaggerated but also not in general justified. Research has shown that Baroness Orczy, A. E. W. Mason, Jeffrey Farnol, Dornford Yates, 'Sapper' and other well-known writers of crime and adventure stories were favourite authors in the twopenny library. The largest number of titles to be found in the twopenny libraries were by the prolific Edgar Wallace ('Have you read this afternoon's Edgar Wallace?' was a stale joke). A colossal 201 of his books were in print. War stories were also greatly in demand as were detective novels. Richmal Crompton's 'William' books and P. G Wodehouse's 'Jeeves and Wooster' books were at the head of the 'Humour' section. Romance was very popular, headed by Ethel M. Dell, who published thirty novels between 1911 and 1939, and by Ruby M. Ayres. Among contemporary novelists, readers wanted Gilbert Frankau and Ursula Bloom, while Zane Grey was the best-known author of Westerns, a genre that, surprisingly, J. B Priestley chooses to tell his readers is the favourite of Miss Spilsby, who lives at the Burpenfield single ladies' hostel in *Angel Pavement*.

If you had seen the film of a novel, you would ask the twopenny librarian if he could get it for you to read. Women read more than men, particularly fiction, and were more likely to visit and borrow books from the twopenny libraries. These were popular also because there was no subscription to pay. You didn't have to leave a deposit. Quite often the library was in a shop that you would go to in any case to buy a newspaper or a packet of cigarettes. If the owner of the twopenny library was sharp, he would acquire a novel that was in demand more quickly than the public library, and he would turn it into a profit while there was still much interest in it. Even if you did borrow some books from the public library eager readers would also get a book that was in demand from the twopenny library and pay 2d. to read it. Esther Simons did both. The local twopenny library occupied a small corner shop at the end of a street near where she lived. The public library was in the same street. In fact, it had become quite easy to borrow a book to read, especially if you lived in a town.

The twopenny libraries took the pressure to acquire light fiction off the public libraries whose librarians were doubtful about using local funds to buy what they judged 'inferior' literature. The twopenny library could be big business. It was indeed so in the Yorkshire city of Sheffield, where the 'Novel Library' opened in 1934. It signed up 5,000 readers for free in its first week. Unlike the public library, the Novel Library was open conveniently from 8 in the morning until 11 at night. It aimed to stock 15,000 books, mostly popular novels by writers such as J. B. Priestley, Edgar Wallace, Ruby M. Ayres and Warwick Deeping, whose *Sorrell and Son* was one of the most-read books of the decade. Sheffield also had a middle-class Boot's Booklovers Library, as well as a central public library, but the latter had the reputation of being intimidating while the twopenny libraries were places to socialise, to discuss what you were reading with other customers and the proprietor. In fact, when the public library changed its buying policy and bought what had previously been considered 'inferior' literature, it increased its issues by 300,000 in a year and added 12,000 readers to its ticketholders. In due course, the Novel Library failed, its role having been taken over by the free public library.

What People Read

The figure of nearly 27 million volumes sold annually suggests that many people bought several books a year. Most were hardbacks, whose usual price was 7/6. Mystery, humour, crime and detective stories sold healthily and made it possible for publishers to produce cheaper editions at 3/6, which was about the cost of the most expensive suburban cinema ticket.

P. G. Wodehouse's Jeeves and Bertie Wooster stories were the leaders in humour. Bertie's background was far more wealthy and idle than that of his readers, but the latter liked to read imaginative or even fantasy literature about people whose lives were highly different from their own.

Nearly as popular as Wodehouse was Richmal Crompton, the mature, unmarried teacher of Latin and Greek, who wrote her William books about a schoolboy's reaction to his conventional, stuffy upper-middle-class family and neighbours, with their maids, cooks and gardeners. She touched the funny bone of a wide range of readers, even though the style and language of the William books made no concession to the ill-educated. They were immensely successful, being almost annually and sometimes more frequently reprinted. *Just William* appeared in May 1922 and by November 1924 was in its eleventh printing. *William the Conqueror* appeared in March 1926 and had been reprinted seven times by August 1929. Nearly a century later people still read the William books with pleasure and joy. They appeal to both children and adults. Robert Barltrop recalled that his Aunt Hilda read them in the thirties. The series began in the 1920s. Starting with *Just William*, they would go on appearing until 1970. William was a relatively new character in fiction: the comic schoolboy. He didn't like to wash his face or brush his hair. His Eton collar was always awry, and his socks were down around his ankles, or at least this was how his illustrator Thomas Henry pictured him in his pen and ink drawings. Henry drew the images for so long that Richmal Crompton must have come to imagine William exactly as Henry pictured him. William is eternal. He's just a boy, untidy, playing with other boys in his gang, which he calls 'the Outlaws', getting himself dirty, and defiantly eloquent in his arguments. He is easily provoked and opiniated. Nevertheless, he scores over the adults around him, whom Richmal Crompton sets up as boring, unimaginative and conventional. He doesn't like school, refusing to learn French or anything else, or church (except when a new curate talks to the Sunday School pupils about the Crusades, which for William means lots of exciting fighting). He dislikes older, patronising people unless they are good for a shilling or two, and he hates 'goody-goody' other children. He thinks girls are 'soppy', though he can be smitten by a beautiful young woman, especially if she takes some interest in what William likes doing. That is how he falls for his brother Robert's girlfriend when she happily takes part in William's Red Indian play-acting.

Classic novels were regularly reissued in different editions and series. The 'kitchen-sink' playright John Osborne recalls that he read Harrison Ainsworth's *The Tower of London*, Edward Bulwer-Lytton's *The Last Days of Pompei*, *Gulliver's Travels*, *Alice in Wonderland* and *Alice Through the Looking-Glass*, and the novels of Edgar Allan Poe. He also read the contemporary and highly admired H. G. Wells. But, like many other boys, he also read the extremely popular Biggles books. Dickens was widely read, as were the other nineteenth-century novelists Trollope and Thackeray. Esther Simons's son read Jules Verne; his favourite books were Dickens's *A Tale of Two Cities* and *David Copperfield*, which his mother had received as a school prize in a rather fine edition.

Adventure, crime and violence were popular genres, particularly John Buchan, who was somewhat less obsessed with racism than other authors of the tough, ex-officer kind, though not free of the customary antisemitism of writers of the time. Another very popular writer was P. C. Wren, whose exotic settings in the French Foreign Legion, particularly his novel *Beau Geste*, reflected the interest in the Middle East and North Africa that had been stimulated by the accounts of the deeds of Lawrence of Arabia during the Great War, followed by the 1920s French and Spanish colonial wars against Moroccan tribesmen. More openly racist and antisemitic was H. C. McNeile, pen-named 'Sapper' whose hero 'Bulldog' Drummond, was extremely popular. Very widely read also were the novels of E. Phillips Oppenheim, a prolific writer of best-selling adventure fiction, featuring glamorous characters, international intrigue and fast action. Notably easy to read, they were viewed as popular entertainment.

However, new genres were emerging. 'Spy-consciousness' seemed to permeate popular reading interest in the latter 1930s, with its themes of secrecy, disguise, conspiracy, treason and assassination. Perhaps the film *The Lady Vanishes*, with Margaret Lockwood and Michael Redgrave, based on a novel of 1936, was emblematic. Here you read about a long journey in foreign trains, with officials who spoke with foreign accents, and a British secret agent, in this case Miss Froy, who was completely unlike any other agent, being neither a man, nor young nor violent, and with a pair of heroes, a man and a woman, between whom there is a soupçon of sexual tension. Added to this, there is a pair of British friends, stolid and reliable, whose only wish is to get back to learn the result of a cricket match. They discover that it has been rained off as they emerge from a reassuring Victoria station at the end of the film. Rather more worrying was the real-life case when three employees of Woolwich Arsenal were charged in 1938 with stealing plans for new naval guns to sell to a foreign power. They were directed by a 'Mr. and Mrs. Stevens', from a flat in London's rather prosaic Edgware Road. Danger to safe old England was coming closer and was now going to be written about.

A genre was arising with novels less about tough ex-officers with right-wing views who beat up Bolshevik villains, and more about ordinary people, often lonely and even frightened, in flight from secret police, using false passports. Unlike earlier thrillers, the enemy was no longer the Bolshevik or the powerful man in the shadows, but the Fascist-type European regimes and British indifference to the dangers they threatened. In Eric Ambler's novels, the refugee or political exile fights the Fascist allied to the capitalist and the arms manufacturer or dealer. Ambler's *The Dark Frontier* of 1936 is set in an invented foreign country, and deals with the danger of huge power, in this case a super-destructive bomb in the hands of a third-rate state. However, in Ambler's *Epitaph for a Spy* of 1938, Nazis are specifically mentioned. The editor of a German Social Democrat newspaper is living as a refugee in a French hotel, having managed to get away from a concentration camp, whose cruelties he describes. A refugee is the main character in Graham Greene's *The Confidential Agent* of 1939. Its hero is an anti-Franco Spaniard though Greene does not actually say so.

In Geoffrey Household's extremely popular *Rogue Male* of 1939, the hero sets out to assassinate someone who, though unnamed, is obviously Hitler. Reality was coming nearer.

In 1933 a new writer had become all the rage. This was Dennis Wheatley, whose *The Forbidden Territory* was reprinted seven times in as many weeks and filmed in 1934. More novels followed. Most of Wheatley's heroes were wealthy and upper-class men, as was usual in adventure fiction, but Wheatley displays no racist or antisemitic prejudice. In fact, one of the groups headed by the Duc de Richleau, which appears in many of Wheatley's thrillers, is the Jewish Simon Aron. Wheatley, like several other British novelists, used the Spanish Civil War of 1936–39 as the background for an adventure, but instead of the very common trope of British people endangered by Spanish left-wing revolutionaries, Wheatley's *The Golden Spaniard* of 1938 is remarkable for its political balance and the author's obvious close knowledge of recent Spanish history. Almost as soon as the Second World War began Wheatley would start to publish his series of strongly anti-Nazi novels, featuring his hero, Gregory Sallust.

In fact, while the prewar cinema was inhibited about portraying Nazism, readers of books were sometimes presented with accounts of its horrors. Christopher Isherwood's *Mr. Norris Changes Trains* of 1935 and *Goodbye to Berlin* of 1939 are set in early 1930s Berlin as the Nazis were forcing their way into power. In 1937, Phyllis Bottome depicted the impact of the Hitler regime on a German family in her *The Mortal Storm*. She warned against Nazi warmongering, antisemitism and its insistence that women should be confined to domestic roles.

One of the most-popular writers of thrillers was Leslie Charteris, whose hero was Simon Templar, alias 'The Saint'. In 1938, Charteris published *The Saint Plays with Fire.* Here the enemy is 'The Sons of France', a Fascist-style organisation of which there were a few in France. They are in alliance with an arms manufacturer, still the typical 'baddy' despite the obvious contradiction that Britain and France needed to rearm rapidly. In *The Saint Plays with Fire*, Charteris includes a British Fascist, who boasts that he beat up a rabbi at a London protest meeting. Simon Templar forestalls an attempted Fascist coup (such an attempt to overthrow the Third Republic had almost been successful in Paris in February 1934). Charteris makes the point that the British working class doesn't understand the violence of Continental right-wing extremists. He declares that it was the Nazis who set fire to the Reichstag in 1933 and blamed it on the Communists as an excuse for imposing emergency legislation. The villain in *The Saint Plays with Fire* is clearly the arms dealer but Charteris also describes one of his characters as 'a little Hitler, boasting to tame dummies in the Reichstag'. The confusion in thriller literature about who the real villains were was influenced by the contradictions in left-wing thought at the time. It was accepted as fact that Nazism and Fascism led to war. But war was not possible without weapons, so the real villains were the arms manufacturers and dealers. However, to deter Nazi and Fascist aggression, the democracies needed to rearm. There were other contradictions that emerged in international thriller literature, reflecting the confusion in public opinion. While some authors did tackle Nazism, other were reluctant to blame Germany. Sympathy for the unfair treatment of Germany by the Versailles Treaty was widespread, and not all readers were necessarily opposed to keeping Jews out of public life and sending socialists to 'labour camps'. There was much British support and even admiration for Mussolini, who had famously 'made the trains run to time'. And at the time of Italy's manufactured grievance and aggression against Abyssinia in 1935–36, some people asked why Italy should not have colonies like Britain and France.

Another genre, where the reader does not know the identity of the villain until the end, was known as the 'whodunnit'. Its detectives were upper-class amateurs, among them the Dorothy L. Sayers's aristocratic Lord Peter Wimsey. The greatest of the whodunnit authors, Agatha Christie, invented the elderly Miss Marple and the Belgian Hercule Poirot, who is very foreign and fussily precise in contrast with the stolidly British Inspector Japp. The amateur detectives make the professional policemen look foolish. Simon Templar makes Inspector Teal look even stupid, as years before Sherlock Holmes had done with Inspector Lestrade. It was all very upper middle class, of course, allowing the readers to imagine themselves in the luxury flat, cruise liner, first-class railway carriage or perfect English country context in which the novels are set. Agatha Christie, Margery Allingham and Dorothy L. Sayers were the bestsellers in this form of detective fiction. Here, the amateurs, Poirot or Miss Marple, use their almost unearthly powers to restore the innocence of the stable, middle-class, well-mannered and well-spoken world in which the murders occur.

Margaret Mitchell's *Gone with the Wind* was the absolute bestseller of the age, but Daphne du Maurier's *Rebecca* must have run it close. In print ever since it appeared in 1938, the reader is still drawn magnet-like into the plot by the haunting iambic pentameters of its opening paragraph, 'Last night I dreamt I went to Manderley again … There was a padlock and a chain upon the gate'. This was very different from the rawness of the great social novel, Walter Greenwood's *Love on the Dole*, which was widely read also. It had three reprintings in 1934 and a further eight by the end of the decade. Ernest Raymond's morally conflictive *We, the Accused* of 1935, which ends with a judicial execution, went on to have multiple editions while *The Citadel*, A. J. Cronin's attack on public medical services, sold a massive 40,083 copies in its first three days.

Similar in that it deals with the sordidness of some aspects of everyday London life was Patrick Hamilton's trilogy *Twenty Thousand Streets under the Sky*. This was a trilogy of three novels published between 1929 and 1935 about the depressed and the distressed of London's dingy streets and how they find shelter in its pubs and dosshouses. It is about the world of shabby hotels and none-too-clean boarding houses, and the pubs where the lonely meet. Another of Hamilton's novels, *Hangover Square*, though published in 1941, is set in 1939. Introducing it, J. B. Priestley said it was 'among the minor masterpieces of English fiction'. Hamilton himself writes that his novel is about 'the whole poisoned nightmarish circle of the idle tippler's existence'. In its depressiveness, *Hangover Square* seems to today's reader to forecast the coming blackness of war.

Today, collections of books inherited from ancestors who lived through the 1930s frequently include the soft- and hard-backed volumes bound in red published by the Left Book Club or LBC. This had been founded in May 1936 by the publisher Victor Gollancz. By 1939 the LBC had enrolled 57,000 members, who engaged to buy a book every month at the reduced price of 2/6d. Monthly sales of left-wing books, selected by Gollancz and the Labour Party members John Strachey and Harold Laski, reached 50,000. The books of the LBC created material for some 1,200 discussion groups. If you were that way inclined, the Left Book Club, its books and its discussion circles would give you some Socialist education and a sense of contemporary issues from a progressive viewpoint.

The Left Book Club issued several books about the Spanish Civil War, then raging. Nazi Germany and Fascist Italy were intervening on the insurgent General Franco's side, while the Soviet Union was aiding the forces of the Spanish Republic which Franco would finally vanquish in March 1939. The Left Book Club was not, however, the publisher of one of the best-known books about the Spanish War published in Britain. This was the famous *Searchlight on Spain* by Katharine, Duchess of Atholl, to which there came a riposte with the title *Daylight on Spain*, published by the Right Book Club, which had been set up as a rival to the Left Book Club.

Searchlight on Spain was one of a series called Penguin Specials, published by Allen Lane in his new imprint called Penguin Books. Having noticed that the choice of reading material at station bookstalls was very poor, Lane resolved to issue a series of paperbacks for the very small price of 6d. in which he would publish high-quality material. They would stand out in colour coding: orange for fiction, blue for biography, green for crime and magenta for travel. Allen Lane aimed to tap a vast new market, an expanding army of earnest, high-minded, self-taught readers, the products of the broader educational opportunities of the later Edwardian and post-1918 age, a new middle class that had some, though not much, disposable income, but could afford 6d. at a time when novels usually cost 7/6d. and even reissued novels cost 3/6d. In the new England of the arterial road, electrical goods, the cinema and J. B. Priestley's so-often-quoted factory girls who looked like actresses, Lane was sure he had a hidden army of curious readers who avoided staid bookshops. He knew that the habit of reading had become enormously widespread among people who also frequented F. W. Woolworth's and other 3d. and 6d. shops. He launched Penguins on 30 July 1935 in Woolworth's. Success was immediate, and Penguins would be followed by Pelicans and other series. They were aimed at readers who would rather buy than borrow books, if they could afford them. At a mere 6d., after all, you could buy on impulse. Allen Lane wanted people to be able to pick up a Penguin at the railway station bookstall or in the local newsagent's. The attractive bindings were clearly designed with their own logo. The titles were middlebrow and came from a successful backlist of authors. The first Penguins included André Maurois's *Ariel* (a biography of the poet Shelley), Ernest Hemingway's *A Farewell to Arms*, a memoir of his experiences in the Great War, Compton Mackenzie's highly successful novel *Carnival*, and two whodunnits: Dorothy L. Sayers's *The Unpleasantness at the Bellona Club* and Agatha Christie's *The Mysterious Affair at Styles*. Allen Lane sold a million Penguins in the first year. A generation later, Penguin would be the first British publisher to issue a cheap and unexpurgated edition of D. H. Lawrence's *Lady Chatterley's Lover*, which previously would probably have been confiscated in Dover or Folkstone if you had bought it in France. Well into the 1950s sharp-eyed customs officers were on the lookout for erotic books in relatively cheap editions coming over the English Channel. Customs officers were understandably less concerned about the privately printed edition of *Lady Chatterley's Lover* or James Joyce's *Ulysses* in a luxury printing, issued at the huge price of 5 guineas in late 1936.

Of course, when Mrs. Blenkinsop in E. M. Delafield's *Diary of a Provincial Lady* of 1930 asks, 'why is there so much sex in books?' she is not thinking of James Joyce's *Ulysses*, *Lady Chatterley's Lover* or other novels available only on the Continent in expensive and often very limited or even private editions. The really sexy book for women had appeared in 1919. It was Ethel Maude Hull's *The Sheikh.* Reading about the desert was a sort of aphrodisiac even though actual sex between a white woman and a man of another colour or race was considered shameful. *The Sheikh* was the basis for the film of 1921 in which heart-throb Rudolf Valentino took the leading part. By the mid-1930s, middle-class typists and suburban ladies might find *The Sheikh* on the respectable shelves of Boot's Library. They could read about the ecstasy of being seduced by a manly Arab chieftain, although he turns out, reassuringly, to be the son of an upper-class British landowner who has 'gone native'. *The Sheikh* led to a spate of novels for women in which 'sex' of a sort featured. By the 1930s the woman's romance had come into its own and was codified into its own false and self-contained world. At this time Mills and Boon's romantic fiction was flourishing. Its most successful author was Denise Robins. A curious woman looking at the cover of her 1928 novel *Women Who Seek* would see a glamorous flapper checking her makeup. So, sex was now the openly suggested come-on to buy a book or perhaps borrow it from a twopenny library. At about the same time, Georgette Heyer was beginning to attract women with her historical and Regency romances. Miss Lilian Matfield, the senior secretary in J. B. Priestley's *Angel Pavement,* likes romantic novels, particularly if they are set in exotic places, with, as she muses, 'Jungles and lagoons and coral reefs and mysterious brown faces,' but at a particular moment, as she is reading on the bus stopping and starting along London's Oxford Street, she wonders, 'Why were all these novels filled with people who spent all their time travelling about to mere resorts and spas, and deciding who to live with next? Nobody ever did any work in them.'

Readers would find sex now in books read by both sexes, and not necessarily only in romantic novels. In *Love on the Dole*, Walter Greenwood writes: 'She murmured his name, her lips sought his and, abandoning themselves, they surrendered to ecstatic oblivion.' In Chapter 7 of Ernest Raymond's *We, the Accused,* Myra Bawne gives in to Paul Presset: 'At last life had its way with her. She turned to him passionately, abruptly, and drew him down, with her eyes closed again and the faint smile back on her lips, welcoming him.' However, 'sexy' writing in light literature in the 1930s still meant no more than suggestion, unlike a generation later, when it would come to mean detailed description.

All the same, highly suggestive sex was present and widely read, perhaps more than anywhere in James Hadley Chase's *No Orchids for Miss Blandish*, published in 1939. This novel, short, vigorous, composed of punchy sentences, would be immensely popular among servicemen in the Second World War, selling 500,000 in its first five years. It portrays a dystopic small town in the US, a world of hotel bars, cheap and sordid rented rooms and all-night driving, interspersed with car chases, drugs, rape, sadistic violence against women as a matter of course, and killing to prevent the victim identifying a criminal. All the novel takes place against a background of baking desert heat, where the men drink rough rye whiskey like water, Crime is widespread, protection rackets flourish and strippers in bars provide the entertainment. The police react with their own brutality, in the context of a legal system that allows monsters like the loose-mouthed, yellow-toothed and long, thin, wolfish-faced kidnapper and rapist Slim Grissom to murder as he pleases.

Peter Cheyney, another British writer, was immensely popular. His books over the next few years would sell in their millions. In Lemmy Caution Peter Cheyney created the blueprint for the tough-talking, hard-drinking pulp fiction detective. In 1937 he published *Dames Don't Care*. Not only is the dialogue americanised but Cheyney also writes the prose as Lemmy Caution would have put his thoughts into words. As for sex, Cheyney tells his readers through Lemmy Caution: 'All of which goes to show you that you never know where you are with dames – especially when they got sex-appeal. The more sex-appeal a dame has got, the more trouble she causes.'

Toward the end of the 1930s the 'lowlife' genre began to emerge. The authors produced gritty portrayals of underground and criminal London. James Curtis published his *The Gilt Kid* in 1935 and Robert Westerby his *Wide Boys Never Work* in 1937. Gerald Kersh's *Night and the City* appeared in 1938, as did John Worby's *Spiv's Progress*. These were novels about the dissolute semi-criminals who haunt the sordid London streets and pubs, and who sleep in furnished rooms or dosshouses. They eat in places like the one where Jim Bankley in *Wide Boys Never Work* goes when he arrives in London. It was 'A grim oasis, badly lit, dirty windows, a dull and cheerless shrine to strong tea and the dusty bun'. The women they meet are typified by one about whom the author tells us, 'you could notice the tired sag to her skin, the dark roots of her hair … as hard as nails … the smell of cheap talcum'. This novel begins with a fight at the dog-racing stadium, where Jim Bankley is invited to join a London gang The first paragraph of James Curtis's *The Gilt Kid* includes the sentence 'the washbasin was full of dirty water, and by the bed stood a slop pail, on the top of which floated a few rapidly disintegrating cigarette butts'. These novels reflected a society of petty criminals, ponces, prostitutes and heavy-fisted policemen in London's West End. The characters have lost interest in everything except getting what they need. Worby's *Spiv's Progress* is about a chancer, a vagrant, a small-time crook, an easy-money man who could probably have found a job but prefers a picaresque style of life.

Magazines

Apart from newspapers and books, British people were avid readers of magazines, as George Orwell described when he published – in *Horizon* in 1940 – his often-quoted essay on boys' magazines. Did Orwell actually go into one of the little newsagents' shops that he describes, with their 'poky little window with sweet-bottles and packets of Players, and a dark interior smelling of liquorice allsorts and festooned with … twopenny papers'? Perhaps he did and took a note of the magazines covering an immense range of hobbies and pastimes, among them gardening, cats, budgerigars, homing pigeons, fretwork, carpentry, chess, stamp collecting, football and other sports, together with the 'buying-and-selling' magazines, *Exchange and Mart* and *Dalton's Weekly*.

As for general and political magazines, middle- and upper-class Conservative opinion read the *Spectator* and on the Left there was the *New Statesman*. If you were interested in reading about something that you had heard on the wireless, you would take the *Listener*. These joined the ubiquitous *Radio Times* which many middle-class homes kept in a special leather or embroidered cover. One or more of the weekly illustrated magazines, with features and often fiction, was read widely. Depending on the particular mixture of features, opinion, illustration and fiction that you favoured, you would buy *John Bull* or *Weekly Illustrated*. Esther Simons's local public library took the rather staid and expensive *The Illustrated London News* (which you had to ask for if you wanted to 'peruse' it, as a notice read), and, for some unknown reason, *The Aeroplane.* The daddy of them all was the humorous *Punch*.

Things were changing in the world of magazines, however. You might be one of the 50,000 who bought a bright new publication in early 1936. This was *Cavalcade*, which was modelled on the American *Time*. In the summer of 1936 *Cavalcade* published pictures and a piece stretching over five columns about King Edward VIII and his suspected mistress Mrs. Simpson, who were enjoying a holiday cruise together. The British press had tacitly agreed to keep the king's affair with Wallis Simpson under wraps, but the gossip was beginning to spread.

In October 1938 a brilliantly edited and illustrated weekly burst on the scene. *Picture Post* was a new sort of publication, using photojournalism in a pioneering way. Its mixture of current affairs, social comment, news and pictures concentrated on ordinary people and day-to-day life. It rapidly reached a circulation of 1.7 million, which suggests it may have been read by several million. Esther Simons's son remembered that he read it in the barber's while he was waiting his turn. It was good value for 3d. Half of it consisted of a pictorial feature. Twice in early 1939 Robert Capa's photos of Spain, strikingly chosen and executed, and accompanied by compelling prose, showed readers what it was like to be defeated in war for women and children fleeing toward France from Catalonia in freezing early February, and for men, the remains of a defeated Spanish army trying to survive hemmed in on windswept French beaches by barbed wire and armed guards. Among other illustrated features in *Picture Post* in those months were a circus, the pope's Swiss Guard, women at the sales, Scotland Yard, the London tea market, and a night in a bus garage, that is a series of disparate subjects made interesting to the reader by the photographs and the accompanying lean prose. *Picture Post* also carried serious full-page articles on current issues. There was a series on great British painters. *Picture Post* published a lot of material on the unemployed, including one piece in early 1939 that followed an unemployed man from the dole queue to his impoverished home, and ended in a picture of a shabby man and his dog disappearing into the mist, as if to say that he had nothing to look forward to. *Picture* Post offered a regular extract from a humorous author, and a generous amount of space to well-written letters from readers. It published an account by the editor, Stefan Lorent, about his imprisonment by the Nazis, and a gripping page by the military expert Captain Liddell Hart about what the defeat of the Spanish Republic at the end of March 1939 would mean for Britain.

In 1937. Stefan Lorant had founded the monthly *Lilliput*. Unlike *Picture Post* this smaller-format but thicker magazine published artistic female nudes, but it was much more than a glamour magazine. It offered ten short stories, ten articles and ten cartoons, and it published in colour. It cost 6d. and appeared monthly. Among many other well-known authors who wrote for *Lilliput* were V. S. Pritchett, Nancy Mitford, H. E. Bates, C. S. Forester and Robert Graves. By early 1939 it was selling 200,000 copies.

To complete up-to-date and informative reading, since May 1938 for a shilling you could have bought the British (and first international edition) of *Reader's Digest*, which gave you a variety of thirty summarised articles from magazines. As the monthly editions mounted up, *Reader's Digest* would join *Punch* and perhaps *Country Life* and *The Illustrated London News* on the table in doctors' and dentists' waiting rooms.

Women's Magazine Reading

The oldest magazine for women was *The People's Friend*. It was aimed at mature women. Besides its fiction it offered readers articles about crafts and general interest. Working-class girls and women would buy *Peg's Paper* for its romances, which often crossed the class boundary. The fictional 'Peg' announced herself in the opening number as a one-time mill girl. There were many other magazines like *Peg's Paper* with names such as *Golden Star, Lucky Star, Red Star Weekly, Silver Star* and *Crystal*. They cost 2d. or 3d. and included long and short stories, serials, agony aunts' columns, some harmless personal guidance and readers' letters. 'Rags to riches'-type stories were popular, but sex and domestic problems were usually avoided. These magazines satisfied the need for women to have fantasies. Margaret Powell, in her memoir of servant's life *Climbing the Stairs*, described the romance magazines in this way:

> the husband is so chivalrous to his bride that he carries her over the threshold, and then they have a lovely candle-lit dinner together. And then they go upstairs and the blushing bride goes into the bedroom, undresses on her own, puts on a lovely chiffon nightdress and sits up in bed with a bow in her hair, and then some sort of veil is drawn over the rest of the proceedings.

At the other end of the social ladder, the upper-middle-class woman found her interests catered for in *The Lady*, with its adverts for high-priced consumer goods and its news about high society and luxury houses. *Ideal Home* and *Good Housekeeping* were expensive and glossy journals, which displayed middle-class gardens, furniture, horses and dogs, wirelesses and holidays. Their advertising portrayed servants and expensive cars. As the working-class wife whose husband was in a well-paid and reliable job moved into the lower middle class, she would explore the contents of several new women's magazines that appeared and became mass-circulation weeklies. The best-known three were *Woman's Own* in 1932, *Woman's Illustrated* in 1936 and *Woman* in 1937. All of them reflected the assumption that a married woman should stay at home and run her house efficiently. Importantly, they did not assume, as had earlier middle-class women's publications, that their readers would have servants. Now the ideal was to be a capable housewife and mother. *Woman's Own* introduced itself in October 1932, proclaiming that it intended to be for the 'up to date' wife and the 'wife-to-be'. *Woman's Own* was, in its own words, 'The home paper that makes any girl worth her salt want to be the best housewife ever – and then some'. That last phrase was a daring American vulgarity. *Woman*, appearing in 1937, was the first woman's magazine to be printed by colour gravure. Women found it compelling, and it became the market leader with a circulation of 750,000.

A woman would buy one or more of these magazines, usually referred to as 'books', or have it delivered. The content was similar in all of them: a romantic story, advice on how to keep your husband happy, fashion, health and how to keep yourself attractive. The editor assumed you lived in one of the new suburban houses, so you would be interested in cookery, wallpaper, knitting, sewing and flower-arranging. And of course, you were interested in glamorous women, and you admired film stars but just as much aristocratic ladies. You wanted to model yourself on the new queen and her two daughters ('So much more suitable than that dreadful Simpson woman,' it was said).

Interestingly enough, although the women's magazines underlined female domestic roles, they actually offered careers to women. Many of their editors and writers were women. They also promoted a child-centred environment that demanded a small and planned family. High-quality and attentive child care within a context of efficient domesticity were the ideals, rather than the uncontrolled family and hand-to-mouth living of the inner-city working class. Not the pub but the home ought to be the place where the father and husband wanted to spend his leisure.

The Bride's Book, in a new and revised edition, published by The Bride's Book Company in London in June 1936, was a hardcover volume that pulled together a variety of information of the sort that would have been found in the advice sections of the women's magazines. So many copies of *The Bride's Book* have survived that it probably had a wide sale. Esther Simons's younger sister, who married in November 1936, had a copy. The book's earlier chapters dealt with preparing for the actual wedding, the invitations, the ceremony and the reception. The trousseau, the bride's outfits, jewellery, beauty preparations and the like occupy several chapters. Then there are chapters on the home, decorations, furnishing, bathroom and 'household hints', which suggest, as was indeed usually the case, that the new wife would not have the benefit of servants, despite further chapters on such indications of upper-middle-classness as cars, holidays and entertaining. The book ends, as one might expect, with motherhood. Sex and contraception, nevertheless, are strikingly ignored.

Children's Reading

Brian Magee, recalling his childhood, writes that, in the 1930s, sweets, the pictures and comics consumed the few pence he received as pocket money. The first nursery comic he read was *Tiny Tots* followed by *Tiger Tim's Weekly*. Then there was *Funny Wonder*, which had its own annual, just as was produced for the cartoon character Rupert Bear, or film comedians such as Laurel and Hardy, Abbott and Costello, or *Radio Fun* once comedy was allowed on the BBC. Annuals of all sorts flourished. Boys were often given *The Boys' Book* of something or other as a birthday or Christmas present.

As for novels, Arthur Ransome's *Swallows and Amazons* series began to appear in the 1930s. It used the trope of a group of girls and boys engaging in healthy outdoor activities, in this case in the Lake District and East Anglia. For children's reading, the 1930s was the world of the comfortable middle class, with its gentle and only slightly unreal fantasy in a universe of security and reassurance, featuring among other characters Mary Poppins, the nursemaid with magic powers, who appeared in several books beginning in 1934, and would be rediscovered and put on film thirty years later. Nearly a century later, Christopher Masters still preserves the books that were given to his father, including a series called *Books of Delight*, a series starting with simple fairy stories and nursery rhymes and ending with more elaborate historical and scientific essays, as well as stories, poems and short plays. The last volume, *Ages and Ages Ago*, was particularly good, containing little stories about a prehistoric man or people in ancient Egypt or Babylon, written as if you were there. Esther Simons's son was given a book called *The Boy Through the Ages*, which had gone through four editions by 1938, and whose author had published *The Girl Through the Ages*, together with similar easily read popular histories.

Boys' Literature

Boys read the Biggles books, about the adventurous airman James Bigglesworth. First flying in 1932, Biggles appears in *Popular Flying* magazine, which had been founded by the RAF officer Captain W. E. Johns, a prolific writer much read by boys. Johns contributed Biggles adventures to *The Modern Boy*, a magazine about rapidly developing inventions such as aeroplanes, locomotives, racing cars and speedboats. *True Adventure* was one of many magazines of that sort, read over his breakfast of eggs and bacon by Percy Boon, the garage attendant in Norman Collins's

London Belongs to Me. Stanley Pool, the office clerk in *Angel Pavement*, reads about the boy aviator Jack Dashwood and Dick Robinson, terror of Mexican bandits, in the twopenny *Boys' Companion*, which Mrs. Cross, the office charwoman, calls in Victorian style a 'Penny Blood'. Robert Barltrop, who would pass the scholarship examination and go to the grammar school, read more demanding material: Dickens, *Tom Brown's Schooldays* and P. G. Wodehouse, but also full-length adventure stories by G. A, Henty, who was getting rather out of date by then, and Percy F. Westerman, who set tautly written stories in exotic places and who was at the height of his enormous productivity in the 1930s. Barltrop also read school stories by Talbot Baines Reed, among them the famous if very dated *The Fifth Form at St. Dominic's* and much other material in the *Boys' Own Paper*. Yet he also read twopenny magazines with their weekly stories. But this did not stop him reading Dickens. One form of reading did not cancel out the others.

Sherlock Holmes, whose adventures were set before 1914, was still popular in the 1930s, but he was outnumbered by the powerful stream of Sexton Blake stories, Sexton Blake was arguably the most popular detective in the boys' story papers. With the success of longer Sexton Blake tales in *The Boys' Friend Library* the publishers decided to give him his own story paper. *The Sexton Blake Library* specialised in longer tales, and at the height of its popularity was published five times a month. In the 1930s, four Sexton Blake novelettes were being published monthly as well as a hundred stories a year churned out by a stable of writers. In the same decade three films were made about Blake and his sidekick Tinker. He appeared also in *Detection Weekly*, and he had an annual devoted to his exploits.

George Orwell's attack, in his essay 'Boys' Magazines', on the school stories in *The Magnet*, which featured Billy Bunter and his companions of the Remove at Greyfriars School, is so well known that it has made them nearly as familiar as they were when they were being published. They have been estimated to have been read by half a million weekly. Orwell criticises their unreality and their unchanging character. They don't reflect the modern world, he complains. To quote Orwell's well-known lines, 'The clock has stopped at 1910. Britannia rules the waves, and no one has heard about slumps, booms, unemployment, dictatorships, purges or concentration camps.' They are of course 'racist', but in a way that nobody in the 1930s would consider unacceptable. If the British were best, Anglo-Saxons were next, then Latins, while Blacks and Orientals were bad. These rather silly and unreal stories about schools attended by a very small minority appealed to the most unlikely readers. Orwell expresses surprise that a lady of years wrote to him saying she read *The Magnet* regularly, and he himself was struck to discover that older, grown men enjoyed reading the unlikely and even absurd exploits of Bunter and the other boys. Yet this seems to be the point. They were indeed complete fantasies. Certainly, nobody at Greyfriars School had heard of the Depression or Fascism. But whether the Bunter stories did really reinforce anachronistic ideas and stereotypes may be doubted. The half a million readers of the Bunter stories could not have helped hearing about Franco, Stalin and Mussolini. Just because they liked to read about Billy Bunter did not mean that they didn't read the newspapers. Plenty of those who would vote Labour into power in 1945 had read the public-school nonsense of *The Magnet*. John Osborne, the 'kitchen-sink' playwright, recalls in his autobiography that he read *The Magnet* and its accompanying and similar paper *The Gem*, but it did not prevent him writing *Look Back in Anger* and creating the character of the Angry Young Man. He also read *The Wizard*, *The Hotspur* and *The Dandy* with their fantasy characters Desperate Dan and Keyhole Kate. The constant repetitions of situations and plots, and of words, phrases and exclamations, those tautologies that surprised Orwell so much, resemble today's weekly comedies on the television, where we expect to see what is no more than a fantasy constantly repeated.

The heyday of *The Magnet* had, however, passed by the late 1930s, by when it had been replaced by 'the big five': *Adventure*, *The Rover*, *The Wizard*, *The Skipper* and *The Hotspur*. Most boys read them. Of 1,850 girls and boys who were questioned in 1930s London, more than half said they read three such papers a week and some even more. Brian Magee read *The Wizard* and *The Hotspur*. He recalls that he learned language from comics that he would not have acquired from the more difficult texts his parents wanted him to read. In 1937 *The Dandy* was launched, followed the next year by the *Beano*. These, however, were comic strips, much frowned on by teachers, but they still functioned as reading texts that taught language.

What Did Girls Read?

Girls also read school stories in magazines such as *Schoolgirls' Weekly*, *School Friend* and others. These were cheap, well illustrated, crammed with stories and part of the daily lives of even poor girls. In her childhood, Esther Simons enjoyed reading about Bessie Bunter, Billy's sister, in *School Friend*, a stablemate of *The Magnet*. Like several others, all of which had similar titles, these novelettes were moral. Smoking, drinking and swearing were out. All the same, the stories often portray rebellious and adventurous girls, which was a new development in the 1930s. Other rather 'hotter' magazines of the type classed as an 'erotic blood' and probably appealing to girls aged over 15 or so included *Silver Star*, with typical stories titled 'Love's Sinner', 'Her way to keep his love', and 'The night she would never forget'. Another of the girls' magazines was *The Oracle* where the fantasy was centred on men and women who were immeasurably wealthier than the readers. All these magazines had a page of personal advice about how to deal with the other sex.

The interwar years specialised in full-length novels for middle-class readers about girls in boarding schools where games and leadership were what really mattered. They were sexless though the young and often attractive games mistress might have had a 'past'. In these stories engaging, outspoken and sometimes naughty fourth formers made their appearance. Angela Brazil's novels were perhaps the most popular, followed by Dorita Fairlie-Bruce's *Dimsie* series. In girls' schools, gentler than the boys' institutions, games were encouraged, but not compulsory. If a homesick girl was seen to cry, she would be comforted by the others. As with the boys' school novels, patriotism is stressed, and there is no time for eccentricities like pacifism or vegetarianism. 'Soppiness', that is schoolgirl 'crushes', are recognised but condemned. The jolly tomboy, often philistine, is praised for her healthy-mindedness. In Angela Brazil's *An Exciting Term*, published in 1936, Miss Davis, the gymnastics mistress, teaches drill and deportment. Formality and feminine elegance are valued. The school is very strict about ladylike behaviour in the street, and the girls are given badges rewarding their high standard. However, the tomboys, who are also praised, are allowed to run around and let off steam in the playground. The uniforms are of course described in detail, and some distress is caused because the colour does not suit one of the girls. However, the girls' school novel underlines that discipline and community are more important than individuality.

The late 1930s was an age in which reading, if not universal, was at least very widespread. Paladins of high culture complained that some writing had indeed become valuelessly commercialised. Popular culture had arguably been dumbed down. But one might also argue that culture had become more widespread, and that readers were able to select their reading according to their interests and requirements. It would be hard to deny that the millions of daily newspapers, magazines and novels consumed meant that people who had never read before were now widening their knowledge as well as their communication skills and critical standards.

Chapter 9

Habits, Leisure and Amusements

In Patrick Hamilton's 1934 novel *Plains of Cement*, Mr. Eccles, a regular at the pub in London's Euston Road where Ella Dawson works, takes her out to a cinema further west near Madame Tussaud's famous waxworks. Leaving the picture house, they go to an ABC cafeteria in Baker Street.

Going to the pictures and eating out at an ABC or at a Lyon's teashop or Corner House were such familiar activities that they are often mentioned in novels of the 1930s. However, there was another amusement, or perhaps habit, that was so common as not even to be mentioned except when you had no money to indulge it. In George Orwell's *Keep the Aspidistra Flying*, Gordon Comstock's daily life is often marked by whether he has enough money to buy cigarettes.

Smoking

Tobacco was big business. Many of the historic tobacco firms had now come under the aegis of the Imperial Tobacco Co. including Wills of Bristol and Player's of Nottingham. They made the cheap Woodbines and Weights, and the smarter Gold Flakes and the very strong Capstans, as well as Player's Navy Cut cigarettes. Two-thirds of all the cigarettes sold in Britain were Player's and two-thirds of these were Player's Medium Navy Cut, with a picture of a bearded sailor of the Royal Navy on the packet. In January 1937, Player's sold nearly 3.5 million cigarettes.

Cigarettes were widely advertised, particularly in the press, at a cost of some £60 million a year. The slogans were everywhere, 'Player's Please' being perhaps the best known. Others included 'Senior Service Satisfy', De Reske's 'Mine's a Minor' and 'Smoke Craven 'A' for your throat's sake'. Some advertising genius had suggested the cigarette card, which led to a widespread mania for collecting sets. There were many of these. They included series on footballers, boxers and cricketers, ships, wild animals, actresses and military uniforms. The cigarette manufacturers gave away albums, so boys tried to persuade their older male relatives to buy another packet to try to complete the series that they were collecting.

Smoking was almost universal. While £42 million had been spent on tobacco in 1914, the figure was £204 million by 1939. The gross output of the tobacco trade quintupled between 1907 and 1937. Consumption per head almost doubled. Smoking was pervasive and a social lubricant. You took out a cigarette and offered the packet or your cigarette case around. If an attractive woman took out a cigarette, several men would dive in to light it for her, and your lighter had to ignite at once, or at least that was the film cliché. Repeated attempts accompanied by muffled curses would make a man look foolish.

Social occasions were thick with smoke. As you sat in the cinema you saw wreaths of it through the ray of the projector. Your hair and your clothes smelled of cigarette smoke. You smoked on the upper deck of the bus even after it was enclosed, and in five out of the seven carriages in London Tube trains. You smoked in a restaurant before, often during and after your meal. You 'lit up' almost without thinking and rarely thought it necessary to ask other people if they minded. It was calculated in 1938 that eight out of ten men and four out of ten women smoked.

The habit had increased enormously among men during the Great War. As women took over men's jobs they adopted the male habit of smoking cigarettes. During the 1930s, advertisements for women's products and clothes often featured the cigarette as an indication of sophistication. When she was up at Oxford the later novelist Barbara Pym chain-smoked Gold Flake cigarettes. In 1936 the song 'These Foolish Things Remind Me of You' included the lines 'A cigarette that bears a lipstick's traces/an airline ticket to romantic places' and this confirmed that smoking was as elegantly sophisticated as taking a plane to, say, Rome or Paris.

Smoking was thought to curb the appetite and thus a way of keeping slim. At least, this was what the Kensitas brand manufacturer, Gallaher, claimed. Packets of Kensitas cigarettes also bore the picture of a butler handing you cigarettes on a tray, which suggested that upper-class people smoked that brand. Carreras proclaimed that the cork tip on their Craven 'A' cigarettes protected your throat and found professional singers who confirmed this. Nobody thought that smoking was dangerous for the health, although in the Billy Bunter and other books about boys' boarding schools the unsporting boys, the cheats and bullies who visited pubs, also smoked. The habit was known to be 'bad for the wind' and explained why they did not play rugger or football. Smoking as well as drinking alcohol was heavily punished in boys' schools, also because it suggested that you were grown-up when the point of school discipline was to keep you, metaphorically at least, in uniform and short trousers for as long as possible.

Opening a packet or taking a cigarette out of a case and lighting it with a lighter, which in turn led to an industry of lighter fillers, was almost a ritualised habit. A silver- or gold-plated, gunmetal or leather cigarette case was what a youth would aim to borrow from his father. He would flip it open and offer a cigarette to his friends or, better still, to a girl. It was even 'cooler', although that word was not used, to put Virginia cigarettes on one side and Turkish on the other. Another habit was to tap the cigarette on the case, although when Mass Observation investigators asked why smokers did this, few could give a satisfactory explanation. It might have been a way of pressing in loose strands of tobacco, but it was noted that smokers did not necessarily place the tapped end in their mouths. If that was the reason for the tapping habit, once corked filter tips were introduced in 1935 it would no longer have been necessary, but smokers continued to perform the ritual tap.

Men, but not women, smoked pipes. The pipe was supposed to help you to think judiciously. It made you seem solid and reliable and very upper middle class, a view of himself that Prime Minister Stanley Baldwin cultivated. Advertisements would show a bewigged judge, a golf player in plus fours or a police inspector with pipes in their mouths. Smoking a pipe had its ritual as much as if not more than the cigarette. First you used a special tool to clean out the ash and dottle, then you took a pipe cleaner to remove the sticky tars from the pipe stem. Next you slowly and meditatively filled the bowl with just the right amount of pressure on the loose tobacco as would be needed to keep the pipe alight. You lit it with a Swan 'Vesta' match, which was reputed not to convey the odour of burning wood to the tobacco. Then you tamped down the burning tobacco so that it burnt slowly. Pipe smoking was an art that many men tried to learn but many also gave up in favour of the easier cigarette.

There was another way to smoke. Esther Simons's elderly uncle 'rolled his own'. He had a little machine, which fascinated his great-nephew as he watched the old gentleman place the cigarette paper in the roller and produce cigarettes from it as if by magic. He used to make several cigarettes at a time. 'I'll be making more in a few days. And you can watch me again,' he assured the wide-eyed little boy.

Drinking

Pre-1914 alcohol consumption had been very high, and during the Great War it threatened to hamper productivity in the armaments factories. In consequence, the government restricted opening hours for pubs. However, the Licensing Act of 1921 relaxed the restrictions and allowed pubs to open on weekdays from 11.30 a.m. to 3 p.m. and 5.30 to10 p.m. and on Sundays for two hours at lunchtime and three hours in the evening. A perceived result of these still quite restricted daytime opening hours compared with the pre-1914 era was that convictions for drunkenness fell from 183,514 in 1913 to 45,954 in 1938, a decline of 75 per cent. Weakening the strength of beer may, however, have had a significant effect also.

However, the drinking culture was still deeply embedded despite the campaigns for teetotalism and the temperance traditions among some religious groups. In England and Wales in the 1930s there were still about 73,000 pubs plus a few thousand more in Scotland and Northern Ireland. In Bolton, the Mass Observation enquirers discovered that there were 300 pubs. In parts of London there was a pub perhaps every 200 yards.

In the early 1930s, drunkenness, violence and a very rough, aggressive and masculine atmosphere were characteristic of many British public houses, especially in the poorer parts of the cities. The pubs were badly lit and ventilated. Women generally avoided the pub except in really rough and poor areas such as the London suburb of Hoxton, where Bryan Magee remembered seeing women of the coarsest kind leaving their babies outside in prams as they drank in the pub. Leslie Halliwell, the later film critic, recalled that he used to bring his mother a jug of stout from the nearby special pub window precisely because she would not go into the pub. He also remembered the raucous and drunken singing of music hall songs such as 'Nellie Dean' and 'Lily of Laguna'. Jack Simmonds remembered women urinating in the street outside pubs in London's East End. The worst sort of pub is described by George Orwell in *Keep the Aspidistra Flying*, when Gordon Comstock and his publisher drop into a pub in the slummy district where the former is lodging: 'It was a filthy, smoky room, low-ceilinged, with a sawdusted floor and plain deal tables ringed by generations of beer-pots. In one corner four monstrous women … were sitting drinking porter …'

Porter, a dark and thick beer drunk by men who hired themselves out to carry burdens, was also called 'stout porter' and is now, in a refined form, called 'stout'. Its best-known version has long been Irish Guinness, which had the reputation of being good for the health. Indeed, pregnant women were recommended to drink it, and frail old men were given it in hospital. 'Guinness is good for you' was a slogan invented in the 1930s by the whodunnit writer Dorothy L. Sayers, who was employed by an advertising agency to compose such sales jingles.

Nevertheless, in the years between the wars, pubs were changing. The 1914–18 wartime restrictions and now investments in other forms of leisure, directed particularly at younger people, were changing drinking habits. The average consumption of beer per person in 1900 had been 26 gallons, a figure that fell in the 1930s to 14 gallons or 112 pints. With the improvement in so many people's housing and the move toward more companionate marriage, by the late 1930s much spending on alcohol took place at the off-licence where you bought drink to take home, not only beer but also wine and spirits. Sanatogen or Wincarnis tonic wine, usually a sweet wine with added herbs, advertised as providing some medical benefit, was also very popular. You bought it at the grocer's, and some housewives became addicted to it.

No longer were there so many dirty drinking dens as in the pre-1914 epoch. Many pubs were becoming places where respectable middle-class couples could spend a pleasant couple of hours without the presence of drunks or having to pass neglected children waiting outside. There had usually been a 'saloon bar' where the beer cost a penny or so more and the company was somewhat better mannered than in the 'public'. There were tables and armchairs where you could sit and read the evening paper, perhaps while you waited for the rush hour to pass, and you could get a seat on the bus home or on the London tube. Ashtrays were provided and you were expected not to spit on the floor, which was carpeted rather than sawdusted. And now pubs were being gentrified. The saloon bar was turning into something like the cocktail lounge in a hotel. As the pub became more attractive to women and a man could take his wife into it without embarrassment, so buying beer from the 'jug and bottle' side of the pub and taking it home to drink became less common. Female customers required their own clean toilets, which led to better facilities for men. In some old 'spit and sawdust' boozers there may not even have been lavatories, but just a concreted channel and a drain in the yard. All the same, for another generation at least, the old boozers were still to be found. Pubs, especially in the public bar, were stuffy and hazy with tobacco smoke, and in some public bars men still spat on the floor. There were no seats. Those 'spit and sawdust' boozers were patronised by labouring men in their working clothes and boots.

In the interwar years, faced with greater demand from women and respectable working-class men, brewers built or renovated 6,000 public houses. Often the new pubs were in town centres next to new railway stations and super-cinemas. They were sometimes called 'hotels', though they did not have bedrooms. The old 'spit and sawdust' boozer became rarer. The 'respectable' working class began to edge out the 'rough' trade. The pub became a place where middle-class couples could spend a pleasant interval without the disturbing presence of rowdy, drunken women and neglected children. The pub became 'gentrified', with a 'lounge' decorated like a hotel, not divided into a public and a saloon bar. There were neat tables and chairs as a matter of course, carpets and clean toilets. There was less standing-up drinking. Often there was hot food on offer, as well as non-alcoholic drinks. There were pub gardens for pleasant summer evening socialising. The new pubs were built in Tudor style in the 1920s and in Georgian style in the 1930s. They were expensively built and architect-designed. They were large because they were intended to be places of mass entertainment. Often the frowsty public bar and the somewhat cleaner saloon bar were merged into one large room with a long bar counter. Some had kitchens and chefs providing food of high quality. No longer places where the working-class male dropped in for a quick pint or to spend the evening downing pots of ale, the new pubs personified bourgeois ideas of high-class and sophisticated leisure where you sat with your spouse at elegant tables and sometimes there was waiting staff to take your orders.

These pubs were aimed at attracting couples who lived in the new suburban estates. George Orwell didn't like them. For him, as he wrote in *The Road to Wigan Pier*, they were dismal sham-Tudor places fitted out by the big brewery companies.

As the new super-pubs got larger, some morphed into what were known as roadhouses. With ample space, allowing the parking of dozens of cars and sometimes boasting a swimming pool and a dance floor, the suburban roadhouse attracted well-heeled middle- and upper-middle-class folk who owned cars and took advantage of the new arterial roads around the capital to visit them. The best-known roadhouses around London were the Ace of Spades on the Kingston Bypass, the Spider's Web in Bushey and the Thatched Barn on the A1. In the roadhouse people seeking entertainment could escape the licensing hours of the pub and spend their disposable income in a nightclub-like atmosphere. Here one could dance to swing bands and cheek to cheek as a crooner sighed into the microphone. During the day, the roadhouse acted as a country club, where the new cult of health and efficiency made mixed bathing acceptable, and there were tennis courts and bowling greens. Later, you would enjoy yourself on the dance floor, dine in one of the restaurants, which had perhaps tempted a top-class chef away from a London hotel, or drink in a sophisticated way in the cocktail lounge. Cocktails were in fact becoming popular as J. B. Priestley noted in his *English Journey*. The roadhouse, which was far out of town, had a somewhat transgressive or 'naughty' air about it. A married man might take his mistress there, or a couple might conduct an adulterous affair. Rumours flew around about 'orgies', naked bathing and 'Americanization'. The roadhouses did indeed suggest the image of the American 'motel' where what you got up to away from home or the office was nobody else's business. In time, the image of the roadhouse became somewhat sordid. As car ownership spread so the social class of patrons of the roadhouse was perceived to decline. However, it could not have been very high if Graham Greene was correct to send 'Pinkie Brown', the vicious antihero of *Brighton Rock*, and his gang to the 'Queen of Hearts' roadhouse on the Brighton Road.

In inner London you could, if you were so inclined, visit any one of many hundreds of nightclubs. At the same time many people were critical of the values of the new London night life, because it was associated with drugs and jazz music (which some people called 'nigger music'), a phenomenon that suggested to many people a collapse in moral values. 'Jitterbug', which arrived at London's Palladium Theatre with Cab Calloway in 1934, was even more alarming.

Gambling

If you wanted to place a bet on a horse race, you had to do it at the course itself or have an account with a licensed bookmaker. Perhaps as many as 4 million people had at least an occasional 'flutter' on the horses, but most of them did it illegally on a street corner or perhaps in a pub with the help of a 'bookie's runner'. This was somebody who accepted bets on behalf of a bookmaker, licensed or not. Being a bookie's runner was a well-known 'nice little earner', especially if you were on the dole. Robert Barltrop remembered one narrow street in the East London district of Hackney that was known as 'the bookies' turning'. Men stood in doorways, passing money to and fro as well as 'betting slips'. These were pieces of paper in which the coins being gambled were wrapped. You wrote your name, or perhaps pseudonym, and the name of the horse and the race and place, on the slip. An elderly man, pretending to read his newspaper, was the lookout. When he gave a signal that a policeman was approaching, the runners disappeared like lightning into local houses and a general store. That particular shop was much more prosperous in appearance and kept a more extensive stock than most others, so it was assumed that the bookmakers paid the owner to allow the shop to accommodate runners hiding from the policeman on his beat. The latter might sometimes take a bribe to look the other way. After all, the law that banned off-course betting was unpopular. Why should only the well-off be allowed to have a little bet? Most bets were only for sixpence or a shilling. Some opinion, of course, thought it was wrong to bet, especially as it was mostly poor people who indulged in the habit and often those who were 'on the dole' at taxpayers' expense. But it was, for those who betted, just another tiny luxury like five cheap cigarettes, a pint of beer, or going to the pictures, and what is more you might perhaps win a lot of money and get something for the family that you would never have enough income to save up for, such as perhaps a seaside holiday. If you won enough over a year to make up for the amount you lost, where was the harm?

The runner collected the bets and paid off the winners. Esther Simons's father was both an occasional runner and an unwise gambler, whose unskilful betting habit impoverished his family. She once turned down a marriage proposal from a suitor whom she liked, just because he was a gambling cardplayer, probably of pontoon. The amateur and middle-class version of cards was bridge, which became almost an obsession and was played with moderate stakes as a social activity, both at home and at bridge clubs.

Apart from widespread street betting on horse races, which gave employment to the bookies' runners and was estimated to entertain about 4 million people, gambling was a big industry. Some £221 million was spent in 1938 on legal gambling, and illegal betting might have added another £100 million to the total. Estimates at the time calculated that as many as 15 million people betted, at least occasionally. Most of the legal betting took the form of small wagers on the football pools, a weekly gamble in which as many as between 5 and 7 million participated. By the late 1930s Littlewood's and Vernon's Pools were taking £800,000 a week and the Post Office was receiving a substantial income from the massive number of postal orders that people sent in with their pools coupons. Older people can still recall the plummy voice of the BBC announcer as he read out the football results on Saturday evening slowly enough for Father to check the pools and see if he had won anything. It was a weekly tradition in thousands of households. And you knew whether a match had ended in a draw because the tone of the announcer's voice changed as he read out the name of the second team.

A popular spectator sport was the 'dogs', which attracted some 19 million admissions a year. Greater London had seventeen dog-racing tracks by 1933. It cost 1/3d. to get in, which was a little above the price of the cheapest seat in the super-cinema. At the dogs you could bet legally, and the race was over in a minute or two, so you got quick results.

Individual and Partnered Sports

Golf and tennis were played at clubs. All you needed was a partner. They were quite markedly middle- and upper-class sports. Young men and women would socialise at the local tennis club, while to be admitted as a member at the golf club was an indication of your social acceptability. In the TV series *Dad's Army*, set in 1939 and 1940, Mr. Mainwaring, though he is the local bank manager, has not managed to gain membership of the golf club, which understandably angers him when his chief clerk, the aristocratic Arthur Wilson, tells Mainwaring that he has been having lunch with the golf club secretary. Although it seems unlikely that a bank manager would not be accepted, golf clubs were notoriously exclusive. At the same time, women were admitted, as were businessmen, and the golf course was often the place to clinch deals.

Team Sports: Cricket and Football

These were very much spectator sports, even though thousands played them, and the done thing was to support your local side. During the summer, the newspapers' sports pages carried full details of most of the county cricket sides' matches. These were read avidly by supporters of specific county teams. If you lived in Kent, for instance, you would examine the sports pages of the daily newspaper to see who had scored most runs or taken most wickets in that county team's recent match. Cricket was in some ways classless. The rural tradition was that in the village team the squire was as good as the ploughman, and the latter might well be the team captain, whose instructions the squire followed. Nevertheless, in county cricket, professional players were socially inferior. Every year there was a match between amateur county players, who were termed 'Gentlemen' and the professional cricketers, called 'Players'. Professionals were referred to on the scorecards, distributed during matches, by their surnames only, while the names of amateurs were preceded by as many as three gentlemanly initials. Professionals and amateurs were often expected to sit at different tables for lunch. Perhaps the most outstandingly class-based aspect of cricket was that no professional could be considered worthy to captain the national side in a test match with one of the cricket-playing Dominions. Nevertheless, many people considered this right and proper. At the same time, cricket was played in poor city streets by boys who chalked stumps on the wall and played with whatever came to hand and could be used as bats and balls. Schools thought cricket should be played imitating the gentlemanly rules and rites of the public schools. Unlike at football matches, at cricket games, even at school, there was no shouting, save the ritual call of 'Howzat!' when you thought the batsman was 'out', usually for the reason known as 'leg before wicket'. But the umpire made the decision, and neither player nor spectator ever uttered any disagreement. The spectators clapped the batsmen of both sides as they went out to the wicket and when they returned to the clubhouse or the 'pavilion' of a school playing field. You clapped a difficult catch by a fielder, even if it meant that a batsman on 'your' side was out. If you were in your school's team you wore the uniform of white flannels. The test matches were broadcast on the wireless and most boys knew the names of the great cricketers of the age: Yorkshire's Len Hutton, Surrey's Jack Hobbs, Gloucestershire's Wally Hammond and the Australian Don Bradman. These were the heroes of bat and ball. The class difference in cricket was underlined by the existence of as many as 129 local teams around Bolton in 1939, who played outside factory working hours, which contrasted with county cricket, whose games could last for three days and were played on weekdays, so that the only people who could watch them were the young during school holidays, the elderly and those who did not need to go to the office or the factory.

The most popular sport was football. Attendances steadily grew. The Cup Final attracted 150,000 spectators in 1923, the first year it was played at the newly inaugurated Wembley Stadium. Since 1914 the king had attended the Cup Final and presented the cup. Yet football retained a working-class image. Rugby was thought to be more appropriate in the upper-class private schools. The saying was 'Football is a game for gentlemen, played by hooligans: Rugby is a game for hooligans, played by gentlemen', though by 'Rugby' was meant Rugby Union and not Rugby League, which was a more proletarian form of the game, played mostly in the North of England. Again, class emerged. Football was growingly professional and seen as somehow tainted by the football pools. Barracking unpopular players and abusing the referee were becoming common, and the crowd kept up a continuous roar, rising to a paroxysm when a goal was scored. Watching the local football team on a Saturday afternoon was the favourite entertainment for tens of thousands, though it was quite expensive. While the pictures cost an average of 7d., football usually cost a shilling to watch the match on the terraces, that is from a standing position, and of course more in the stands, where, paradoxically, you sat. There was also some tendency to violence and swearing at football matches, though if women were present, men would silence a foul-mouthed spectator. Football had a real 'star' in Stanley Matthews, who played for Stoke City. Despite his fame, he was paid only £8 a week, which still was more than twice what the average working man earned. Matthews was admired, among other reasons, for never having been booked or sent off in his entire career.

Rambling, Skating and Swimming

There were, in addition, many participatory and non-spectator sports, for which you didn't need much competence or equipment. For rambling, or the more purposeful hiking, you hardly needed more than proper clothes, which you probably had in any case, and you could do it in a social group or on your own. You didn't need a piece of equipment such as a bicycle, and you could do it without charge, unlike using a swimming pool.

Unlike golf and tennis, there was nothing class-based about rambling and hiking. These were also courtship activities, because both men and women engaged in them, but at the same time they were not age limited. Many a middle-aged person was still walking miles every weekend in an open-necked shirt and a pair of shorts. Rambling was a well-established pastime in the northern cities, where you could get out easily to the Moors or the Peak District. In his *English Journey*, J. B. Priestley describes the large group of hikers he came across on the Yorkshire Moors, looking almost German in their seriousness. Manchester's Central Station on a Sunday morning saw crowds of ramblers, with rucksacks and boots, waiting for the train to take them out to the countryside.

Rambling was not class-divided, but ramblers and landowners did clash over rights of access. The events on Kinder Scout in Derbyshire are still the stuff of legend among hikers. Kinder Scout is a moorland plateau at the highest point in the Peak District, in Derbyshire. It was there that a mass trespass took place in 1931 which led to fighting between militant ramblers and gamekeepers. Five prison sentences were imposed for violent affray and grievous bodily harm. Some limited rights of access were later granted by Parliament, but ramblers were disappointed. On the other hand, landowners and many country-dwellers did not want to see hikers singing raucous songs, and girls in shorts, with the concomitant introduction of cafés and picnic spots. Farmers feared fires and gates left open. To some extent, the conflict was eased if not solved by the expansion of the Youth Hostel Association. By 1939 there were 380 hostels in Great Britain; the YHA boasted 83,417 members. In each hostel there was a 'Country Code' posted up, instructing ramblers and hikers how to respect the countryside.

Figure skating became increasingly popular in the 1930s. While previously women had skated in long skirts, the Norwegian Sonia Henie, who dominated the sport, winning the Olympic winter sports championship in skating in 1936, wore a knee-length skirt, as had already become common in tennis. It became the style and allowed women skaters to display their bodies and the elegance of their movements. Henie, a ten-time world champion, brought a new elegant and fluid style to figure skating, which became ever more popular. In addition, her smooth and unlaboured movements were a major advance for figure skating. She became a film star and made three films in the 1930s. As a result, many skating rinks opened in Britain. In Cricklewood, a suburb of north-west London, it cost a shilling or 1/3d. to go in, depending on the day and time, but you could hire skates and even get free tuition.

Another physical entertainment was swimming or sunbathing in an open-air pool, known as a lido. Both sexes could enjoy it together, and it required only a special costume, which allowed women to display the shapeliness of their bodies. Swimming didn't need great skill, unless you wanted to swim and dive well. You no longer needed to go to Brighton, Blackpool or Bournemouth to get a fashionable tan. The lido was as much about sun-bathing as serious swimming and diving skills, which were better catered for in the older indoor pools that were open all the year round. Nearly 200 lidos were opened over the country in the 1930s including at Prestatyn, Blackpool, Plymouth, Exmouth, Skegness, Hastings and St Leonards, New Brighton and Wallasey, Brighton, Penzance, Morecambe and Weston-Super-Mare, to name only a few. There were sixty-four in London, including two in the borough of Hackney alone. Some lidos were built alongside beaches. These charged for entry, of course, but they had the advantage that you could sunbathe or float on your inflatable mattress, called a Li-Lo, without the nuisance of sand, the tide, or uncomfortable pebbles, and there were changing rooms and a café.

Dancing

Activities that both sexes could practise together were becoming more popular. Dancing was one that in addition implied physical contact between men and women. It was also an activity that required some essential skill. Local newspapers advertised dancing lessons, although many people, including Esther Simons and her sister and brothers, seemed to know the steps instinctively and could keep to the beat of the music. The Mass Observation commentators in Bolton calculated that more people went to the dance halls on Saturday night than attended church and chapel the next morning. When, during his motor tour around England, the novelist J. B. Priestley looked in at a Leicester dance hall (charging 1/6d. to go in and 3d. for the cloakroom), he watched the mostly young patrons dancing foxtrots and quicksteps, but also the newish Latin American rumba and the older waltz.

Dancing was also one of the most popular ways of meeting a marriage partner. The atmosphere in a dancehall could be intoxicating, because you were among perhaps hundreds of young people. Dancing was also the courting activity par excellence because men and women touched, at least the man held the woman by the waist and the hand. But couples also danced 'cheek to cheek'. 'Cheek to Cheek' was the title of a song written by Irving Berlin in 1934–35, specifically for the star of the musical *Top Hat*, Fred Astaire, who sings 'dancing cheek to cheek' as he dances with Ginger Rogers:

> *Heaven, I'm in Heaven,*
> *And my heart beats so that I can hardly speak;*
> *And I seem to find the happiness I seek*
> *When we're out together dancing, cheek to cheek.*

There were twenty-three dance halls in London in 1933 but 498 licences were issued in that year for dancing in other halls. A book called *Modern Ballroom Dancing* was published in 1939 and sold 100,000 copies in its first year. Its author was Victor Sylvester, who had opened a dancing academy in London, and then formed his own band and later orchestra. In time he would become the most successful dance band leader in British musical history. His signature slogans were 'Slow, slow, quick, quick, slow' and 'Strict Tempo'.

Quite different from ballroom dancing was the 'Lambeth Walk', which was just that, a sort of rhythmic, springy and swaggering walk, supposedly the strutting gait of London working-class males. It was all the rage in 1938 and 1939. It was very often to be seen when the London County Council introduced open-air dancing in the parks of working-class districts of the capital in August 1938. Some 3,000 people were observed 'doing the Lambeth Walk' in Myatt's Fields, Camberwell, one day in August that summer and 20,000 at Highbury Fields three days later. Unlike the steps of the ballroom dances, the Lambeth Walk was very easy to learn, so dancing began to be something that was relaxed, especially because men did not have to invite women to dance, and women did not have to wait to be asked. The origin of the 'Lambeth Walk' was a song in a musical comedy of 1937 called *Me and My Girl*. It went like this:

Anytime you're Lambeth Way
Any evening, any day
You'll find us all
Doing the Lambeth Walk, Oy!
Every little Lambeth gal
With her little Lambeth pal
You'll find 'em all
Doing the Lambeth Walk, Oy!

Everything free and easy
Do as you darn well please-y
Why don't you make your way there?
Go there, stay there!

And indeed, everything was 'free and easy' as the lyrics said. You danced in a line. In a sense, the 'Lambeth Walk' was a forerunner of the end of formalised dancing a generation later. There was also another dance that you performed in a long, snaking line, holding the waist of the person in front of you, called the 'Hokey Cokey'. The words were:

You put your left leg in, your left leg out,
In, out, in, out, shake it all about.
You do the hokey cokey and you turn around.
That's what it's all ...

It was a long way from the foxtrot, the quickstep and the tango, not to speak of the Viennese waltz.

Going on Holiday

By the late 1930s more than two-thirds of the British population lived in massive conurbations, so a brief time away in the country or at the seaside became ever more desirable. One could go independently, but organised holidaymaking made things easier. The Youth Hostel Association was just one of several voluntary recreational organisations whose numbers doubled in the 1930s. These included the Co-op Holidays Association, the Holiday Fellowship, the Workers' Travel Association, the Camping Club of Great Britain and the Cyclists' Touring Club. These were mostly middle-class, because many working-class people did not have paid holidays. In addition, with the growth of motor transport and the increase and improvement in road construction, more facilities for travel became available. Roads to seaside resorts were already crowded at weekends. By the latter 1930s cars themselves were getting more reliable. Furthermore, if you did break down, motorists could rely on the Automobile Association or the Royal Automobile Club to provide a skilful mechanic to get them out of trouble. The car also offered a chance to explore parts of the countryside that were otherwise inaccessible. Moreover, it provided greater income to rural communities. Motorists stopped at a farmhouse for tea or asked if there was a bed available. On the other hand, the car contributed to the process of de-ruralising the countryside. Petrol filling stations were built, and advertising hoardings appeared.

The upper middle-class and the well-off went in for one of the 280 sea cruises on offer in 1939. They also visited casinos at Le Touquet and Deauville on the French coast or played golf and tennis at exclusive clubs. Staying with friends at castles in the country or Ireland or shooting in Scotland were the usual holiday activities of high-class families. Skiing became popular. It was said that the Prince of Wales had done as much to popularise winter sports in Switzerland as the Prince Regent had done over a century earlier to make Brighton fashionable.

If you went abroad the exchange rate was usually favourable to the pound sterling. You could stay in a Belgian hotel for about 12s. a day. Ten days with complete board was offered at the Caux Palace Hotel in Montreux in 1934 for £12.10s. Some 17,000 British motorists were reported to have driven on French roads that summer, while hotels in Saint-Malo and Dinard reported 15,000 British visitors. You could go for a weekend to Paris without a passport, as several hundred men did on their way to Spain to fight in the International Brigades for the Spanish Republic against the insurgent General Franco. Sir George Mounsey, a Foreign Office mandarin, had toured Spain by car a few months before the civil war. And Esther Simons, single until 1933 and earning a reasonable wage in an office, was able to treat herself to a weekend in Ostend.

However, most people, if they managed to get away, stayed in England. Middle-class families went to the same places year after year, and sometimes to the same boarding-houses at St. Annes in Lancashire, Southwold on the East coast or Bexhill in Sussex. The Vaughans of New Malden in Surrey, who were quite well off, always went to Cliftonville, the posher part of Margate, and others would go to Hove, a mere few hundred yards from the more proletarian part of Brighton. Another habit of less well-heeled people was to rent a room and buy the food, which would be cooked for them by the landlady and her servant. This was complicated, because, as the later film critic Leslie Halliwell describes in his autobiography, the landlady had to keep the food of the various families separated. A strange custom was to make a charge for the 'cruets', that is the containers of salt and pepper.

London working-class people who could afford it went to Brighton, which by the late 1930s was very busy indeed. Brighton always had something raffish about it, and in the late 1930s the protection rackets were giving the town a nasty reputation, which was reinforced by Graham Greene's novel *Brighton Rock* and his psychotic villain 'Pinkie' Brown. In the North, Blackpool was attracting 7 million holidaymakers a year, and Southend in the Thames Estuary received five million. Nearly 3 million went to Hastings, 2 million to Southport, a million to Ramsgate and a million to Eastbourne, though most probably stayed no longer than a week.

The one-week holiday habit gradually spread until it was estimated that in 1937 15 million or one-third of the population, that is the upper and middle class and those members of the working class who could afford it, enjoyed a holiday. If you couldn't afford to stay in a boarding house, you might go and stay with relatives in the country. For poor London people, going to work in the harvest in the Kent hop fields, while hardly restful, did at least allow the children a week in the open air. There was a Children's Country Holiday Fund for which parents contributed a penny a week toward the 10s. that it cost. Esther Simons remembered sadly that things were so tight when she was a girl that her parents had to ask for their money back.

What was it like to go and stay at a boarding house by the seaside? You might go on the train, but not everywhere had a railway station and the coach was usually cheaper. If a large group went together, they might hire a charabanc, called a 'chara', though this vehicle was becoming out of date by the late 1930s. On 31 July 1938 the press reported that 15,000 trains and 2,000 coaches had left London that weekend.

Going for a week to Margate or Scarborough or Great Yarmouth was pleasant enough if the weather was good. But even high-quality boarding houses and hotels lacked the facilities that a guest in the twenty-first century considers indispensable. If it was chilly you had to put a shilling in the gas meter and light the gas fire. J. B. Priestley noted in his *English Journey* that his hotel room in Coventry had stained wallpaper. It had no running water and the basin in the washstand was chipped. Standards and facilities in English boarding houses and even hotels were poor. En suite bathrooms and lavatories were unknown except in newly built and very expensive hotels. Not all boarding houses had even hot and cold running water. None of them had individual lavatories. In Norman Collins's *London Belongs to Me,* the Jossers stay at the high-quality Medusa Private Boarding Establishment in Brighton, but they must put a shilling in the meter for the gas fire and there is a washstand rather than hot and cold running water. The Jossers paid £5.5s. for a week for two. And, at the seaside, if it rained there was nothing to do except stay in your room, if the landlady allowed you to, sit in a shelter on the promenade or perhaps kill time over a cup of tea in a café.

Holidays with Pay

Most working people did not have the benefit of holidays with pay, but even with pay a man on the average of £3.15s. a week could not save enough to pay for a week away with his wife and children. This was investigated in June 1939 by the *News Chronicle*. Of men earning £4 and over per week, almost all could afford an annual break, but of those earning less, only a third could manage to get away. For two adults and two children the week away could cost at least £7–£8. To this you had to add the costs of travelling and the spending money needed when you were there.

A great advance came about in April 1938, when a parliamentary committee that had discussed holidays with pay reported its findings. This led to the Holidays with Pay Act of 29 July 1938, which recommended, though it did not mandate, that everyone should have the right to a week's holiday with pay. At the time, 7.75 million out of 18.5 million employed people earning under £250 per year already enjoyed a holiday with their wages paid, but nearly 11 million did not. One year later, the figure receiving pay had risen to 11 million.

'Happy Campers'

Another great change had come about in 1936, when Billy Butlin opened his first holiday camp at Skegness on the North Sea coast. Amy Johnson, the famous aviatrix, was invited to open it formally. Butlin's boast was 'A week's holiday for a week's wage'. He charged £3 in the high season and

35s. in the off season. But this included all the amusements, the swimming pool, dancing, sports, in fact everything except drink. In addition, you stayed in private chalets. The problem of what to do if the weather was bad had been solved, for at Butlin's everything was indoors as well as free.

Unsurprisingly, the first Butlin's holiday camp was completely booked up almost at once. Today, it might be thought over-organised. True enough, you were woken up at 7.45 by loudspeakers, but you were not obliged to get up, though you might risk losing your breakfast if you stayed in bed. Nor were you obliged to take part in any of the organised activities, although that was the whole point of being there. The entertainment in the evening was a major plus. By 1938 Mantovani and Lew Stone's bands were in residence; Butlin's engaged stars such as Gracie Fields and the comedians George Robey and Ethel and Doris Waters. They were probably paid for by the money that the visitors spent in the bars. Large and welcoming pubs were available on site, so there was no point in going out to look for one. There were beauty contests, quizzes and talent shows going on all day until 11.45 p.m., and the staff, called 'Redcoats', were there to see that everything went smoothly. Even better, you could have your children taken off your hands and provided with their own entertainment. In 1939 another Butlin's was opened at Clacton in Essex and one more at Filey on the Yorkshire coast. By now 100,000 'Happy Campers' a year were coming to Butlin's. It was the great success of the age. But it was still too expensive for a family where the father earned poor wages. He still had to pay the rent even if he was away on holiday. His holiday wages would cover his own stay at Butlin's, but he would be unlikely to have been able to save another £7 or so if he had children or if his wife was not earning. There were no holidays for the poorest or the unemployed.

Going abroad, especially by air, was well into the future, long after the coming war, which would put an end to many of these leisure activities. The seaside would be inaccessible and lined with barbed wire against the danger of an enemy invasion. Nevertheless, going away for a week's holiday had become a hugely more common activity than it had been a mere twenty years earlier.

Chapter 10

Communications

By 1930, most residents in North and West London had access to the Underground, known as the Tube, while most in the south and east of the capital had access to a tram, and almost everyone lived close to at least one bus route. An investigation concluded that only one in a hundred Londoners lived more than 560 metres from a public transport stop or station. In Norman Collins's novel *London Belongs to Me*, with its compelling picture of Londoners just before the Second World War, Connie Coke looks after the cloakroom in a West End gambling club. It closes very late, so Connie must make her way back to Kennington in South London after the buses have stopped running. She walks down Regent Street to Piccadilly Circus, then to Trafalgar Square and down Villiers Street by the side of Charing Cross Station until she reaches the Embankment. This was a terminus point for numerous tram routes. Here she can get an all-night tram to Kennington.

Double-decked, noisy, swaying trams were still running – there were 2,000 of them in London – and would continue to do so until well after the Second World War in many British cities. The Irish poet 'Æ' called them 'those high-built, glittering galleons of the street', but J. B. Priestley, who took a tram in Birmingham during his tour around England, complained that it 'lumbered and groaned like a sick elephant'. Esther Simons recalled that a journey of any length on a swaying tram made her feel seasick. Robert Barltrop paid only a halfpenny to ride to school on a tram. The tram did not overcome its association with the working class. Consequently, the middle and upper classes avoided it as much as they could, although in the 1920s Liverpool introduced some first-class tramcars furnished with carpets and cut-glass lampshades.

The trams' rails caused problems for motorised as well as horse-drawn vehicles, not to speak of bicycles whose wheels got stuck in the rails. When the tram arrived at a stop, you had to step out into the road to get on it, which was dangerous and held up other traffic. Consequently, when the centralised London Transport was formed in 1933, its management decided to replace the trams with modern trolleybuses, which were more manoeuvrable and certainly quieter. You sat in them and heard the smooth whine of the electric motor as the trolleybus accelerated.

There were 6,000 characteristic red buses in London in the mid-thirties. None had open tops, but some still had open stairs to the upper deck. The new six-wheelers, however, were all enclosed. The routes were being extended all the time along the new arterial roads into the newly built suburbs. From the early 1930s onward, you would be growingly likely to board the RT model, looking surprisingly modern in photographs of the time. It had a diesel engine that produced a characteristic smell. On the upper deck, often full of smokers, the atmosphere could become unbearably stuffy. It carried fifty-six passengers, including a few who were allowed to stand. That load was the most that London Transport considered manageable by the conductor, whose task it was to control the number of passengers and to collect the fares.

There were conventions that all passengers, at least in London, understood. Some bus stops were white. Here the bus had to stop. At others, coloured red, the waiting passengers had to raise their hand to signal that they wanted the driver to stop. If you wanted to get off at the red-coloured 'request stop' you rang the bell. Another convention was that, if the conductor was still 'on top' when you wanted to get off ('alight' was the formal word), you gave your fare to somebody and asked them to pay it for you, such was the level of public honesty.

You boarded and got off the bus at the back. It was open and people often jumped on or off between stops. When the bus came to a halt at a bus stop the conductor would stand at the entrance, and perhaps shout 'Seats outside!', which meant on the upper deck, or 'Seats both sides!' This meant on both decks. Perhaps he would shout, 'Standing room only!' Since only a certain number of passengers were allowed to stand, during the morning and evening rush hours you might often have to wait for the next bus. This meant that orderly queueing at the bus stop was expected. Queue-jumpers were very unpopular.

The bus conductor's life was known to be healthier than that of the sedentary driver because the conductor ran up and down the stairs many times during his shift. It was a demanding job, for not only did the conductor have to control the number of passengers who boarded the bus, but he was responsible for shouting 'Hurry along!' and 'Hold tight!' before ringing a bell to signal the driver to depart. The conductor also had the difficult job of collecting passengers' fares, for which he shouted, 'Any more fares, please!'

and 'I thank you!' He carried a leather bag of change and a wooden frame loaded with tickets for values ranging from the single penny for the shortest journey that a child would take, up to the maximum fare covering the whole journey from one end of the route to the other, which might be as much as a shilling for an adult. The tickets, in various colours, were printed with the names of the places that constituted the fare stages, so the conductor had to be able to know the fare between any two places. He also had to keep in mind where individual passengers had got on and what value ticket they had bought, though he was helped by the hole that he punched into the ticket with a machine which made a characteristic 'ping'. The conductor's mental arithmetic skills had to be sharp. A passenger who got on at one stop with perhaps his wife and two children would say something like 'Two and two halves to such-and-such a place' and the conductor would have to calculate the total of the fares, issue the ticket and produce change. For this purpose, he usually kept a handful of pennies in his hand. Passengers who proffered bank notes were understandably not popular. For this very demanding job the bus conductor earned over £4 a week, which put him high up in the scale of working-class wages, but he worked shifts lasting eight hours and a six-day week.

The London bus driver earned £4.6.6d., but his job was extremely stressful. Not only did he have to negotiate the crowded streets of the capital, but he had to keep to time. The new six-wheeler buses with their enclosed staircase could travel at 30 mph, so the driver now was expected to cover the route faster at the same time as he was faced with traffic lights, pedestrian crossings and many more slow-moving passengers getting on and off these larger-capacity vehicles. London bus crews went on strike in 1937, demanding better conditions. The facts were alarming. Rising at 4 a.m. for the early shift, or, if they were on a later shift, not getting home until 1 a.m., plus the stresses of the job, were leading many drivers and conductors to retire early with illnesses, and an excessive number were dying prematurely.

Esther Simons's son attended a boarding school. She took him there on the Green Line bus, through the country to the provincial town where the school was located. Over thirty Green Line routes took you way out of the capital to Windsor and Hampton Court on trips to see the royal palaces. Green Line buses used the new arterial roads on numerous routes to places like Watford, Maidenhead, Welwyn Garden City and Guildford, enabling Londoners to ride through the 'Green Belt', in which development was limited, to visit historic towns, and bringing people right into the centre of the capital to see the sights or for shopping.

If you travelled on the London Underground or Tube, you bought your ticket at the booking office or in busier stations from automatic machines. Commuters bought season tickets, which was part of the budget of monthly costs, especially for those people who were buying their houses in one of the new suburbs into which the Tube lines were extending. As you began your journey you went through a barrier to go down the escalator – people still called them 'moving stairs' – where a uniformed man clipped your ticket, thus making it impossible to re-use, and another collected it as you left the arrival station, scrutinising it to make sure you had paid the correct fare. A commuter who wanted to reduce his daily fare could get a workman's ticket, but to do so you had to reach your destination by 8 a.m. In London, the Metropolitan Railway, which took you home by electric train through 'Metroland' as far as Buckinghamshire and Hertfordshire, had the luxury of a Pullman carriage, where an attendant served you breakfast or an alcoholic drink in the evening. Similar Pullmans were operated for businessmen travelling into London from Brighton. Well-off men (it would almost always be men) in different parts of the country had similar facilities provided for them. All this would come to an end when the Second World War began.

The new suburbs in the north-west of London, in the south and around other big cities, such as Glasgow and Manchester, were served by overground electrified railway lines, but many commuters still came into the cities on steam-hauled trains, which in London brought them into main-line stations such as Liverpool Street and St. Pancras These were, in consequence, very smoky and dingy. The stations themselves, even on electrified lines, were very much as they had been before 1914. In Graham Greene's *The Confidential Agent* of 1939, his character 'D' waits on a dark Sunday morning on a station platform lit by oil lamps. There is a waiting room with a large table, a coal fire and sepia photographs of places taken early in the twentieth century. On the platform is a slot machine that offers matches and raisins. It jams when 'D' inserts a coin. At the end of the platform is a signal-box. 'D' watches the signalman emptying a teapot out of the window. Platforms, even in inner suburban London, were usually built of wood. There was a booking-office clerk, and a porter, who would double as the ticket collector. He would also be responsible for seeing that all the doors were closed before the train started off again. As a result, at every station there was a lot of banging of doors and shouting. Even on the London Underground, where the doors were closed by a guard who pressed a button from the rear carriage, 'Mind the doors!' was the warning that punctuated your journey because it was shouted by the station employees.

Stations on overground lines such as the one near where Esther Simons and her family lived in London were very similar. In the winter a coal fire burned in the waiting room. Paul Johnson's autobiography describes the 'Loop Line' which was run by the London Midland and Scottish Railway (the LMS) in the Potteries district of the Midlands. It was out of date but ran a reliable service every fifteen minutes. The plush seats of the carriages were dusty, and the stations had, like so many permanent metal advertisements for Virol, Horlicks and Guinness.

Besides the LMS, there were three other major railway companies: the London and North-Eastern Railway or LNER, leaving London's King's Cross Station and going up the East Coast route to Scotland; the Great Western, leaving Paddington for Wales and the West Country; and the Southern Railway, with its 600 miles of electrified track and advertisements with pictures telling you where you could walk in the Kent, Surrrey or Hampshire countryside. The Southern, with its green-painted trains, 60 per cent of which now ran on electrified lines, was very much used by commuters who came into Waterloo, London Bridge, Victoria, Charing Cross, Cannon Street, Holborn and other London stations.

During the school holidays boys took sandwiches and a bottle of fizzy pop in their school satchels and stood at the end of platforms by the locomotives as they collected the numbers and noted them down in books that were specially printed for the purpose. Schoolboys crowded round the LNER's locomotive *Mallard.* If you had seen *Mallard* on 3 July 1938 speeding along the East Coast route at 120 mph and touching 126 mph near Grantham (Lincolnshire) you would remember it all your life. Collecting bus numbers (each make of bus had a code and each vehicle had a number) was less popular than locomotives but many boys did it at busy London bus terminals or even in the local high street.

Main-line trains were getting faster and the services on them ever more luxurious. The route from London to the major Scottish cities had taken over eight hours to cover the 400 miles. Now Nigel Gresley's *Flying Scotsman* travelled at 100 mph. *Silver Jubilee*, celebrating the twenty-five years of George V's reign and coloured silver like a bullet to give the impression of extreme speed, had hit 112 mph in September 1935 on the route from London to Newcastle, and *Coronation Sco*t touched 114 mph on its journey from London to Glasgow. Nevertheless, in many, especially local, trains, the absence of corridors and lavatory or refreshment facilities was recognised as a drawback. For many journeys, the coach was becoming an acceptable alternative. In 1934, J. B. Priestley observed that there seemed to be coaches to all destinations.

The Air

The Prince of Wales and future Edward VIII was the first British monarch to be a qualified pilot. He created the King's Flight in 1936 to provide air transport for the Royal Family's official duties. He bought a de Havilland Dragon Rapide which could carry five to seven passengers, flying it to London, as the poet John Betjeman wrote, and arriving

At the new suburb stretched beyond the runway
Where a young man lands hatless from the air.

Thomas Cook, the travel agents, first offered holidays by air in 1937, but for the time being small aircraft like the Dragon Rapide were sometimes chartered for business or pleasure use. In July 1936, the year of Edward VIII's accession, a Dragon Rapide was chartered from Olley Air Services at London's Croydon Airport, and flown with a small group pretending to be on a luxury tourist jaunt, including a couple of attractive young women, to the Canary Islands where they picked up General Francisco Franco and flew him to Spanish Morocco to lead the professional forces of the Spanish Army in an uprising that was to become the Spanish Civil War.

Britain had a national air carrier. This was Imperial Airways, which sought economies of size in 1938 by merging with British Airways to form British Overseas Airways Corporation. Not only did it carry officials on urgent business all over the Empire, but ordinary people could now communicate by air mail in a few days with their friends and family in Canada, Rhodesia or Australia and New Zealand. You could get to the Cape of Good Hope in thirty-nine hours. In October 1934 two British pilots flew to Australia in just under three days, exactly seventy hours and forty-five minutes' flying time. Passengers on standard flights, however, spent several nights in different cities and took ten or eleven days to reach Sydney. In early 1939, Pan-American's 'Yankee Clipper' flew 2,500 miles from Baltimore to the Azores, continuing via Lisbon, Bordeaux and Marseilles to Southampton. Ten crew flew the aircraft and looked after eleven passengers. In May of 1939 a regular air service carrying twenty-one began from New York to Britain. It would not last long.

Air travel for pleasure or business was increasing, but for ordinary people, to see an aircraft in the sky was not very common. You might, however, visit an airport, as they were known, such as Heston or Croydon, as a pleasant summer's day outing, to watch the aeroplanes (that was the usual word) arriving from Paris or leaving for Brussels. For 5s. a pilot would fly you around the perimeter. Royal Air Force aerodromes, such as Hendon just north-west of London, held open days where you could reassure yourself about Britain's defences.

1936 to 1939 saw intense development of new airport terminals at Liverpool, Manchester and Birmingham, whence you flew to the international hub at Croydon. If you flew from there to Amsterdam, you could get connections to forty European cities, probably on Germany's Lufthansa airline, which covered more routes than most other European airlines put together. However, passenger aircraft were not pressurised, so they flew at low altitudes and were often bounced about by wind and weather. Air sickness was common. For British prime minister Chamberlain to fly to Germany to meet Hitler several times for the first time in his life, at the age of 68, was a brave enterprise. Flying was still for only a very small proportion of the travelling public.

Personal Transport

Buses and underground and surface railways could not, however, take you everywhere, and they were costly for the family man. A single person could cycle, and very many people did so all over the country. Bicycles were fundamental and widely used for suburban and rural mobility. Women did their shopping with baskets fixed to the front of their machines, children cycled to school, men put cycle clips around their wide-bottomed, flapping trousers, donned waterproof capes if it was raining and cycled long distances to and from work. Cycling was also a leisure activity in itself, and the cycle, sometimes the two-seater tandem, or the motorcycle, took you to where you were going away for a few days, camping for example. Cycling in the 1930s evokes George Orwell's famous vision in his *The Lion and the Unicorn*, where he speaks of 'Old maids biking to Holy Communion through the mists of the autumn mornings'. W. H. Auden's poem *Spain* includes the evocative lines:

> *To-morrow the bicycle races through the suburbs on summer evenings.*
> *Today the struggle*

If you belonged to the expanding middle class you were probably buying your house; you had a wireless or a radiogram, a gas cooker, and some other domestic electrical items. You probably owned a bicycle. The next thing you would aspire to was a small saloon car. With a car you could travel longer distances without depending on non-existent or rare public transport. You could drive to a better and bigger choice of shops, cinemas, pubs and perhaps even roadhouses. More importantly for the family man, to transport your wife, children and perhaps parents, in comfort, protected from the weather, at a time which suited you, to wherever you wanted, there was no substitute for the private car. The 1930s would see a major expansion of roads and a huge increase in the number of private cars.

The Car

The statistics are telling. In 1931 there were 1,076,128 private cars on the roads of Great Britain. In 1938 the figure had increased by nearly 80 per cent to 1,916,226. In the same year close on 2 million people held driving licences. According to another calculation, one in five families had the use of a car. If you lived in the Midlands, you might well work for car manufacturers Austin or Morris, while in the South-East Ford was a major employer in Dagenham (Essex).

Over the country as a whole, real income was about 30 per cent greater in 1938 than in 1920. Esther Simons's husband was able to buy a second-hand car for about £5, his average week's wages. The Barltrop family, who had a small business, drove regularly from where they lived in north-east London to Southend on the Thames Estuary. In London, of course, unemployment was rarer than in most of Britain. And in Surrey, with its large population of middle-class suburbanites, one-third of families had cars by 1938. At the same time, the prices of cars fell because of faster methods of production. As a result, the cost of owning a car was calculated to be 40 per cent less in 1938 than it had been in 1924. Road tax was £6 a year and insurance about the same. Together they came to about 5s. a week. Petrol cost 1/7½d. per gallon or about 5d. a litre. All those charges had to be considered when calculating how much it would cost to run a car. The expenditure was within the budget of a couple like Esther Simons's younger sister, who had a responsible job managing an office and whose husband worked in an estate agent's firm, but for a man whose wife did not work, with a mortgage and children to bring up, it would not have been so easy. Cars were rare in the mining and shipbuilding areas of the North-East, South Wales and Central Scotland, where over a million were still unemployed by the time war broke out. Despite the increased number of cars on the roads, over the country as a whole, only one in fifteen people owned one.

In 1990, the historian and university chancellor Lord Annan looked back in a book that he called *Our Age*. In it he pictured the typical motorist of the generation of the 1930s as an ex-Great War officer who opens a garage. He drives out on a summer evening to a roadhouse on a new arterial road and discusses different makes of the high-powered cars that he sells to wealthy young men who like driving at speed. In reality, by 1938 the typical motorist was more likely one who drove along one of the 'bypasses' that were under construction. He might have bought his eight horsepower car second hand. If he felt sufficiently well off to buy a new car, he could acquire an Austin Seven for £108–£129, an Austin 'Big Seven' for between £137 and £150, or an Austin Ten for £175 to £189, all depending on the extras the car might include. By 1939 you could buy a Morris Ten for £175. For another £10 you could have it with a sliding roof. These prices were half those of the 1920s. Robert Barltrop's Aunt Hilda's husband was in a good job in the design section at Ford's in Dagenham. Strangely enough, he owned, not a Ford, but a 'Baby' Austin, costing £122. This car could reach a rather uncomfortable speed of 52 mph and could travel for fifty miles on a bare gallon of petrol. Some of the masters at Barltrop's grammar school in north-east London were motorists. The head had a 'modest' Ford, by which Barltrop probably means a Ford 'Popular', which sold at £125. Another had a Morris Cowley with two seats and a 'dickey' seat behind. This was a well-upholstered seat that folded out from the back, where the boot would usually be. It was open, so if it rained you got wet. Perhaps the most popular of all small and mass-produced cars was the Morris Eight.

A man on a salary of £250 a year, that is slightly above the higher working-class and just inside the lower middle-class range of income, could probably just afford a car, at least a second-hand one. His new house might have space for a garage or at least a place to park the car off the road. His car would be suitable for the family, that is not an open-top. It would have a self-starter so that he would not risk breaking his wrist turning the motor with a starter handle. However, in the winter, the quality of car batteries was such that he might often have to start the car by turning the engine with the handle. He would belong to the AA or the RAC and his car would bear the badge of one of those organisations, whose motorcyclist patrolman would salute him on the road and do a running repair for him if he broke down on the bypass or arterial road.

The bypass and the arterial road were the features of the new highways that were being built. Some £10, £13 and £14 million pounds were spent on roads in 1937, 1938 and 1939 respectively. Around Greater London sixteen new arterial roads stretched for 266 miles. The Eltham–Sidcup Road, the

North Circular Road, Eastern Avenue and the Barnet Bypass were some of them. Those roads had been intended to allow vehicles to drive non-stop at an even speed for hours on end, but planning regulations were so lax that much housing and industrial development took place along them. This was called 'ribbon development'. The Kingston Bypass, to the south-west of London, which was extended as far as Esher in the 1930s, is an example of this, with houses and light industry along its entire length, in a similar way to the Great West Road and Western Avenue. These highways were well designed with dual carriageways and only gentle curves. The intention was to allow higher speeds, but when ribbon development created long lines of houses along the arterial road, crossings had to be provided, as well as traffic lights and suitable stopping places for vehicles. Ribbon development was not controlled until the Restriction of Ribbon Development Act of 1935. Consequently, there would be no real non-stopping 'motorways' for another twenty-five years.

Some observers liked the arterial roads for themselves, as well as their convenience. Here is one cyclist's paean to such a road: 'Then the Great West – a really glorious road by night – all colours of lights. All the wonder-factories floodlit, some in varying colours. Some have grand fountains playing … one long avenue of palaces …'

The contemporary poet Louis Macneice was, however, hostile:

Along the North Circular and the Great West Roads
Running the gauntlet of impoverished fancy
Where housewives bolster up their jerry-built abodes
With amour propre and the habit of hire purchase.
The wheels whistled in the wet, the flashy strings
Of neon lights unravelled ...
Rubbish dumps,
Bungalows in lath and plaster, in brick, in concrete,
And shining semi-circles of petrol pumps,
Like intransigent groups of idols.

So, motoring represented modernity and progress. The car transformed people's lives. Their leisure, their shopping and often their journey to work became easier and more enjoyable. 'Bypass man' joined the fast-moving traffic and instead of waiting for a bus, drove with his wife and family to the new neon-signed super-cinema. However, for some, the fast motor road and people driving along it in little metal boxes, going nowhere of any real value, reflected undesirable materialism and an attack on traditional values.

Driving was in general a male activity. Although the enclosed saloon car of the late 1930s was more friendly to women than the open tourer of the 1920s, it was still poorly ventilated in the summer and cold in the winter. Furthermore, at a speed of over 50 mph the car could be hard to control. Few women held licences before the war. As a result, driving the car, especially at speed, and tinkering with the engine, became linked with concepts of masculinity. Only men were interested in the technicalities of the motor. Men talked about their cars as fifty years later they might similarly exchange jargon about computers. To drive required some physical effort, especially if you had to use the starting handle, which might be necessary in the winter. Punctures were quite frequent and to change a wheel required muscular strength.

While motoring was steadily becoming a mass-consumption activity in which women could take part if men allowed them to do so, it also became linked with freer attitudes to sex. A car and the arterial road would take you and your lover out to an expensive roadhouse. At the other end of the income and social scale, in Walter Greenwood's novel *Love on the Dole*, Sam Grundy the bookmaker urges Sally Hardcastle to get into his car, the only one in that wretchedly poor part of Manchester. She obstinately refuses to do so until in the end she succumbs to Sam's propositions. Readers of *Love on the Dole* would know what getting into a man's car meant.

The lack of both clear legislation and decisiveness on the part of local magistrates tended to encourage bad driving. Driving too fast and aggressively had been typical of certain men ever since the early years of the motor car. In 1908, Kenneth Grahame published his famous *The Wind in the Willows*, in which one of the main characters is the boastful and reckless Mr. Toad, who has become the archetype of the badly behaved car driver. Bad, mostly male, driving led to accidents. 6,560 people were killed on the roads in 1936, compared with a much-reduced 1,560 in 2021, even after a vast increase in the mileage driven. The average annual number of traffic-involved injuries in the later 1930s was 227,000, compared with a much smaller 135,00 eighty years later. In the 1930s the deaths and injuries on the roads of Britain was becoming a major scandal. The unsatisfactory conditions for driving and the necessary maintenance of cars demanded very careful attention by drivers, but they did not receive it. Furthermore, the law and its administration clearly needed strengthening.

In the 1930s many roads were narrow and badly surfaced. There were very few dual carriageways, none for instance for the entire distance between London and Newcastle. The lighting was often scarce and poor. Motorists drove too fast for the conditions and pedestrians were unaware that drivers could not always stop in time. However, there was an influential motorists' lobby, and the government was unwilling to antagonise wealthy car-owners and the manufacturers of powerful cars. Nevertheless, the rising accident rate brought middle- and upper-class people into conflict with the police for the first time. Even so, in the absence of speed cameras and given the custom of Automobile Association patrolmen of warning drivers of speed 'traps' ahead, evidence against speeding motorists was so easy to contest that prosecutions were rarely successful. The new arterial roads encouraged speeding, as Paul Vaughan notes in his autobiography, speaking about the Kingston Bypass near where he lived as a boy. There were few traffic lights, no protected pedestrian crossings, no white lines in the road, no cat's eyes, and no non-skid surfaces. Cars did not have the powerful brakes that would be fitted later. They were often poorly serviced or not at all. Drivers and passengers did not have seatbelts. In addition, in the absence of driving tests many drivers were simply incompetent as well as selfish and inclined to take risks.

It was not only drivers and their passengers who ran risks on the roads. About half the number of traffic-involved deaths were of pedestrians and cyclists. So great was the need for reform that in 1934 the minister for transport, Leslie Hore-Belisha, introduced the Road Traffic Act. This brought in a speed limit for cars of 30 mph in built-up areas, rather than the 20 mph limit that had been abolished in 1930 just because it was frequently ignored. The new Act made a driving test compulsory for all new drivers from 1 June 1935. It also strengthened legislation relating to insurance for drivers. Hore-Belisha's name is preserved in the 'Belisha' blinking beacons that stand on both sides of a pedestrian crossing. So, by the end of the 1930s motorists and pedestrians were getting used to the stricter regulation of driving. Headlights had to be dipped before oncoming traffic, your windscreen wipers had to work properly, and you had to use hand signals and the mirror. Pedestrians and particularly children were the target of a sustained campaign to take care on the road, in which the famous film star and singer Gracie Fields recorded a jingle:

All you little boys and little girls will,
When you leave the schoolroom,
When you're at your play,
Look to the left and look to the right,
Then you'll never get run over

By 1938 close on 450,000 cars were produced annually in Britain. Even so, most deliveries to houses were still carried out by horse and cart.

Until 1938 Esther Simons's husband had been a local milkman in London's East End. He went from house to house, perched high on a cart drawn by two shire horses and carrying twelve churns of milk. But in 1938 the private dairy for which he worked was taken over by one of the big chains, the Express or the United Dairies, which delivered milk in bottles, although still by horse and cart. Coal was also delivered and refuse taken away by horse and cart. The whistling errand boy on his heavy bicycle still delivered groceries. Horses would be seen on city streets until a long time after the Second World War, together with the dung they produced and the flies that it attracted.

Letters, Telegrams and the Telephone

These came under the responsibility of the Post Office and the Royal Mail. If you wrote to a government department such as the Inland Revenue, you wrote the letters OHMS (On His Majesty's Service) at the top of the envelope and you did not have to stick a stamp on it. The telegraph boy in his uniform and characteristic round cap brought telegrams, that is urgent messages that had been transmitted by the telegraph, whose posts lined the railway lines. It cost an expensive 6d. a word to send a telegram, but it would arrive within an hour or two, announcing a death perhaps, or more happily a birth or some words of congratulation that would be read out, perhaps at a wedding breakfast.

The much more usual form of communication at distance was the letter or the postcard. Letters cost 'three haypence' or a penny and a halfpenny for two ounces. You would expect post to be delivered early in the morning, at mid-morning and in the afternoon, by a postman wearing a dark blue uniform and a peaked cap. He could carry all the letters in a mailbag over his shoulder. Mailbags were traditionally sewn by convicts. It was kinder than making them break stones.

Because letters could be relied on to reach their destination the day after posting and given that the telegram was delivered in a matter of hours, the telephone, which business and government had begun to use well before 1914, did not expand its domestic service to the degree that might have been expected. Upper- and middle-class households, of course, usually had the telephone. It was a convenient way to order goods from local shops. But the costs dissuaded lower-middle-class households from installing the 'phone. So, statistics showed that in well-off areas such as Bournemouth and Epsom in the south-east there was a telephone for every 3.5 households, while in unemployment-beset Merthyr Tydfil in South Wales the figure was only one telephone for forty-seven households. Nobody in Esther Simons's family, who all lived in London or in the outer suburbs, had a private telephone, although the milk bar that she and her husband opened in 1938 had a public telephone already installed that customers could use. This arrangement was quite frequent and signalled by a notice that read 'You can telephone from here'. You were rarely far away from a public phone box. In the United Kingdom there were 48,168 telephone 'kiosks', as they were called, for public use. They were painted bright red. Big railway stations and hotels had rows of them, and there was usually at least one or two in a London Tube station. American films often showed a character whose telephone conversation had been cut off. He jiggled the receiver up and down angrily shouting 'Operator!' Doing this in Britain would not help. However, you might perhaps dial '0' and be lucky enough to persuade the operator to reconnect you for no charge. It cost twopence to make a call. You put two pennies in the slot and dialled the number you wanted. If and when the person picked up at the other end and said 'Hello', you pressed 'Button A', you heard the two pennies fall into the metal box and you began your conversation. If the line was 'engaged' (not the Americanism 'busy') or otherwise unobtainable you pressed 'Button B' and your two pennies were returned to you. Telephone kiosks had directories (consisting of four large volumes in London) in case you did not know the number of the person you were ringing (you said 'ringing', not the Americanism 'calling', which at that time in England usually meant visiting personally). If you wanted to make a long-distance phone call you had to ask for the operator to connect it for you. If you were in a kiosk the operator would tell you how much to put into the slot for your three-minute conversation. This would be ended by warning pips.

At home more and more people had the modern 'Swedish' or Ericsson style of telephone set installed. In this, the earpiece or receiver rested on the apparatus. When you lifted it off, it emitted the purring sound that told you that you could dial a number. Some houses, however, still had older telephones called 'candlesticks'. They had a base with a vertical pole about ten inches high, on top of which was a microphone. There was a hook on the side on which an earpiece was hung. You put it to your ear and grasped the neck or the 'pole' of the apparatus with your other hand. In the boarding school to which Esther Simons's son went there was a 'candlestick' telephone in one of the classrooms. It had probably been installed before the large house had been converted into a school. It rarely rang and was infrequently used.

To make local calls, the telephone had a rotary dial on the handset with letters and numbers, with which you dialled the combination of the name of the exchange and the number which were required to contact the person to whom you wanted to speak. In London the names of the exchanges were abbreviated to three letters (so 'Maida Vale' was MAI) followed by four numbers. As for extra services, the 999 emergency service was introduced on 30 June 1937. If information to do with a crime or witnesses was required, the BBC news reader encouraged you to help Scotland Yard by ringing WHI (for Whitehall) 1212. There was also a speaking clock for which you dialled the letters TIM. You could send a telegram over the telephone. Telephone capacity was, however, insufficient and sometimes you had to be content with a 'party line' which meant that only one of the subscribers could use the line at a time. You paid by monthly bill for the rental of the phone itself and your calls, which were not limited in time. Esther Simons could spend a whole hour talking to a friend. Like the cinema, the telephone had become familiar to her as she grew up, though she didn't have private access to one until the late 1930s.

So, the telephone allowed immediate communication, and public transport, at least in the cities, was abundant, while the motor car was fast becoming available to ever wider sectors of the population. Twenty years earlier, travelling either to work or for leisure, was mostly a middle- and upper-class practice. Now, more and more working people took the bus, the London Tube, or suburban railways. But the Second World War, as in so many aspects of life, would put a temporary stop to the spread of car driving and a halt to the expansion of railways in general.

Chapter 11

Will There Be War?

People who remembered the later 1930s used to say that war had been 'inevitable'. However, at the time, the views of the general British public about whether Britain should use force for any purpose at all were mixed, confused and sometimes contradictory, and often depended on what people had read that morning in the newspaper, as well as on their general attitudes and opinions. One of these was the general British sense of insularity and even their ignorance and scorn for 'abroad'. 'I know how to deal with foreigners,' sneers Captain Mainwaring of TV's *Dad's Army*.

Relatively few British people travelled abroad. Concern with what went on in other countries had been quite limited until October 1935, when Fascist Italy launched its attack on Abyssinia. Disquiet increased in March 1936, when the Nazi government, which had come to power at the end of January 1933, contravened the 1919 Treaty of Versailles and remilitarised the demilitarised zone of the Rhineland. Next, Germany intervened without justification in the Spanish Civil War of 1936–39 in favour of General Franco's insurrection against what was in most British people's view a liberal and progressive republic. Yet British opinion did not in general see the new Nazi Germany as a threat to Britain or indeed to European peace, especially after Britain came to an agreement with Germany about the relative sizes of their navies, which maintained the superiority of the Royal Navy. While there was some discomfort about newsreel pictures of British footballers giving the Nazi salute when playing in Germany, Nazi attacks on German Jews, Socialists, Communists and trade unions did not provoke widespread outrage until the destruction of synagogues on 9 November 1938, known as *Kristallnacht*. Not until Nazi Germany demanded parts of Czechoslovakia and it seemed that Britain might be drawn into war did British anxiety increase substantially. Great relief came with the Munich agreement of 30 September 1938, followed by Prime Minister Chamberlain's return from Germany with what became known as his 'little piece of paper' containing an apparent accord that Britain and Germany would never go to war with each other again.

Relief lasted until March 1939, when Hitler invaded Czechoslovakia. British public opinion turned against Germany. As a result, civil defence preparations, which the government had begun earlier, now turned into widespread and practical action. Even then, it was widely hoped and often declared that there would be no war. The contradictions in British people's views and emotions over pacifism as a national policy and about the appeasement of German grievances, the general dislike for Hitler and the Nazis, together with unwillingness to engage in a war that some considered to be for the sake of other countries, were overlaid by fear not only of another huge loss of young men such as had been experienced in 1914–18, but of a new sort of war, characterised by the mass air bombing of civilians. All these emotions and anxieties increasingly marked life in Britain through the latter part of the 1930s.

Disarmament and Appeasement

There had been alarm when Italy attacked Abyssinia in October 1935. The epoch was one of pervasive pacifism and trust that the League of Nations, in which Britain and France took leading positions, would solve international tensions peacefully. British armed forces had been allowed to decline while Italy had quadrupled its naval construction programme. This obliged the Admiralty to tell the prime minister, Stanley Baldwin, that the Royal Navy would not be able to tackle Italy if the Abyssinian crisis led to war.

From another point of view, many in Britain saw Italy and Germany as less threatening than the Soviet Union and its influence over the working classes in Western Europe. Of course, some people were prescient and realised that the essential of Fascism and Nazism was war, but few would have foreseen the Nazi conquest of most of Europe. Some in Britain were shocked at the Nazis' attacks on Germany's Jewish citizens, but plenty of others, in a world where both genteel and working-class antisemitism was widespread, as well as a basic tenet of the British Union of Fascists under Oswald Mosley, thought and even said that the Nazis were doing the right thing. Auschwitz and the Holocaust were unimaginable.

Few British people, even the best educated, knew a foreign language. The vast majority had never left the British Isles. Neville Chamberlain's description of the Czech crisis as 'a quarrel in a far-away country between people of whom we know nothing' has echoed down the years. Many

British people were drawn to justify Nazi behaviour as anti-Bolshevist, but friendly to Great Britain, as indeed Hitler insisted he was. Persuading influential British opinion of German friendliness was the aim of Joachim von Ribbentrop, Nazi ambassador to Britain. German propaganda, guided by Ribbentrop's *Dienstelle* or private agency that he ran behind the back of the German Foreign Ministry, strove to bring leaders of British society into sympathy with Germany's demands. The Prince of Wales, later Edward VIII, made friendly pronouncements about Nazi Germany, which disturbed the British Foreign Office, and did so even more after the Abdication when in October 1937 Edward, now Duke of Windsor, and the duchess, previously Mrs. Simpson, were almost apotheosically received by the Nazis.

The Great War had ended only twenty years before. It was in the memory of probably most of the British population. For the children, widows and parents of men who had been killed, the possibility of another such conflict was a constant dread. When the 18-year-old Francis McFarland, a civil service clerical officer, said that Hitler would have to be fought, his older colleagues, men who had seen war at close quarters, told him not to be so eager. Pacifism was a common stance. The United Kingdom remained a strong supporter of the League of Nations even when the League failed to prevent Italian aggression against Abyssinia in 1935–36 and was ineffective over the intervention of foreign powers in the Spanish Civil War of 1936–39.

In Britain pacifism was accompanied by strong feelings of objection to an arms race and to rearmament in general, as well as a dislike of military alliances. In literature, pacifism was encouraged by works that were widely read and admired, such as R. C. Sheriff's play *Journey's End* of 1928, Erich Maria Remarque's 1929 novel *All Quiet on the Western Front*, which was made into a film in 1930, Robert Graves's memoir *Goodbye to All That* of 1929, the poetry of Wilfred Owen, published in 1931, and Vera Brittain's *Testament of Youth* of 1933. 1933 also saw the success of the Oxford University Union motion 'This house will in no circumstances fight for its King and country'. In 1934 the League of Nations Union organised a 'peace ballot'. An overwhelming number of the respondents supported arms reduction and the use of economic or other sanctions rather than the threat of war to deter aggressors. However, a distinct majority also supported military measures if necessary. This would, of course, require an appropriate volume of rearmament, so pacifists tended to say that they supported rearmament to the limited extent that would be necessary to carry out a theoretical League of Nations vote to use force against an aggressor. The prime minister, Stanley Baldwin, had made a speech in November 1932, in which he said, 'the bomber will always get through', suggesting that rearmament would lead to an arms race and to a universally destructive war. Labour opinion was pacifist, and in Parliament Labour MPs voted against the military estimates. The largest pacifist organisation in Great Britain was the Peace Pledge Union, supported by large numbers of influential public figures. People who joined it signed a pledge: 'We renounce war and never again will we support or sanction another.'

In July 1938, John F. Kennedy, the later president of the United States, came to Britain, where he stayed with his father, who was the American ambassador. He travelled in Continental Europe and was back in the United Kingdom when war began. In 1940 he wrote a book with the significant title *Why Britain Slept*, in which he concluded that the United Kingdom had a visceral opposition to armaments, even to the extent that much opinion was in favour of Britain disarming unilaterally. Almost all opinion held that Britain should rearm only to be able to carry out the decisions of the League of Nations. The statements of the British government, wrote Kennedy, either encouraged or reflected the view that disarmament was the ideal and that a peaceful settlement with Hitler's Germany was possible. Too many people in Britain, said Kennedy, were ignorant of Nazi psychology. They also thought that the Hitler regime would not be tolerated by the German nation, and that the German economy would collapse under the strain of arms spending. In addition, they assumed that the Royal Navy was sufficient to assure Britain's defence, and they were too trustful of French military power and the famous 'Maginot Line', a set of fortifications that were thought to ensure complete protection against a German invasion. All this, claimed Kennedy, explained why Britain did not rearm sooner than it did.

British weakness in the latter 1930s in the face of Hitler's actions and demands is called 'appeasement'. However, 'appeasement' did not, at least originally, mean weakness. There was considerable public sympathy with Germany, a nation that much British opinion thought had been harshly dealt with by the Versailles Treaty. To be an appeaser did not mean that one supported the Nazis; merely that Germany had legitimate grievances, and that Britain and France should try to accommodate them. Those who sympathised with Hitler's demands described the remilitarisation of the demilitarised zone of the Rhineland as Germany 'going into its own back garden'. There was even sympathy with the *Anschluss* or the union of Austria with Germany of March 1938. At the height of the September 1938 crisis over Czechoslovakia, *The Times*, which was a leading exponent of the appeasement of German demands, went so far as to advocate the cession of the Czech-ruled Sudetenland to Germany. After all, the inhabitants of that territory, said many people, were Germans. Should they be prevented from joining other Germans?

The problem was that Hitler's territorial demands could be satisfied only at the expense of Poland and Czechoslovakia, countries whose security was supposed to be internationally guaranteed. So, 'appeasement' eventually came to mean the abdication of British power and international prestige, and having to grant the unpleasant Hitler what he wanted in the face of his threats. The noisy clash of opinions did not see with perhaps enough clarity that international affairs were not to be conducted by Hitlerite bullying but by long and patient diplomatic negotiations, followed by keeping one's word. It took time for British opinion to understand that Hitler did not think in this way.

'Appeasement' included the opinion that war was not inevitable. It was thought and certainly hoped that Hitler might be suitably appeased and even 'brought to reason' by British rearmament and the threat of naval blockade. William Woodruff, who lived through the thirties and later became a noted historian, writes perceptively in his autobiography that 'In an Oxford untroubled by threats of war … people like me, who came hurrying back from Germany with a note of alarm in their voice, were called prophets of doom'.

Moreover, it was widely held that Britain ought to remain aloof from agreements with the Soviet Union. It was feared that such an agreement, known at the time as 'collective security', would alarm Hitler because it would seem that Britain and France were ganging up with Hitler's stated enemy: Soviet Bolshevism.

Spain

The civil war in Spain had widespread influence on many ordinary British people's opinions on international matters as well as on their emotions. On the one hand, there was overwhelming support, at least according to public opinion polls, for the non-intervention policy, established by Britain and France in the hope that other countries would not furnish arms to either Spanish party. When, on 1 November 1936, Hitler and Mussolini signed the 'Rome–Berlin Axis', declaring their joint support for Franco, British anxiety increased.

The war in Spain allowed large numbers of British people to throw themselves into political campaigning to an extent that was unparalleled in its intensity in interwar Britain. They did not limit themselves to the traditional forms of political protest but also explored the field of large-scale humanitarian endeavour, not only at a national level through the National Joint Committee for Spanish Relief, but also by means of countless local committees organised by individuals, parties, trade unions, churches and other groups of activists. What at first had been seen as an distant conflict in a backward and hardly known country developed, after widespread attacks by Franco's largely Italian air force against British merchant shipping, the destruction by German bombers of the Basque town of Guernica, and the Italian bombing of Barcelona over three days in March 1938, into a tide of rising consciousness of the conflict between democracy on the one hand and Nazism and Fascism on the other. Scenes of the war in Spain were shown regularly on cinema newsreels and thus entered the conscience of literally millions of people weekly. Nevertheless, newsreels were subject to government-advised manipulation. They emphasised the horrors of modern war and insisted that Britain should not involve herself. The newsreels failed to warn the public of the danger of a Franco put into power by German–Italian military force.

Bombing

Prime Minister Stanley Baldwin's remark in the House of Commons on 10 November 1932 that 'the bomber will always get through' and that the only answer was to bomb the enemy in reply, assumed that there was no defence against the bomber and ignored the roles of fighter aircraft and of civil defence. Baldwin's statement had the effect of strengthening the atmosphere of pacifism. Fear of air raids spread and multiplied. George Orwell, writing *Keep the Aspidistra Flying* in 1935, described Gordon Comstock imagining 'the whole western world going up in a roar of high explosive'. Fear increased, particularly after people read about Italian aircraft dropping poison gas from the air in Abyssinia, and when the cinema newsreels showed scenes of bombs falling on Madrid and Barcelona and when the small town of Guernica was razed to the ground by bombers on 26 April 1937. Such events seemed to confirm the reality of the 1936 film *Things to Come*, which had portrayed air bombing in a future world war and had caused widespread anxiety.

Beginning in 1935, local authorities were charged with organising ARP, the abbreviation for Air Raid Precautions. Doctors and policemen were given extra training, and a corps of Air Raid Wardens was established. The message was clear. Simulations of air raids stressed that war was most certainly on the horizon, and the country had to be prepared for heavy air raids. As a Birmingham local newspaper reported on an ARP exercise:

> The latest devices for detecting and locating hostile aircraft were employed in the demonstration. In one part of the park an instrument for picking up the sound of approaching aeroplanes was stationed, and a search-light was erected, while two guns and a mechanism for predicting the position of the aerial target were placed in another position.

The *Willesden Chronicle* of 14 January 1934 announced that there would be a display of searchlights later that month. In July 1937, the mayor of the London borough of Hampstead was appealing for volunteers to participate in ARP. What were needed were men and women wardens, first-aiders, cyclists to carry messages, experienced building workers to rescue people trapped in bombed buildings, and specialists who knew how to decontaminate water supplies.

Nevertheless, much pacifist opinion was hostile to ARP. The *Willesden Chronicle* published a letter on 24 July 1937 insisting that ARP was useless against the threat of incendiary bombs. This exchange began a debate. Was there a defence against the bomber? Scare stories were widespread about cataclysmic poison gas and bomb attacks delivered on cities from the air, as well as mysterious death rays, bacteria-laden bombs, gliding bombs and pilotless aircraft. However, civil defence exercises were carried out, often in the face of ribaldry and joking, by men and women wearing unfamiliar uniforms, sirens blaring from ambulances and fire engines, and other people pretending to be victims being succoured by first-aiders.

Two years later, in June 1939, Orwell's character George Bowling in *Coming Up for Air* imagines London under a hail of bombs. At about the same time, Nevil Shute's novel *What Happened to the Corbetts*, a thousand copies of which were distributed free to air raid wardens, imagines the effect of aerial bombing on Southampton, the major southern port of Britain. In this novel, war begins after a surprise aerial bombing of twenty other British cities. It is the first of many attacks. The sewage system is destroyed, which causes widespread cholera. The gas and electricity supply collapses. The telephone system is knocked out, the roads are full of craters, and there is neither post nor newspapers. The hospitals are overwhelmed. Shute describes populations abandoning the cities and setting up encampments in the countryside. Food and fuel become scarce. The author claims through the mouth of his leading character that German navigation is highly skilful. British anti-aircraft fire is useless against German bombers, which can fly in very bad weather, when British fighters cannot locate them.

The novel is frightening. Shute does, however, offer solutions. He writes about food rationing, the evacuation of civilians and mass inoculation against disease. One can make, he says, a gasproof room, prepare pumps and buckets of sand against incendiary bombs, and wear oilskins as a protection against mustard gas. To some extent his novel is prescient. Shute was trying to explain the worst possible effects of bombing and how they could be faced. Nevertheless, the novel must have alarmed if not terrified most of its readers.

Their fears would have already been aroused by the statement from the Air Ministry that Germany had 2,909 first-line aircraft compared with Britain's 1,550. The official assumption was that every ton of bombs dropped would cause fifty casualties and that the first week of war would result in 83,000 civilian deaths. Some rumours spoke of thousands of German bombs being dropped daily causing 250,000 casualties and £100 million of damage in the first week of war. Those who feared a sudden knockout blow, with hundreds of thousands of deaths followed by social disintegration, were unaware of the difficulty of carrying out a campaign of sustained bombing. Not considered properly were the general inaccuracy of bombing, the power of fighter defences and anti-aircraft artillery, as well as civilian resilience and the benefit of the efficient provision of air raid shelters. In reality, the total of British civilians killed by enemy bombing throughout the entire six years of the Second World War would be 61,000, a heavy figure, but only a fraction of the deaths that had been foreseen.

1938, however, also saw the publication of two sober books about bombing: Professor J. B. S. Haldane's work *ARP* and John Langdon-Davies's *Air Raid*. Both were based on their authors' study of the bombing of Spanish cities. Cheaply priced, they were probably widely read.

Haldane claimed that official precautions in Britain were insufficient, but that the scare stories were exaggerated. His advice was good. He explained that a direct hit on an air raid shelter would be fatal to all in it, but it would be very unlikely to happen. In contrast, flying debris and glass presented real dangers, so it was essential to build shelters and to evacuate women and children from cities. It was also important to develop a warning system of the approach of bombers and to have a disciplined regime of taking shelter so that people would not be caught in the open. He was pointing out that well-organised ARP could save many lives. The Italian bombing of Barcelona over the three days of 16–19 March 1938 killed 1,300, a much lower figure than those that were being bandied about, even though Barcelona was undefended by fighter aircraft, overcrowded with refugees from other parts of Spain, and without sufficient bombproof shelters. Haldane listed other features of adequate defence, among them blackouts, barrage balloons, anti-aircraft artillery and searchlights.

Many people who read these two books must have been to some extent reassured that even heavy bombing of London would not be quite as nightmarish as pacifist propaganda was indicating.

Rearmament

The Italian attack on Abyssinia of October 1935 showed that if effective sanctions against an aggressor nation were to be applied, major powers such as Britain would probably be dragged into some sort of conflict and would have to be suitably rearmed. On 19 July 1934 the prime minister had already announced a programme of defence spending, including forty-one more squadrons for the Royal Air Force. Nevertheless, defence spending remained cautious. The British army was weak and probably unable to field significant manpower in a Continental war. The Royal Navy was powerful but overstretched if it was to defend the Empire in the Far East, combat Italy in the Mediterranean and protect merchant traffic in the Atlantic. The Royal Air Force was far behind Germany in bomber aircraft. However, after the Munich agreement in September 1938 and as the optimism that had been created by the apparent solution to the crisis waned, more and more people grew pessimistic about the possibility of appeasing Germany and resisting Hitler's aggressive demands. Britain would have to fight and therefore to rearm.

Despite the pervasive opposition to rearmament, between 1933 and 1938 Britain spent £1,200 million on arms, mostly on warships and warplanes. In the motor industry, spending on tanks and armoured cars brought significant re-employment. In Castle Bromwich, near Birmingham, for instance, a new factory was begun where Lord Nuffield, using his existing labour force for aircraft rather than cars. would eventually produce thousands of Spitfire fighters.

In Neville Chamberlain's 1936 budget broadcast, filmed by the Pathé and Gaumont-British cinema newsreels, and thus seen by several million people, he said that each of his previous budgets had been 'a little better' than the previous one. He had hoped that this one would be better still. 'However,' he continued, 'instead of that…' He went on to say that Britain couldn't disarm when her potential enemies were rearming. Nevertheless, said Chamberlain, the money to be spent on weapons would provide employment at good wages for years. Rearmament spending increased when in May 1937 Chamberlain became prime minister. He realised that it was useless to take a strong line with Hitler and Mussolini if they knew that Britain did not have sufficient armed force to back it up. Decisively, Chamberlain's government raised defence expenditure from £137 million in 1935–36 to £186.7 million. Germany, however, was reputed to be spending 25 per cent of its national income on war material. John F. Kennedy later described British rearmament policy as 'apologetic'. Yet some British opinion feared that it might be seen as 'aggressive' by Germany. The Labour Party was still hostile to spending on rearmament rather than social programmes, even though rearmament would offer work to many of the current unemployed. For people in Britain who paid income tax, the cost of rearmament was evident in their salary cheques. To pay for the spending on the armed forces, income tax steadily increased in those years. It had been 4/6d. in the pound on taxable income. It now rose to 4/9d. and it would increase in annual increments to 7/6d. (37.5 decimal pence) by 1939.

Munich

'Munich' is the general term for the agreement that Chamberlain and French premier Daladier made with Germany to settle the Czech question. France had been bound by treaty to come to the aid of Czechoslovakia if Germany invaded the Sudetenland, the part of Czechoslovakia that Hitler was claiming. Britain would be drawn in to any war that threatened France. On Wednesday, 14 September 1938, 'Cassandra', the *Daily Mirror*'s columnist, published an article illustrated by a picture of a ruthless man sticking a dagger into Prague, which probably had an important influence on the millions who read the paper. When the crisis became acute, Chamberlain flew three times to meet Hitler. Tension reached its height on the night of Tuesday, 27 September. By this time fear had spread over Britain that the country would be at war in a day or two. The *Daily Mirror* set its headlines in large type

WAR UNLESS BRITAIN IS STRONG.

By now, ARP personnel had been mobilised, cellars and basements had been requisitioned for air raid shelters, school children and hospital patients had been evacuated from London, and 40 million gas masks had been distributed. Trenches were being dug in the parks. On 28 September the Royal Navy was mobilised. Tension and anxiety reached their height.

Immense relief spread on the afternoon of 28 September when at 4.15 p.m. Chamberlain, giving a long speech in the House of Commons about his efforts, suddenly announced that Hitler had invited him to a further meeting the next day. He flew to Munich where agreement was reached at 2.30 a.m. on Friday, 30 September. The Czechs were to hand over the Sudetenland to Germany. Neither Britain nor France would back the Czechs if they resisted. The *Mirror*'s front page blazed:

IT IS PEACE. HITLER ACCEPTS NEW PLAN AND WITHDRAWS ULTIMATUM.

Chamberlain became the national hero. He received over 20,000 letters and telegrams of congratulation. Commemorative plates and cups were manufactured. Movietone's cinema newsreel proclaimed, 'Our words of admiration are exhausted for the man who prevented Armageddon'. As Chamberlain returned to an ecstatic London one cynical observer later wrote, 'I thought they were going to grovel on the ground in front of him.' *The Times*'s editorial for 1 October commented, 'No conqueror returning from victory on the battlefield has come home adorned with nobler laurels than Mr Chamberlain from Munich yesterday.' The Archbishop of Canterbury called for a national day of thanksgiving in British churches. In a BBC broadcast on the evening of 2 October the archbishop told of an old farmer who, pointing upward to the wide heavens, said quietly, 'There's a God up there.' Chamberlain was invited to appear with the king and queen on the balcony of Buckingham Palace before the massive and emotional crowds. Godfrey Winn, an actor and columnist and a well-known public figure in later years, wrote in the *Sunday Pictorial*, imitating a scriptural verse: 'Let us now praise ourselves … for the last few weeks we have walked in the Valley of the Shadow of Death and we have been afraid.' A letter was published in a Bolton newspaper remarking that Chamberlain was 'above all earthly beings'.

Chamberlain himself, brandishing on his arrival of a piece of paper bearing his and Hitler's signatures as proof that Germany and England would never go to war again, seemed to believe what was written on it, but Edouard Daladier, the French premier, commented as he was driven past the cheering Parisian crowds '*Ah! Les cons! S'ils savaient!*' ('The idiots. If they knew!'). The *Daily Telegraph* published a piece by Winston

Churchill, who had warned repeatedly about Hitler's intentions. The future war leader wrote, 'Only the most blunt, plain, even brutal language will make its effect' ... 'This is no time for bluff'. One Minister – Duff Cooper, First Lord of the Admiralty – resigned, and others were thought unhappy about the agreement. In the post-Munich debate in the House of Commons thirty Conservatives abstained from voting in support of the government, including three future prime ministers: Churchill, Eden and Harold Macmillan.

It had seemed that the Munich agreement was received with great rejoicing by most of the British nation. And yet in a series of by-elections that took place during October and November 1938 in which foreign policy played a major role, the government fared badly. In every contest the opposition increased its percentage of the poll and in two the Conservatives lost their seats. On 3 October 1938 Major Attlee, leader of the Labour Party and another future prime minister, spoke in the Commons of 'a gallant and civilised democratic people betrayed and handed over to a ruthless nation'. That autumn the discrepancy grew between the extreme admiration expressed for Chamberlain and the shame felt about the betrayal of Czechoslovakia. The economist J. M. Keynes expressed the contradictions in a personal letter: 'Intense relief and satisfied cowardice join with rage and indignation, plus that special emotion ... of having been swindled as never before ... in [our] history.'

In the eleven months between Munich and the outbreak of war, observers noticed a steadily lessening of support for appeasement, which was replaced by views demanding a firmer policy. While the Munich Agreement had been received with optimism mixed with a sense of guilt and shame, the German occupation of Prague in March 1939 delivered a profound shock. There was a sense that Britain had been deceived by Hitler and by the diplomats who had been saying that things were quietening down. Gallup polls of public opinion changed radically, from the 74 per cent who in February 1939 thought that Chamberlain's policy would keep Britain out of war, to the 76 per cent in July 1939 who responded that Britain ought to go to war in defence of Poland, where Hitler was making demands.

The occupation of Prague and the rest of Czechoslovakia by German forces on 15 March 1939 was followed by a speech by Chamberlain saying that he could not trust Hitler not to invade other countries and by his announcement on 31 March of a guarantee to defend Poland if Germany invaded. He received support from all the parliamentary parties.

The marked increase in official activity as war became ever more likely was reflected not only in the widely read press and in cinema newsreels, but also in what could be seen all around as preparations increased in urgency. People began to understand that war would affect individuals personally, as Doris Josser in Norman Collins's novel *London Belongs to Me* learns when Bill, now a recently qualified doctor, tells her that Britain will be at war soon and that he could be conscripted and sent abroad.

Almost everybody in Britain now accepted that war was coming or at least that the country should prepare seriously for it. The government responded by a series of energetic preparations, including a limited form of conscription. The Military Training Act of 27 April 1939 announced that single men of 20 to 22 years old were to be conscripted and known as 'militiamen' to distinguish them from the regular army. The first of 200,000 were 'called up' in July 1939.

In October 1938, Sir John Anderson had been put in charge of Civil Defence. His appointment, accompanied by a vastly increased budget, must have signalled that the government was taking the likelihood of war seriously. Now, in the second part of 1939, new regulations, schemes, official bodies and plans were being announced almost daily, as the nation geared up for war. Some 2 million men and women were to be occupied in civil defence services of one kind or another.

Gas masks had been issued in 1938. People were now instructed to get used to them by wearing them for ten minutes every day. In 1939 2.7 million specially made masks were announced as being ready for infants. This was perhaps the most terrifying aspect of war preparations, followed by uncertainty about what would have to be done about household pets. Larger public shelters were now prepared. In Ramsgate, for example, a mile of railway tunnels and several miles of tunnels in the chalk cliffs were prepared for the accommodation of 60,000 people. Older men were told to enrol in the ARP, as wardens, or ambulance drivers, and in the Police Reserve. Jack Simmonds, a big, tall man, applied for the Police Reserves, but was rejected when it was discovered that his father had been born in Germany, although he had arrived in Britain at the age of 6 and had been naturalised as a boy. Jack was directed to work on the railway where he spent the war loading and unloading parcels. ARP drills now became compulsory in factories and offices. Other aims included creating 250,000 extra hospital beds and organising the mass evacuation of 3 million children from big cities as well as mothers with babies under the age of 5.

For those people who were to remain in the cities, the plan, announced in December 1938, was to offer 10 million 'Anderson' shelters. These were made of curved panels of corrugated iron, to be assembled by the householder. To be fully effective, the shelter had to be dug into a four-foot-deep pit in the ground, with the soil being heaped on top to provide cover against falling debris. Blackout became compulsory. Street lighting and motor vehicle lights would be dimmed, and no lights were to be shown from houses. In drills people became used to ARP wardens shouting, 'Put that light out!' Nevertheless, there was a general dislike of officious wardens, which years later would be reflected in the character Mr. Hodges, the greengrocer, who is the chief ARP warden for 'Warmington-on-Sea' in the TV series *Dad's Army*.

A grand-scale Civil Defence exercise was held in the London district of Chelsea on 19 June 1939. Many people still thought it was foolish. The gas masks of September 1938 had been put away. People felt silly at having to pretend to be injured and submit to rather amateur bandaging before an imaginary ambulance arrived. A major nationwide blackout exercise was conducted on 8 August 1939. Kerbs and the bases of tree trunks in London were painted white to help pedestrians find their way in darkened streets. To offset the effect of blast people were advised to stick strips of brown paper over windows and this was done on buses also. The National Gallery was closed and its pictures evacuated to a mine in distant Wales. Houses in the country, sneeringly referred to by many as 'boltholes' were advertised in the more expensive press. Sandbags were filled and placed against walls all over the capital. On 24 August 1939 Parliament voted the government emergency powers. The last hopes of peace faded. On the same day the agreement between Nazi Germany and Soviet Russia was announced. If war broke out over Poland, the USSR would not intervene to support Britain and France in their guarantee to protect Poland.

On 3 September 1939, in his reedy voice Neville Chamberlain made his sad declaration that Britain was now at war. All cinemas and theatres were closed because a bomb could cause hundreds of casualties. As the national anthem was played on the wireless the air raid sirens were sounded. People, shepherded by wardens, went obediently to the street shelters. Calm-natured people thought that bombing would cause some damage but few deaths while nervous minds thought of the apocalyptic scenes in the film *Things to Come*. Esther Simons's husband, unruffled, went up to the roof to see if aircraft were coming, but her nervous sister fled in panic to the countryside. However, she would return and during the heaviest bombing in 1940 would make her way bravely through the centre of London, amid the crash of bombs and anti-aircraft fire, to the building occupied by the firm where she managed the office to save the essential files. When the sirens sounded on 3 September 1939, nothing happened and, in a few minutes, the 'all-clear', a long blast on the siren, sounded over the capital. It had been a false alarm.

In 1939, Noël Coward composed a play that he called *This Happy Breed*, quoting Shakespeare's *Richard II*. It was Coward's picture of a British family in the interwar years. The play was about to be staged just as the Second World War began and was made into a film in 1944. In it, two of his characters consider the immense relief felt in Britain by the Munich agreement of September 1938. The leading character, Frank Gibbons, says:

> I've seen something today that I wouldn't believe could happen in this country. I've seen thousands of people – British people, mark you – carrying on like maniacs, shouting and cheering with relief for no other reason but that they've been thoroughly frightened. And it made me sick and that's a fact. And I only hope to goodness we've got guts enough to learn one lesson from this and we shall never find ourselves in a position again where we have to appease anybody.

His sister Sylvia retorts:

> All you men ever think about is having guts and being top dog and killing each other. I'm a woman. I don't care how much we appease so long as we don't have a war. War is wicked and evil and vile. Them that live by the sword shall die by the sword. It's more blessed to give than to receive.

Sylvia doesn't care how much Britain appeases Hitler, because she doesn't understand that Nazism will never be satisfied. Frank seems to be saying that Britain must be strong enough not to have to appease any other country's demands. These succinctly expressed views sum up the opinions and emotions of large sectors of British public opinion about the European crisis of the late 1930s.

Conclusion

The aim of this book has been to describe the material and social progress of Britain that was rapidly taking place in the latter part of the 1930s at the same time as mass unemployment was only slowly easing. However, when Britain declared war on 3 September 1939, the feeling spread that the rising expectations of social and economic progress that had been evident since about halfway through the decade were now about to be paralysed. As George Orwell wrote in *Coming Up for Air*:

> Ordinary chaps that I meet everywhere, chaps I run across in pubs, bus drivers, and travelling salesmen for hardware firms, have got a feeling that the world's gone wrong. They can feel things cracking and collapsing under their feet.

Was this, then, the end of a period in which a large proportion, though not all, of the British population had enjoyed better food, paid holidays, ever-cheaper motor cars, and, for very large numbers of families, greatly improved housing, in other words a distinct betterment of their quality of life and an upward movement of social class? It certainly put a stop to progress in education, for 1 September 1939 was the day on which the school leaving age was to be raised to 15. This would have given large numbers of children an extra year in school and would have opened the door to some secondary education for all, a significant advance that would now be delayed for years. Were all those improvements not only about to come to a halt, but would they disappear completely in another world war, which in addition to repeating the huge human losses of 1914–18, would bring the collapse of society under the assault of thousands of bombers and clouds of poison gas?

Neville Chamberlain had feared that this would happen, though he had also hoped that rearmament would keep Britain away from war. Years before, in 1934, Chamberlain had been able to declare a budget surplus and restore many of the previous spending cuts. He had told the House of Commons, 'We have now finished the story of *Bleak House* and are sitting down this afternoon to enjoy the first chapter of *Great Expectations*.' But by 1935, faced with a resurgent Germany, he was convinced of the need for rearmament. Money that should have gone to social improvements would now have to be spent on fighter aircraft and new warships.

During the war of 1939–45, a brake would have to be put on some of the advances made in the latter 1930s, but, under war conditions, much progress was made in assuring full employment and improving social welfare. More rapid and intensive improvements would come about when Labour came to power in 1945 and would be continued by progressive Conservative administrations in the 1950s. What stands out when one considers the later 1930s is the widespread concern with improvement and the serious attempts to advance British society, based on the embryonic beginnings that had already been seen in the years just before the Great War.

The advances being made in the later 1930s did not, however, alter the fact that the question of class coloured most aspects of life, and so 'class' is a word that has frequently appeared in this book. British governments were clearly upper class, either by noble descent or by having risen through the commercial or industrial bourgeoisie or the law. In society in general class differences were clearly apparent. In areas where work was least attractive and poorest paid, and where many had no entitlement to welfare benefits, it was evident that odd jobs, petty thieving, running bets, hiring babies as aids to begging and the like were preferred. This was the characteristic of the 'rough' lower class. There was a difference between what was called 'rough' and 'respectable 'Respectable' meant that you deferred your gratification, you paid your rent punctually and didn't just 'do a midnight flit', that is leave with rent unpaid. On your way into the middle class, with a job for which you wore a collar and tie and laid aside your cloth cap, you expected your train to town to be on time, because you yourself had to be punctual and reliable. Middle-class life meant perhaps buying your own house and adopting 'suburban' values. In the suburbs where people were buying their houses, the developers strove to keep the lower-class council estate at a distance. Even in the cinema, which all classes attended, the manager in evening dress and the uniformed commissionaire were reassuring sights for the patrons who were paying for the better seats. Many shops retained their shopwalker, who approached ladies with the deference that they expected and offered them a seat. Behaviour, the way you and your spouse dressed and your children behaved, clearly marked your class. The lower-middle-class voice that aimed to be 'posh' was very noticeable. Voices in television's *Dad's Army*, which is supposed to be happening in 1939–41, mark class very clearly. Captain Mainwaring, whose social origins are lower than he would like to be thought, has adopted an authoritarian tone, while his chief clerk, Arthur Wilson, who is aristocratic, has a gentler, refined note in his voice. Mrs. Pike, however, with whom Wilson lodges, has a lower-class tone overlaid with a pretentious attempt at refinement. The lady who runs the tearoom in Carnforth Junction Station in the film *Brief Encounter* is an even more noticeable example of artificial enunciation intended to suggest that she is socially superior.

Contrasting occupations, and patterns of spending, accompanied by clearly defined differentiations of behaviour, values, dress and voices, remained, despite some changes. And yet, the latter were massive. Priestley's famous factory girls looked like actresses even though they did not quite speak like British film actresses. All who could afford it could visit Lyons Corner Houses or Harry Ramsden's fish and chip restaurants and be served by a waitress. If you wore a collar and tie, and a hat, instead of a muffler and a cap, if you saved up a deposit, found a reliable job and began to pay off a mortgage, and strove to imitate what had previously seemed 'posh' habits in your speech, your ambitions for your children, your choice of leisure activities, and many other apparently minor but really quite significant changes, all these would mark your transition to a higher class. Spread over millions of people, such behavioural changes had by 1939 changed Britain into a country where the lower middle class was probably close to a majority.

One of the most marked changes was in relations between the sexes. Many years later the poet Philip Larkin would date the previously unknown freedom of sexual relations in Britain as beginning in 1963:

> *Between the end of the Chatterley ban*
> *And the Beatles' first LP.*

Yet, in Orwell's *Keep the Aspidistra Flying*, published in 1935, a young couple do not seem to think that their unmarried coupling is out of the ordinary. In addition, *Lady Chatterley's Lover*, with its erotic scenes, did not become available for all to read until 1960, but *No Orchids for Miss Blandish* with its sexual violence had already appeared in 1939. Again, homosexuals had to wait until 1967 for their activities to be decriminalised, but Christopher Isherwood's novel *Goodbye to Berlin*, with its homosexual undercurrent, had been published a generation earlier in 1939.

Social history is a slow process. Many other new aspects of the latter 1930s, such as frequent cinema-going and the seaside holiday, would still be familiar even twenty years later, but at the same time, much that one would think appeared only sometime after 1945 had also been, at least embryonically, apparent a generation earlier, in the latter 1930s … before the war.

Sources

Full details of works mentioned here can be found in the bibliography

General

For statistics I have relied mostly on Branson & Heinemann. For basic information and many factual details Keesing's Contemporary Archives is most useful. Stevenson and Marwick are major sources on the 1930s, together with Mowat for more detail and Seaman for somewhat less. McKibbin and several of the essays edited by Gloversmith are often enlightening. More popular works include Cartland, Gardiner, Pugh and Graves & Hodge. Blakeway's book on 1936 is valuable, as are other books on specific years such as Caffrey, Kee & Law (2018).

I have made much use of the various works based on Mass Observation's study of Bolton, particularly Barron on education and the anthology *Speak for Yourself* published in 1984.

Autobiographies of people who lived through an epoch are valuable. I have used Annan, Robert Barltrop, Margaret Powell's account of life as a domestic servant, Brian Johnson's upbringing in the Potteries, Brian Magee's description of his childhood in a poor London district, Paul Vaughan's suburban childhood and the early lives of later distinguished academics such as William Woodruff and Harold Perkin. J. B. Priestley's *English Journey* was enlightening.

Popular contemporary novels are valuable, because not only do they reveal what people were reading, but they also frequently give details of daily life. Among many others, I have quoted Norman Collins's *London Belongs to Me*, A. J. Cronin's *The Citadel,* Pamela Frankau's *The Devil We* Know, Walter Greenwood's *Love on the Dole*, Patrick Hamilton's *Twenty Thousand Streets under the Sky*, Ernest Raymond's *We, the Accused*, and George Orwell's *Keep the Aspidistra Flying* and *Coming Up for Air*.

Specific

Chapter 1, *Unemployment and Work*. Major sources were Burnett (1994), Beddoe and John Boyd Orr.

Chapter 2, *Income, Expenditure and the Cost of Living*. Here I used Burnett (1966), The *New Survey of London Life and Labour*, Gazeley (2003), Jackson (1991), McGrandle, McKibbin & Massey.

Chapter 3, *Housing*. I found Burnett (1980), Jackson (1973), Keun, Weightman & Humphries (1984), and Oliver, Ryan & Scott (2013) valuable.

Chapter 4, *Eating and Dressing*. Major sources included Burnett (1966), Crawford, Dickson-Wright, Oddy & Miller, Purkiss (2022) and, on fish and chips, Walton (1992) and Harding on J. Lyons & Co.

Chapter 5, *Health and Education*. Among others, I used essays by Virginia Berridge on Health and Gillian Sutherland on Education in the *Cambridge Social History of England,* Bruce (1968), B. Harris (2004), Lawson & Silver and Barron (2021 & 2022).

Chapter 6, *The Other Half*. My sources were Adam, Barron, Beddoe, Haste, Jethcott. J. Lewis and Rice. On sex specifically, I used Blakeway, Ferris and the deeply researched work of Szereter & Fisher, as well as Kate Fisher's own study, Cook and Steve Humphries.

Chapter 7, *Cinema*, MacKibbin, Richards, Landy and Norden were useful.

Chapter 8, *Reading*, I have used Bingham, Hart-Davis and Cudlipp on the press; McAleer and Black on public libraries; Ferrall and Jackson on juvenile literature; Croom and Bloom on fiction; Mary Cadogan on girls' fiction, and Homberger and Lassner on spy thrillers. Much information emerged from reading novels by Eric Ambler, James Hadley Chase, Peter Cheyney, Phyllis Bottome, D. Fairlie Bruce, Angela Brazil, Norman Collins, Richmal Crompton, A. J. Cronin, Graham Greene, George Orwell. J. B. Priestley and Ernest Raymond. I used Dancyger and White on women's magazines.

Chapter 9, *Leisure*, I used Harrisson and Gutzke on pubs, Gutzke & Law on roadhouses, on motoring O'Connell, and on holidays Pimlott and Walton. On leisure in general I found Jones (1986) valuable.

Chapter 10, *Communications*, I have used O' Connell on motoring, Barker & Robbins on London Transport, Gavin & Humphreys, *Transport in British Fiction* and Jackson (1991), Gardiner, Graves & Hodge, Weightman & Humphries, and Law (2014 & 2018)

Chapter 11, *Will There Be War?* Among the major sources were Keesing's Contemporary Archives, Kee, Mowat, Eatwell, Hucker and Self.

Bibliography

Place of publication is London unless otherwise stated

ADAM, Ruth, *A Woman's Place 1910-1975*, Chatto & Windus, 1975

ADBURGHAM, Alison, *A Punch History of Manners and Modes*, Hutchinson, 1961

ALDGATE, Anthony, *Cinema and History: British Newsreels and the Spanish Civil War*, Scolar Press, 1979

AMBLER, Eric, *Epitaph for a Spy*, Hodder & Stoughton, 1938

_____________, *Cause for Alarm*, Hodder & Stoughton, 1938

ANNAN, Noel, *Our Age: Portrait of a Generation*, Weidenfeld & Nicolson, 1990

BARKER, T. & Robbins, M., *A History of London Transport*, Allen & Unwin, 1963

BARLTROP, Robert, *Growing up in London Between the Wars* (2 vols.), London Borough of Waltham Forest, 1984–85

BARRON, Hester & LANGHAM, Claire, *The Class of '37: Voices from Working-Class Girlhood*, Metro, 2021

BECKER, A. P., 'Housing in England and Wales during the business depression of the 1930s' in *Economic History Review* Vol. 3 (3), 1951, pp. 321–41

BEDDOE, Deirdre, *Back to Home and Duty: Women Between the Wars*, Pandora, 1984

BERRIDGE, Virginia, 'Health and Medicine' in *The Cambridge Social History of Britain* Vol. 3, Ch. 4, Cambridge University Press, 1990

BINGHAM, A., *Gender, Modernity and the Popular Press in Interwar Britain*, Oxford: Clarendon, 2004

BLAKEWAY, D., *The Last Dance: 1936, the Year of Change*, John Murray, 2010

BLACK, A., *The Public Library in Britain 1914–2000*, British Library, 2000

BLOOM, C., *Bestseller. Popular Fiction Since 1900*, Basingstoke: Palgrave, 2002

BOTTOME, Phyllis, *The Mortal Storm*, Faber, 1937

BOYD-ORR, J., *Food, Health and Income, a Survey of Adequacy of Diet in relation to Income*, Macmillan, 1936

BRANSON, Norma & HEINEMANN, Margot, *Britain in the 1930s*, Weidenfeld & Nicolson, 1971

BROWNING, H & SORRELL, A., 'Cinemas and cinema-going in Great Britain' in *Journal of the Royal Statistical Society,* Vol. 117 (1954) part 2, pp. 133–70

BRUCE, Dorita Fairlie, *Dimsie Goes Back*, Oxford University Press, 1935

BRUCE, M., *The Coming of the Welfare State: English Social Policy*, Batsford, 1968

BUCHANAN, T., *Britain and the Spanish Civil War*, Cambridge University Press, 1997

BURKE, T., *London in My Time*, Rich & Cowan, 1934

BURNETT, J., *Plenty and Want: A Social History of Diet in England from 1815 to the Present Day*, Nelson, 1966

_____________, *Idle Hands: The Experience of Unemployment 1790–1990*, Routledge, 1994

_____________, *A Social History of Housing 1815-1985*, Methuen, 1990

BUS FARE (eds. Elborough & Kerr), Basingstoke: AA Publishing, 2018

BYRNE, Paula, *The Adventures of Miss Barbara Pym*, Collins, 2021

CADOGAN, Mar., *Just William Through the Ages*, Macmillan, 1994

CADOGAN, Mary & CRAIG, Patricia, *You're a Brick, Angela*, Gollancz, 1976

CAESAR, A., *Dividing Lines: Poetry, Class and Ideology in the 1930s*, Manchester University. Press, 1991

CAFFREY, Kate, *'37, '39. Last Look Round*, Gordon & Cremonesi, 1978

CAMBRIDGE SOCIAL HISTORY OF BRITAIN 1750–1950 (ed. F. M. L. Thompson), Cambridge University Press, 1990

CAREY, Tanith, *Never Kiss a Man in a Canoe: Words of Wisdom from the Golden Age of Agony Aunts*, Boxtree, 2009

CARTLAND, Barbara, *We Danced all Night*, Hutchinson, 1970

CEADEL, M., 'Popular Fiction and the Next War' in GLOVERSMITH, F., *Class, Culture and Social Change: A New View of the 1930s*, Brighton: Harvester, 1980

CHARTERIS, L., *The Saint Plays with Fire*, Hodder & Stoughton, 1938

CHASE, J. Hadley, *No Orchids for Miss Blandish*, Jarrolds, 1939

CHASE, Mary Ellen, *In England Now*, Collins, 1937

CHEYNEY, P., *Dames Don't Care*, Collins, 1937
CLEEVE, B., *1938: A World Vanishing*, Buchan & Enright, 1982
COCKETT, R., *Twilight of Truth: Chamberlain, Appeasement and the Manipulation of the Press*, Weidenfeld & Nicolson, 1989
COLLINS, N., *London Belongs to Me*, Collins, 1945
'CONSTANTINE, M.', (Murdekin, Katherine), *Swastika Night*, Gollancz, 1937
COOK, Hera, *The Long Sexual Revolution: English Women, Sex and Contraception 1800–1975*, Oxford University Press, 2004
CRAWFORD, SIR W., *The People's Food*, Toronto: Heinemann, 1938
CROFT, A., *Red Letter Days: British Fiction of the 1930s*, Lawrence & Wishart, 1990
CRONIN, A. J., *The Citadel*, Gollancz, 1937
CUDLIPP, H., *Publish and be Damned: The Astonishing Story of the Daily Mirror*, A. Dakers, 1953
CUNNINGHAM, V., *British Writers of the 1930s*, Oxford University Press, 1988
CURTIS, J., *The Gilt Kid*, Jonathan Cape, 1936
____________, *They Drive by Night*, London Books, 1938
DANCYGER, Irene, *A World of Women: An Illustrated History of Women's Magazines*, Dublin: Gill & Macmillan, 1978
DAWES, F. W., *Not in Front of the Servants*, Wayland Publishers, 1973
DELAFIELD, E. M., *Diary of a Provincial Lady*, Macmillan, 1930
DICKSON WRIGHT, Clarissa, *A History of English Food*, Arrow, 2012
EATWELL, R., 'Munich, Public Opinion and the Popular Front' in *Journal of Contemporary History*, Vol. 6, No. 4, 1971, pp.122–39
ELLACOTT, S. L., A *History of Everyday Things in England*, Vol. V 1914–68, Batsford, 1968
FAVIEL, Frances, *A Chelsea Concerto (Just before the War)*, Cassell, 1959
FERRALL, C. & JACKSON, Anna, *Juvenile Literature and British Society 1850–1950*, Abingdon: Routledge, 2010
FERRIS, P., *Sex and the British*, Michael Joseph, 1993
FISHER, Kate, *Birth Control, Sex and Marriage in Britain 1918–1960*, Oxford University Press, 2006
FOWLER, D., *The First Teenagers: The Lifestyle of Young Wage-earners in Interwar Britain*, The Woburn Press, 1995
FUSSELL, P., *The Great War and Modern Memory*, Oxford University Press, 1975
GARDINER, Juliet, *The Thirties: An Intimate History*, Harper Press, 2010

GATHORNE-HARDY, J., *Doctors: The Lives and Work of GPs*, Weidenfeld & Nicolson, 1984

GAVIN, Adrienne & HUMPHREYS, A. F., *Transport in British Fiction, Technologies of Movement*, Basingstoke: Palgrave Macmillan, 2015

GAZELEY, I., et al., 'How hungry were the poor in late 1930s Britain?' in *Economic History Review* Vol. 75 (1) February 2002, pp. 80–110

GAZELEY, I., *Poverty in Britain 1900–1965*, Basingstoke: Palgrave, 2003

GLADSTONE, D. & GREEN, D., *Before Beveridge*, IEA Health & Welfare Unit, 1991

GLOVERSMITH, F., *Class, Culture and Social Change: a New View of the 1930s*, Brighton: Harvester, 1980

GOTTLIEB, J., 'War on Nerves' in *History Today*, September 2018

GRANDY, Christine, 'Heroes and Happy Endings: Class, Gender and Nation in Popular Films and Fiction' *in Interwar Britain*, Manchester University Press, 2014

GRANZOW, Brigitte, *A Mirror of Nazism; British Opinion and the Emergence of Hitler*, Gollancz, 1964

GRAVES, R. & HODGE, A., *The Long Weekend: A Social History of Great Britain, 1918–1939*, Faber, 1940

GREENE, G., *Brighton Rock*, William Heinemann, 1939

____________, *The Confidential Agent*, William Heinmann, 1938

GREENWOOD, W., *Love on the Dole*, Jonathan Cape, 1933

GRIFFITHS, R., *Fellow Travellers of the Right*, Oxford University Press, 1983

GURNEY, P., *The Making of Consumer Culture in Modern Britain*, Bloomsbury, 2017

GUTZKE, D., *Pubs and Progressives; Reinventing the Public House in England 1896–1960*, N. Illinois: Dekalb, 2006

GUTZKE, D. & LAW, M., *The Roadhouse Comes to Britain: Drinking, Driving and Dancing 1925–1955*, Bloomsbury, 2017

HALLIWELL L., *Seats in All Parts. Half a Lifetime at the Movies*, Glasgow: Grafton Books, 1986

HALL, Leslie A., *Sex, Gender and Social Change in Britain since 1880*, Basingstoke: Palgrave Macmillan, 2013

HAMILTON, Patrick, *Twenty Thousand Streets under the Sky*, Constable, 1935

____________, *Hangover Square*, Constable, 1941

HARDING, T., *Legacy: One Family, a Cup of tea and the Company That Took on the World*, Heinemann, 2019

HARRIS, B., *The Origins of the British Welfare State,* Basingstoke: Palgrave Macmillan, 2004

HARRISSON, T. (ed. J. Sommerfield), *The Pub and the People*, Gollancz, 1943

HART-DAVIS, D. *The House the Berrys Built: Inside the Telegraph*, Hodder & Stoughton, 1990

HASTE, Cate, *Rules of Desire: Sex in Britain, World War 1 to the Present*, Chatto & Windus, 1992

HEATH ROBINSON *see under* ROBINSON

HEWSON, Val, *The Twopenny Library* www.reading Sheffield.co.uk, accessed 29 May 2024

HERBERT, A. P., *Holy Deadlock*, Methuen, 1934

HILTON, J. *Rich Man, Poor Man* (*Sir Halley Steward Lectures 1938*), Allen & Unwin, 1944

HOMBERGER, E., 'English spy thrillers in the Age of Appeasement' in *Intelligence and National Security* 5(4), 80–91

HORN, Pamela, *Life Below Stairs in the 20th Century*, Stroud: Sutton Publishing, 2001

HORWOOD, Catherine, *Keeping up Appearances: Fashion and Class Between the Wars*, Stroud: Sutton Publishing, 2001

HUCKER, D., *Public Opinion and the End of Appeasement in Britain and France*, Farham: Ashgate, 2011

HUGHES, M. V., *A London Family between the War*s, Oxford University Press, 1940

HUMPHRIES, S., *A Secret World of Sex: The British Experience 1900–1950*, Sidgwick & Jackson, 1988

ISHERWOOD, C., *The Berlin Novels*, (inc. *Mr. Norris Changes Trains* and *Goodbye to Berlin*), Vintage, 1995

JACKSON, ALAN A., *Semi-detached* London, Routledge, 1973

_____________, *The Middle Classes 1900–1950,* Nairn, David & John Thomas, 1991

JAMES, R., '"Literature acknowledges no boundaries": Book Reading and Social Class in Britain 1930–1945' in *Journal of Social History* 51, 1, Fall 2017, pp. 80–100

JAMES, R., *Popular Culture and Working-Class Taste in Britain 1930–*1939, Manchester University Press, 2010

JEACLE, I., 'Going to the Movies: Accounting and Twentieth Century Cinema' in *Accounting, Auditing and Accountability Journal*, Vol. 22, 5, pp. 667–708

JETHCOTT, A. P., *Girls Growing Up*, Faber, 1942

JOHNSON, P. *The Vanished Landscape: A 1930s Childhood in the Potteries*, Weidenfeld & Nicolson, 2004

JONES, S. G., *Workers at Play: A Social and Economic History of Leisure 1918–1939*, Routledge & Kegan Paul, 1986

KEE, R., *The World We Left Behind: A Chronicle of the Year 1939*, Weidenfeld & Nicolson, 1984

KEESING'S CONTEMPORARY ARCHIVES: 1938 & 1939

KELLY, T., *Books for the People: An Illustrated History of the British Public Library,* André Deutsch, 1977

KENNEDY, J. F., *Why Britain Slept*, New York, Wilfred Funk, 1940

KENNEDY, P., *The Realities behind Diplomacy*, Fontana, 1981

KEUN, Odette, *I Discover the English*, The Bodley Head, 1934

KORDA, M. *Charmed Lives: the Fabulous World of the Korda Brothers*, Allen Lane, 1980

LANDY, Marcia, *British Genres: Cinema and Society 1930–1960*, Princeton University Press, 1991

LANGDON-DAVIES, *Air Raid*, Routledge, 1938

LASSNER, Phyllis, *Espionage and Exile: Fascism and Anti-Fascism in British Spy Fiction and Film*, Edinburgh University Press, 2016

LAW, M. J., *1938: Modern Britain, Social Change and Visions of the Future*, Bloomsbury, 2018

____________, *The Experience of Suburban Modernity*, Manchester University Press, 2014

LAW *see also* GUTZKE

LAWSON, J. & SILVER, H., *A Social History of Education in England*, Methuen, 1973

LETHBRIDGE, Lucy, *Servants: A Downstairs View of Twentieth Century Britain*, Bloomsbury, 2013

LEWIS, Jane, 'In search of a real equality: women between the wars' in Gloversmith cit. pp. 208–39

____________, *Labour and Love: Women's Experience of Love and Family,* Oxford: Basil Blackwell, 1986

McALEER, J., *Popular Reading and Publishing in Britain 1914–1950*, Oxford: Clarendon Press, 1992

McGRANDLE, L., *The Cost of Living in Britain*, Wayland, 1973

McKIBBIN, R., *Classes and Cultures: England 1918–1951*, Oxford University Press, 1998

MAGEE, B., *Clouds of Glory: A Hoxton Childhood*, Cape, 2003

MARWICK, A., *Class: Image and Reality*, Collins, 1980
MASSEY, A., 'The expenditure of 1,260 middle class households in 1938–39' in *Journal of the Royal Statistical Society* Vol.1 05, No. 3, 1942, pp. 159–96
MAYHEW, Madeleine, 'The 1930s Nutrition Controversy' in *Journal of Contemporary History* Vol. 23, 3, 1988, pp. 445–64
MILES, P. & SMITH, M., *Cinema, Literature and Society: Elite and Mass Culture in Interwar Britain*, Croom Helm, 1987
NEW SURVEY OF LONDON LIFE AND LABOUR (e. H. Llewellyn Smith), London School of Economics and Political Science, 1935
NORDEN, D., *Clips from a Life*, Harper Perennial, 2009
O'CONNELL, S., *The Car and British Society: Class, Gender and Motoring 1896–1939*, Manchester University Press, 1998
ODDY, D. & MILLER, D., *The Making of the Modern British Diet*, Croom Helm, 1976
OLIVER, P., DAVIS, I. & BENTLEY, I., *Dunroamin: The Suburban Semi and its Enemies*, Barrie & Jenkins, 1981
ORWELL, G., *Keep the Aspidistra Flying*, Gollancz, 1935
____________, *The Road to Wigan Pier,* Gollancz, 1937
____________, *Coming Up for* Air, Gollancz,1939
OSBORNE, J., *A Better Class of Person: An Autobiography 1929–1956*, Faber, 1981
PERKIN, H., *The Making of a Social Historian*, Athena, 2002
PHELAN, Nancy, *The Swift Fool of Time: An Australian in England 1938–45*, Melbourne: Quartet, 1983
PIMLOTT, J., *The Englishman's Holiday: A Social History*, Faber, 1947
POWELL, Margaret, *Below* Stairs, Peter Davies, 1968
____________, *Climbing the Stairs*, Peter Davies, 1969
PRIESTLEY, J. B., *Angel Pavement*, William Heinemann, 1930
____________, *English Journey*, William Heinemann, 1934
PUGH, M., *We Danced All Night: A Social History of Britain Between the Wars*, Vintage, 2009
PURKISS, Diane, *English Food: A People's History*, Harper Collins, 2022
QUENNELL, Marjorie, *A History of Everyday Things in England*, Batsford, 1968
RAYMOND, E., *We, the Accused*, Cassell, 1935
____________, *The Kilburn Tale*, Cassell, 1947
REED, Eleanor, *Women's Weekly and Lower Middle-Class Domestic Culture*, Liverpool University Press, 2023
RICE, Marjorie Spring, *Working-Class Wives: their Health and Conditions*, Penguin, 1939

RICHARDS, J., *The Age of the Dream Palace: Cinema and Society in Britain 1930–1939*, Routledge & Kegan Paul, 1984
RICHARDSON, D., 'J. Lyons & Co. Ltd.: Caterers and Food Manufacturers. 1894 to 1939' in Oddy & Miller cit. pp. 161–72
ROBINSON, W. HEATH, *How to Live in a Flat*, Hutchinson, 1936
RYAN, Deborah S., *Ideal Homes 1918–39: Domestic Design and Suburban Modernism*, Manchester University Press, 2018
SAVAGE, J., *The Creation of Youth*, Chatto & Windus, 2007
SCOTT, P., *The Making of the Modern British Home: the Suburban Semi and British Life Between the Wars*, Oxford University Press, 2013
SCOTT, P., 'The Twilight World of Interwar Hire Purchase' in *Past and Present* No. 177, November 2002, pp. 195–225
____________, 'Marketing Mass Home Ownership and the Creation of the Modern Working-Class Consumer in Interwar Britain' in *Business History* Vol. 50, No.1 January 2008, pp. 4–25
____________, 'Managing door-to-door sales of vacuum cleaners in Interwar Britain', in *The Business History Review* Volume 82, No. 4, Winter 2008, pp. 761–88
SEAMAN, L. C. B., *Life in Britain Between the* Wars, Batsford, 1970
SELF, R., *Neville Chamberlain: A* Biography, Aldershot: Ashgate, 2006
SHUTE, N., *What happened to the Corbetts?* William Heinemann, 1939
SPEAK FOR YOURSELF: A Mass Observation Anthology 1937–1949 (eds. Calder & Sheridan), Cape, 1984
SPRING RICE *see under* RICE
STEVENSON, J., 'Myth and Reality: Britain in the nineteen-thirties' in Sked, A. & Cook, C, *Crisis and Controversy*: *Essays in Honour of A.J. P. Taylor*, Macmillan, 1976, pp. 90–110
STEVENSON, J., *British Society 1914–1945*, Allen Lane (Penguin), 1984
STOTE, Dorothy, *The Bride's Book*, The Bride's Book Co., 1936
STRUTHER, Jan, *Mrs. Miniver*, Chatto & Windus, 1939
SUTHERLAND, Gillian, 'Education' in *Cambridge Social History of Britain* cit. pp. 119–69
SZERETER, S. & FISHER, Kate, *Sex Before the Sexual Revolution: Intimate Life in England 1918–1963,* Cambridge University Press, 2010
TAYLOR, D. J., *Bright Young People: The Rise and Fall of a Generation 1918–1939*, Chatto & Windus, 2006
TODD, Selina, 'Domestic Service and Class Relations in Britain 1900–1950' in *Past and Present*, No. 203, May 2009, pp.181–204
TROUBRIDGE, Lady, *The Book of Etiquette*, The Associated Bookbuyers' Company, 1931

VAUGHAN, P., *Something in Linoleum: A Thirties Education*, Sinclair-Stevenson, 1994

WADDINGTON, G. T., 'An idyllic and unruffled atmosphere of complete Anglo-German misunderstanding. Aspects of the operation of the *Dienstelle Ribbentrop* in Great Britain 1934–1938' in *History* Vol. 82, No. 165, pp. 44–72

WALKOWITZ, Judith, *Nights Out: Life in Cosmopolitan London*, New Haven & London: Yale University Press, 2012

WALTON, J., *Fish and Chips and the British Working Class 1870–1940*, Leicester University Press, 1992

WALTON, J. K., *The British Seaside: Holidays and Resorts in the Twentieth Century*, Manchester University Press, 2000

WALVIN, J., *Beside the Seaside: A Social History of the Popular Seaside Holiday*, Allen Lane, 1978

WARD, M. & N., *Home in the Twenties and Thirties*, Ian Allan, 1978

WEBSTER, C., 'Healthy or Hungry Thirties?' in *History Workshop*, 13, Spring 1982, pp. 110–29

WEIGHTMAN, G. & HUMPHRIES, S., *The Making of Modern London 1914–1939*, Sidgwick & Jackson, 1984

WESTERBY, R., *Wide Boys Never Work*, Arthur Barker, 1937

WHITE, J., *Campbell Bunk: The Worst Street in North London Between the Wars,* Pimlico, 2003

WHITEING, Eileen, *Anyone for Tennis?: Growing up in Wallington Between the Wars*, London Borough of Sutton, 1979

WHITE, Cynthia, *Women's Magazines 1693–1968*, Michael Joseph, 1970

WOODRUFF, W., *Nab End and Beyond*, Little Brown, 2003

WORBY, J., *Spiv's Progress*, Dent, 1939

Index